The Correspondence of Stephen Crane
Volume I

Stephen Crane in Athens, May 1897. The inscription is to Sam S. Chamberlain, Managing Editor of the New York Journal. *(Collection of Stanley and Mary Wertheim)*

The Correspondence of Stephen Crane

Volume I

Edited by
Stanley Wertheim and
Paul Sorrentino

Columbia University Press
NEW YORK   1988

LIBRARY OF CONGRESS CATALOGING-IN-PUBLICATION DATA

Crane, Stephen, 1871–1900.
The correspondence of Stephen Crane.
Includes indexes.
1. Crane, Stephen, 1871–1900—Correspondence.
2. Authors, American—19th century—Correspondence.
I. Wertheim, Stanley. II. Sorrentino, Paul.
III. Title.
PS1449.C85Z48   1988   813'.4[B]   87-25628
ISBN 0-231-06002-5 (set)
ISBN 0-231-06652-X (v. 1)
ISBN 0-231-06654-6 (v. 2)

COLUMBIA UNIVERSITY PRESS
New York   Guildford, Surrey

Copyright © 1988 Columbia University Press
All rights reserved
Printed in the United States of American

Hardback editions of Columbia University Press are
Smyth-sewn and printed on permanent and durable acid-free paper

To the Memory of

R. W. Stallman
Lillian Gilkes
Melvin H. Schoberlin

Contents

Acknowledgments ix
Introduction 1
Editorial Practice 15
Chronology 21

THE CORRESPONDENCE 27

APPENDIX A
Letters in the Writings of Thomas Beer 661

APPENDIX B
Establishing the Text of Crane's
Letters to John Northern Hilliard 693

TEXTUAL APPARATUS 697
Textual Record 697
Word-Division 737

Index of Correspondents of
Stephen Crane and Cora Crane 741

General Index 747

Illustrations appear as a group
following page 114

Acknowledgments

Our primary debt is to Alfred A. Knopf, Inc., for permission to publish Stephen Crane letters and inscriptions. We also thank the heirs and executors of Joseph Conrad, Ford Madox Ford, Hamlin Garland, Edward Garnett, William Dean Howells, Elbert Hubbard, Henry James, and H. G. Wells for permission to publish the letters of these literary correspondents of Stephen and Cora Crane.

The editors owe an enormous debt of gratitude to the libraries that have granted us permission to use their letters and the librarians who have aided our research. To the following individuals and their libraries, special thanks are due: Lola L. Szladits, Patrick Lawler, and Brian McInerny, The Berg Collection, The New York Public Library; Kenneth A. Lohf, John Aubry, Bernard Crystal, Rudolph Ellenbogen, Alison Scott, and Henry Rowan, Rare Book and Manuscript Library, Columbia University; Mark F. Weimer, Carolyn A. Davis, and Edward Lyon, The George Arents Research Library, Syracuse University; Mildred K. Abraham, Robert Hull, and Richard H. F. Lindemann, University of Virginia Library; George H. Butterick and Richard Schimmelpfeng, University of Connecticut Library; John Schweoke, Dartmouth College Library; Nicholas B. Scheetz, Georgetown University Library; William R. Cagle, The Lilly Library, Indiana University; Richard Everett and Ronald E. Robbins, David Bishop Skillman Library, Lafayette College; Frank Walker, Fales Library, New York University; Alan K. Lathrop, University of Minnesota Library; James Stuart Osbourn, Newark Public Library; Robert A. Tibbetts, The Ohio State University Libraries; Richard N. Wright, Onondaga Historical Association; Hilda Pring, The University of Pennsylvania

Library; and Kimball Higgs, Grolier Club, New York City. Other libraries and institutions that furnished copies and granted permission for the publication of letters and inscriptions contained in this volume are identified in the list of Location Symbols.

We also thank Mrs. Laura Schoberlin, who permitted Sorrentino to first examine in Hawaii her late husband's Crane collection. Maurice F. Neville, Miriam Roelofs, Daniel G. Siegel, and Deborah Berlo generously provided letters and inscriptions from their private collections. Kathleen (Kate) Donahue granted us permission to examine the papers of her late husband, John Berryman. James B. Colvert, David J. Nordloh, Michael G. Squires, James R. Vitelli, James L. W. West III, and Ames Williams gave advice and encouragement. For important information and insight into the publishing history of Crane's writings, we are indebted to the Introductions by J. C. Levinson and the Textual Histories and Analyses by Fredson Bowers in The University of Virginia Edition of *The Works of Stephen Crane*, 10 vols. (Charlottesville: The University Press of Virginia, 1969-76). The Print Shop at Virginia Polytechnic Institute and State University helped immensely in the preparation of the manuscript.

Others who have helped immeasurably over the years, either by example or in the subtle ways that make a work of this type possible, are Richard J. Jaarsma, Harrison T. Meserole, Sal Noto, Carl F. Strauch, and Robert E. Wilkinson.

To Mary Conroy Wertheim the gratitude for a lifetime of support and encouragement usually inadequately expressed to the wife of a scholar can only, once again, be inadequately expressed.

The preparation of this volume was made possible in part by a grant from the Division of Research Programs of the National Endowment for the Humanities. The administrations of William Paterson College and Virginia Polytechnic Institute and State University responded generously with grants of research time and travel funds. Special recognition must be given to Dean Tobin Barrozo of William Paterson College, whose charting of the path through potential bureaucratic obstacles was invaluable, and to the President of the College, Dr. Arnold Speert. Finally, we express our appreciation to our editors—William P. Germano, Vincent Duggan, and Jennifer Crewe—and to the staff of Columbia University Press.

The Correspondence of Stephen Crane

Volume I

Introduction

1

Four full-length biographies of Stephen Crane have appeared—Thomas Beer's impressionistic montage, John Berryman's critically perceptive but tendentious psychoanalytic study, R. W. Stallman's imperfectly integrated assemblage of fact and fallacy, and James B. Colvert's terse, objective narrative.[1] Yet Crane remains, as he knew he would, largely unexplained, the relationship between his life and art still obscure. He was a flamboyant personality who was anomalously both reclusive and mercurial, retaining his inner identity while projecting varied images of himself to others. Since the revival of interest in his writings in the early 1950s, he has been variously categorized as a realist, a naturalist, an impressionist, a symbolist, a "visionist," and even a romantic. This with some justification, for he employed all of these perspectives in different works and at times in the same work. Crane's elusiveness has intrigued critics and biographers and has made him the most controversial American author of the late nineteenth century.

Crane's letters do not often reveal the literary stylist and the imaginative artist, but they are the primary documents for understanding his life and work, evincing many of the paradoxes that have puzzled biographers and critics. They show him to be alternately shy and self-deprecatory, egocentric and generous, irresponsible and conscientious, ingenuous and cynical, ethical and dishonest, rebellious and overly concerned about his reputation. They clarify his attitudes toward literature and the creative process, and they document the circumstances of his life and the composition and publication of his works more coherently and accurately than has been achieved in the biographies.

Not least in importance, the letters provide fascinating and at times troubling insights into the circumstances of the American writer at the turn of the century, both on his native ground and as an expatriate in England. Crane was at the center of the literary life of his time in both countries. He was immensely popular as a personality, if not always as a writer, and was extensively written about in the newspapers and magazines of the day. He knew and corresponded with Hamlin Garland, William Dean Howells, Irving Bacheller, S. S. McClure, Elbert Hubbard, Harold Frederic, Henry James, Joseph Conrad, William Heinemann, Robert Barr, William Blackwood, H. G. Wells, Ford Madox Ford, Edward Garnett, and many other writers and publishers. Nevertheless, except for a short period following the publication of *The Red Badge of Courage,* Crane could not live securely on the emoluments of literature. In part, no doubt, this was in his last years the result of his and Cora's extravagance, but, as letters to the Cranes from the prominent writers who were his friends demonstrate, relative poverty was the common plight of authors who did not pander to the popular demand for romance in fiction. The constantly reiterated demand for money, money, money in Crane's letters to his publishers and literary agents and his final deterioration into hackwork suggest what his future might have been had he survived his twenty-ninth year.

2

Although Crane has achieved recognition as a major American author, scholars who work with his letters have had to rely upon R. W. Stallman and Lillian Gilkes' incomplete, inaccurate, and out-of-print *Stephen Crane: Letters*.[2] The present edition silently corrects errors in the text and dating of *Letters* and relegates to an appendix letters with no other sources than Thomas Beer's biography and articles on Crane. Despite widespread suspicion that many of these letters might be apocryphal or extensively edited, Stallman and Gilkes gave them equal authority with those for which manuscripts or other more reliable sources were available. This new edition brings together for the first time all currently known letters and book inscriptions from Crane, letters to him, and Cora's correspondence relative to his life and career. Of the more than 780 letters and inscriptions included here, almost 400 were not collected by Stallman and Gilkes. Among them are some 170 by Crane and more than 20 by Cora. A number of the new letters have appeared since 1960 in journals and books, most notably the *Stephen Crane Newsletter* (1966-70) and the ten-volume University Press of Virginia edition of Crane's works (1969-76). Others are in institutional or private collections previously unavailable to or overlooked by scholars.

No edition of correspondence is ever complete. The extant letters occasionally refer to missing letters. While Stephen Crane's letters are scarce, they surface from time to time on the rare book and manuscript market and no doubt will continue to do so. Most Crane collectors generously shared their holdings with us; but we were denied access to a few private collections, one of which, we suspect, might contain some of Crane's letters to Cora, none of which have been found.[3] References in Cora's correspondence suggest that Crane wrote or wired her occasionally from Cuba. Cora assiduously saved letters and telegrams, and she would most likely not have discarded Stephen's. There has been speculation that items were removed from Cora's papers while they were stored in Florida before being sold to Columbia University, and some of Crane's letters might have been among these.[4] As did *Letters*, this edition excludes the mawkish epistolary rhapsodies in Cora's notebooks that Lillian Gilkes believed were probably drafts of letters to Crane.[5] Some aspects of these passages may be related to Cora's relationship with him, but others seem to be imaginary or refer to someone else, perhaps Poultney Bigelow, the controversial political historian and journalist with whom she was briefly infatuated. The context of the passages is confused, they cannot be dated with any certainty, and it is sometimes difficult to determine where a "letter" ends and other reflections begin.

3

The new letters and inscriptions in this edition describe and clarify Crane's dealings with his friends, relatives, lovers, editors, literary agents, and publishers. Stallman and Gilkes and subsequent scholars did not have access to the largest group, which is part of the massive research collection of the late Commander Melvin H. Schoberlin, USN, assembled during the composition of his unpublished Crane biography,

"Flagon of Despair." Unearthed by Paul Sorrentino and brought to Syracuse University in November 1984 with Sorrentino's help, the collection includes sixty-two letters by Crane and thirty-two by Cora. Fourteen of the Stephen Crane letters and four inscriptions in books were previously unknown. Among these are engaging letters to two friends of Crane's youth, Armistead ("Tommie") Borland and Louis C. Senger, and to Corwin Knapp Linson, a young artist already established in a private studio who in 1893 befriended the nearly destitute Crane. Of great importance also in the Schoberlin Collection are the letters to Crane's literary agents, Paul Revere Reynolds and James B. Pinker, hitherto available only in typescripts at Syracuse University; copies of Crane's lost letters to Post Wheeler; sections of Agnes Crane's diary dealing with the days when she cared for and taught her younger brother; Borland's autograph albums, which contain much information about Crane's schoolmates and activities at Claverack College and Hudson River Institute; letters of publishers of Crane; and voluminous secondary material, especially Schoberlin's correspondence with Crane's family and friends and the memoirs of these relatives and loved ones.

Another significant group of letters unavailable to Stallman and Gilkes and previously uncollected is Crane's correspondence with Amy Leslie now in the Dartmouth College Library.[6] Amy Leslie, an actress and later drama critic of the *Chicago Daily News*, sued Crane in January 1898 for recovery of money she had ostensibly given him more than a year before when they were involved in a love affair. At the same time that Crane was wooing Cora Taylor, hostess of Jacksonville's notorious Hotel de Dream and later his common-law wife, he was writing fervent expressions of devotion to Amy Leslie. These letters, like others in these volumes, illustrate Crane's occasional tendency toward duplicity and help to dispel the legend of the naive artist crushed by a philistine society or that of the defaithed Christian gentleman lost in a world he never made—views perpetuated by some biographers.

Transcriptions of Stephen and Cora Crane's letters to Sylvester Scovel, a fellow correspondent with Crane in Greece and head of the *New York World*'s staff during the Cuban War, were found in John Berryman's papers at the University of Minnesota, previously unexamined by Crane scholars. The originals of these letters, now lost, belonged to Scovel's wife, Frances Cabané Saportas of Saint Louis. Only partly quoted in Berryman's biography, they offer revealing glimpses of the Cranes' life at Ravensbrook, Surrey, where they lived shortly after settling in England in the spring of 1897. The Berryman Collection also contains Mrs. Saportas' detailed reminiscences of her experiences with Crane as well as many memoirs by other persons. Portions of a cloth-covered diary kept by Stephen's father, Jonathan Townley Crane, from 5 April 1876 through 15 February 1880, transcribed by Berryman, contain new details about Crane's childhood.

Individual letters collected here for the first time offer new insights into Crane's interactions with friends, admirers, and relatives. When *Letters* appeared, little was known about the connection between Crane and John D. Barry, editor of *Forum* magazine. Early in Crane's career Barry convinced others to take the young writer's poetry seriously by reading excerpts from it at the Uncut Leaves Society and by encouraging Copeland and Day to issue *The Black Riders*. On 22 March 1893, a little more than a year before the reading, Barry wrote Crane (No. 18) to complain about *Maggie* because it "painted too black a picture." Despite this admonition, Barry ended the letter positively by acknowledging that "there is horror in your book" and by urging Crane to attempt psychological analyses of his characters in subsequent works. Barry encouraged Crane when the young author's first novel had failed commercially. Like Garland and Howells, virtually the only critics who saw value in *Maggie,* Barry recognized Crane's talent before it was fashionable to do so, and apparently Crane remembered Barry's advice "to study the thoughts as well as the acts of characters" when he wrote *The Red Badge of Courage*. Crane's delight in a highly perceptive review of *The Red Badge* by George Wyndham, a Member of Parliament, expressed in letters to his English publisher, William Heinemann (Nos. 189 and 208), contrasts markedly with his rather deprecatory attitude toward praise of the war novel by American critics who he felt were ignoring or undervaluing his other works.

In other letters, Crane's contradictory nature reveals itself in sharply divergent self-appraisals. His stilted protestations of virtue to Nellie Crouse are contradicted by his stark disclaimer in a letter to Daisy Hill (No. 210): "I am clay—very common uninteresting clay. I am a good deal of a rascal, sometimes a bore, often dishonest." Writing to his older brother William from Greece in April 1897 (No. 315), Crane expresses delight over the possibility of attaining military glory in "a position on the staff of the crown Prince. Wont that be great? I am so happy over it I can hardly breathe. I shall try—I shall try like blazes to get a decoration out of the thing. . . ." The irony that a writer who had exposed the futility of war and had treated heroic exploits cynically should lust for glory in battle seems to have escaped Crane, who was a master of irony; but Crane knew that his conventional brother would value high position and decorations, and he skillfully manipulated people from whom he wished to borrow money.

Also collected here and reproduced for the first time in this volume are Thomas Beer's typescripts of letters from Crane at Brede. Some of these were available to Beer at the time he wrote his biography, while others were not obtained until after the book had appeared. According to his sister Alice, he returned the originals to their owners shortly after he had transcribed them. We owe their preservation primarily to Schoberlin and Berryman, whose copies were sent to them by Alice Beer. These letters are especially significant for their comments upon such other writers as Harold Frederic, Oscar Wilde, Henry James, and Joseph Conrad. According to Crane, whose letters only occasionally reveal the sardonic sense of humor so pervasive in his literary works, Ford Madox Ford "patronized his family. He patronizes Conrad. He will end up by patronizing God who will have to get used to it and they will be friends" (No. 537).[7] Mrs. Humphrey Ward is "an old cow! She has no more mind than a president" (No. 547).

4

While the originals of the letters in the "Thomas Beer Papers" have never surfaced, their provenance is considerably better than many of those quoted in Beer's sparsely documented biography, which contains much of what still passes for the basic facts of Crane's life. Beer, who was primarily a novelist, quotes a number of important letters, all but two of which have mysteriously disappeared,[8] and, equally suspicious, offers basic "information" unverifiable elsewhere. His book is more an impressionistic literary history of the late nineteenth century than a biography; and when Beer does treat Crane, he is often interested in quieting rumors that he was an alcoholic, a drug addict, and a frequenter of bawdy houses. To strengthen his argument, Beer suppressed what he knew about Crane's love affairs with Lily Brandon Munroe, Amy

Leslie, and Cora Taylor. While Beer maintained that his information was derived largely from interviews and correspondence with Crane's contemporaries, the question of what happened to most of the letters and other documents he used remains unanswered. Beer admits that "this book is probably filled with errors" but contends that "my variations from partial biographies have been made on the testimony of Crane's few letters," from which he removed "some hasty estimates of living people in England and America."[9] When only a single letter from Crane cited in the biography had turned up by 1963, Stallman concluded that Beer had probably destroyed the rest, an unlikely surmise since Beer was a bibliophile who idolized Crane and knew the value of his letters to literary history. When a letter from Cora quoted by Beer appeared a few years later, it seemed that others might eventually surface, but to date they have not.[10] A copy of a letter from Wilson Follett to E. R. Hagemann (12 April 1962, ViU), however, suggests that many of the letters and other documents may never have existed and that portions of Beer's book may be fictional:

The rock-bottom truth is that Tom Beer had an imagination like no other that ever flourished on this continent—or any other, to my knowledge. Things that never were became as real to him, once his mind had conceived them [,] as the rising of the moon or a drink at the Yale Club in the prohibition era. He could quote pages verbatim from authors who never wrote any such pages; sometimes from authors who never lived. He could rehearse the plots of stories never written by their ostensible authors, or by anybody, repeat pages of dialogue from them, and give you the (nonexistent) places and dates of publication. He could no more help the way his imagination worked than he could help the smoky red soldier in his wonderful eyes. When he came to troublesome lacunae in Crane's life[,] he lived through them with that same imagination, quite as if he were Crane; and his imagination could document every happening if he were challenged. He was not a liar in any sense that has a jot of meaning; he did not fake the material of scholarship. What he saw with the eye of his imagination was as real to him as anything that registered on his retina. He would talk with great rapidity for hours in a level monotone, in a highly finished style—his own—about imaginary occurrences that to him were history. And—the point that always escapes an assailant of his biography—he *loved* Crane, humbly idolized him, and was incapable of setting down a syllable about him prompted by any force except that love and idolatry. Nobody who did not know him well and spent much time with him will ever be able to conceive that he was as he was. The folk in his stories are miraculous enough; he was more miraculous than all of them rolled into one. And I suppose his chronicle of Crane asks to be taken in the long run, not primarily as the earliest biography, but as a devotional elegiac poem in prose.

Follett was editor of the twelve-volume *The Work of Stephen Crane* (1925-27). As a close friend and colleague of Beer (who wrote one of the introductions to the edition) and as the editor of a collection of Beer's short stories, Follett would have had more than a passing knowledge of Crane's life and work and of Beer's personality. Other acquaintances of Beer who reviewed his biography also noted that Beer identified strongly with Crane and that there was probably a fictional dimension to his book. Mark Van Doren commented upon "Mr. Beer's identification with his subject" and speculated that "if the book is indeed a novel, and it reads like one from the first page to the last, it is the sort which Crane might have written about himself had he the inclination and had he known as much about himself as his biographer."[11] Ernest Boyd, who knew Beer well, also recognized the similarity between Beer and his characterization of Crane. Boyd considered it "within certain limits, a complete expression of [Beer's] personality"; what emerges from the book is "a personality which is stamped as clearly upon his life of Stephen Crane as if it were his own story."[12] To his credit, Beer tried to gather biographical material, but he became so frustrated he wrote in one of his own letters that "Crane might as well have died in the 18th century as in 1900 for all the tracks he left." If Follett is right in calling Beer's book "a devotional elegiac poem in prose," all but two of its letters must be treated with less, if any, authority until verifiable documents appear.

Unfortunately, for almost fifty years Crane scholars, though admitting Beer's unreliability, have accepted the letters in his biography and articles as factual. As a result, misreadings have occurred. A good example is the Crane-Helen Trent relationship in 1891, as treated by Beer, the only source of the story, and by Stallman in his biography. In 1923 Beer supposedly interviewed Trent and read Crane's letters to her. Beer mentions that soon after her relationship with Crane, she married in London an English surgeon, Dr. Charles Goodsall. The General Register Office in London, however, has no record of the marriage anywhere in England or Wales between 1891 and 1899. If she pretended to be engaged simply to discourage Crane's infatuation with her, Beer does not imply any such interpretation. Or if she married elsewhere or someone else in London, Beer had no reason to write otherwise. Because the biography was published in 1923, the same year as the interview, the facts should have been fresh in his mind. Beer also claims that she showed him every bit of correspondence Crane had written her. Yet he says that when in 1900 Crane was pointed out to her as a famous person, she did not know why. It seems odd that someone would keep an admirer's letters for many years, especially after she had married, but not know of his reputation. If she kept the letters out of fond remembrance of a youth in love with her, somewhere in her reading or conversation she would necessarily have learned something about Crane. In the 1890s he was more famous than his works.

Another instance in which letters and documents cited by Beer that have no other origin have established a "fact" of Crane's life that should be reconsidered is the question of his ostensible sojourn in New York City and its environs in November-December 1898. Crane's biographers agree that he left Havana in the latter part of November and spent from four to six weeks in New York before returning to England.[13] The story of Crane's visit to Delmonico's with James Huneker and the fight between Richard Harding Davis and a certain Thomas McCumber occasioned by that visit, the letter Crane supposedly wrote to Mrs. William Sonntag to the effect that he and Cora were "carrying on a duel at long range with ink" as to whether she should come to the United States or he should return to England, and the anecdote about his near arrest in the first week of December as he was leaving a theater with Mrs. Sonntag, her son, and a cousin who was a priest, all find their source in Beer's biography or his article "Mrs. Stephen Crane." There are no extant Crane letters from New York City, Hartwood, or Port Jervis for the period November-December 1898, and two inscriptions in Crane books indicate he was probably in Havana on 24 and 26 November. Most important, according to a detailed transcription made by Schoberlin, the passenger manifest of the *City of Washington*, which sailed from Havana on 24 December and arrived in New York on the morning of 29 December,[14] lists Stephen Crane as passenger No. 15, designates his port of embarkation and his destination, and gives an accurate personal description that leaves no doubt as to his identity. Crane spent only two or three days in New York City before he sailed on the *Manitau* for England, and the statement in his letter to his brother William, written shortly after he arrived on 11 January, that he had not established contact with his family while he was in America because "my position in England was near going to smash and I rushed to save it as soon as I could get enough money to leave Havana" (No. 446), should be taken at face value and not assumed to be a subterfuge.

Like other accounts cited by Beer and supposedly derived from letters and interviews, the Crane-Trent relationship and Crane's late 1898 stay in New York should be challenged. Admittedly, Beer, like every other Crane scholar, realized that details about Crane's life are sketchy because of few primary documents. Years later, when Louis Zara tried to write a biography, he too became so frustrated by the mysterious lacunae in Crane's life that he wrote a fictionalized biography, but he stated outright that he was writing a novel.[15] Because of the circumstances surrounding Beer's book, his documentation should also be treated as at least partly fictional until new evidence suggests otherwise. Until then, scholars should heed Thackeray's advice in *The Newcomes*:

Where dialogues are written down, which the reporter could by no possibility have heard, and where motives are detected which the persons actuated by them certainly never confided to the writer, the public must once for all be warned that the author's individual fancy very likely supplies much of the narrative; and that he forms it as best he may, out of stray papers, conversations reported to him, and his knowledge, right or wrong, of the characters of the persons engaged. And, as is the case with the most orthodox histories, the writer's own guesses or conjectures are printed in exactly the same type as the most ascertained patent facts.[16]

5

At present, there is little separation of fact from fiction in Crane biography. R. W. Stallman's introduction to *Letters* (p.xii) criticizes John Berryman for drawing most of the facts for his *Stephen Crane* from Beer. Yet Stallman's *Stephen Crane: A Biography* is also undiscriminating in this regard, giving Beer's unsubstantiated accounts of incidents and relationships equal authority with those for which reliable documentation is available and, as in *Letters*, not distinguishing between Beer's probably apocryphal or bowdlerized letters and those for which originals are extant. Neither does James B. Colvert, in his otherwise excellent short life in the Harcourt Brace Jovanovich Album Series, observe these essential differentiations. Clearly, the authoritative biography of Stephen Crane remains to be written; and toward that end this edition of his correspondence, along with the approximately eighty reminiscences by friends and acquaintances published or in manuscript dealing with virtually every aspect of his literary career, will serve as *ur*-biography.

From the letters, the most complete and accurate record of that career, a demythologized Stephen Crane emerges. He was not, as sentimentalists would have it, the ghost of Chatterton, not, in Amy Lowell's words, "A boy spiritually killed by neglect."[17] Within the less-than-five-year period between the book publication of *The Red Badge of Courage* and the end, Crane enjoyed a high measure of fame as well as notoriety. Yet his contemporary reputation depended almost exclusively upon the war novel, and he felt that his talent had ultimately been misjudged. *Maggie* was almost entirely ignored when it appeared pseudonymously in 1893; and *The Black Riders*, although well received by a number of American reviewers, was frequently derided. The works of fiction published subsequent to *The Red Badge* were invariably compared with it and judged repetitious or inferior. In his letters, Crane lamented the obsession of the critics with "the damned 'Red Badge' " (No. 115) and "the accursed 'Red Badge' " (No. 165) and hoped desperately that readers might "discover now that the high dramatic key of The Red Badge cannot be sustained" (No. 190). But it was all to no avail. The core of praise remained focused upon his one great success, and whatever else he wrote seemed anticlimactic.

Crane was famous at twenty-four and dead at twenty-eight. From the beginning to the end of his short career, his letters reflect a fierce inner struggle between actuality and ideals, but he was older than his years and, for the most part, reconciled to compromises with reality. Unlike Melville, who virtually abandoned literature for a sinecure in the New York Customs House when he realized he could not live by his pen, Crane insisted upon remaining a writer to the end, although he had to produce inferior hackwork that was easy to write and sell. *The Third Violet* is remarkable only because Stephen Crane wrote it; *Active Service* is a slipshod and clumsy potboiler. The syndrome of advances from agents and publishers and futile efforts to keep up with them became the monotonously dominating theme of his correspondence in the final year and a half of his life and resulted in an embarrassing amount of uninspired journalism. Nevertheless, the quality of Crane's best work improved appreciably between 1893, when he wrote *The Red Badge of Courage*, and 1897, when he wrote "The Open Boat." If he had been healthy and affluent, he might have written even more important fiction. His ability to compose "The Monster," "The Bride Comes to Yellow Sky," and "The Blue Hotel" in later years makes it seem probable that his talents were not depleted and that he could have continued to develop as an artist had he not been forced to grind out stories and sketches for magazines. As it is, his reputation must ultimately rest upon the strength of *The Red Badge*, five or ten short stories, and a handful of poems.

Notes

1. Thomas Beer, *Stephen Crane: A Study in American Letters* (New York: Knopf, 1923); John Berryman, *Stephen Crane* (New York: Sloane, 1950; rpt. Cleveland: World-Meridian, 1962); R. W. Stallman, *Stephen Crane: A Biography*, rev. ed. (New York: Braziller, 1973); James B. Colvert, *Stephen Crane*, HBJ Album Biographies Series (San Diego: Harcourt, 1984).

2. R. W. Stallman and Lillian Gilkes, eds., *Stephen Crane: Letters* (New York: New York University Press, 1960), hereafter referred to as *Letters*.

3. Although Stallman and Gilkes considered the "To C. E. S." items (Nos. 289 and 309) in the Columbia University Crane Collection as letters from Crane to Cora, they are apparently inscriptions written on flyleaves cut from books. Cora had the unfortunate habit of removing inscribed flyleaves from books for easy storage. A number of such cut flyleaves in the Collection have inscriptions by Joseph Conrad, Henry James, Irving Bacheller, and Charles Whibley, and the "To C. E. S." inscriptions resemble these.

4. Lillian Gilkes, "The Stephen Crane Collection Before Its Acquisition by Columbia: A Memoir," *Columbia Library Columns*, 23 (November 1973), 20-21.

5. *Cora Crane: A Biography of Mrs. Stephen Crane* (Bloomington: Indiana University Press, 1960), pp. 361-62.

6. One of the letters to Amy Leslie (No. 288) is in the possession of Robert Stallman, Jr., New York City.

7. Beer, pp. 239-40, quotes a version of this letter from Crane to (Arnold) Henry Sanford Bennett, written about 13 August 1899. His quotation, however, was derived not from the complete text of the letter in the "Thomas Beer Papers" but from another version. Beer's quotation from Crane's letter to Bennett characterizing Oscar Wilde also differs considerably in text from the lost original, which he apparently copied after his biography had been published (No. 547). Beer might have simply tampered with his sources, but to what end in these instances it would be difficult to conjecture.

8. Possibly Beer, p. 141, did not have access to the original of the single extant letter from Crane that he quotes. The letter to William Howe Crane, 29 November 1896 (No. 285) had been published in part in the *Newark Evening News*, 3 November 1921, p. 6, and may have appeared complete elsewhere. The second letter quoted by Beer that has emerged is from Cora Crane to Edward Garnett, 10 January 1899 (No. 445).

9. Beer, pp. 246, 247.

10. Neither have the fascinating letters from Cora Crane quoted in Beer's article "Mrs. Stephen Crane," *American Mercury*, 31 (March 1934), 289-95.

11. Review of Beer's *Stephen Crane*, in *Nation*, 16 (January 1924), pp. 66-67; rpt. in *Stephen Crane: The Critical Heritage*, ed. Richard M. Weatherford (London: Routledge & Kegan Paul, 1973), p. 321.

12. *Portraits: Real and Imaginary* (1924; rpt. New York: AMS Press, 1970), pp. 214, 216.

13. Beer, pp. 200-8; Berryman, pp. 232-34; Stallman, pp. 437-42; Colvert, p. 138.

14. The record of the Fiscal Branch of the National Archives specifies that the ship arrived on 28 December, but the *City of Washington* actually entered New York harbor at 5:00 on the morning of the 29th *(New York Times*, 29 December 1898, p. 3).

15. *Dark Rider: A Novel Based on the Life of Stephen Crane* (Cleveland: World, 1961).

16. *The Newcomes*, 2 vols. (London: Bradbury and Evans, 1854-55), I, 226.

17. Introduction, *The Work of Stephen Crane*, VI (New York: Knopf, 1926), p. xxix.

Editorial Practice

This edition assembles all of the known extant correspondence of Stephen Crane, his inscriptions, and selected correspondence of Cora Crane. The material is arranged chronologically and as fully and accurately as possible. Letters appearing in the publications of Thomas Beer are arranged chronologically in Appendix A. For an explanation of the displacement of Beer's letters, see the Introduction. The letters and inscriptions are generally presented as clear text, with no bracketed cancellations, interlineations, or the use of *sic*. Wavy brackets are used for the few occasions to editorially reconstruct destroyed or partly illegible text or to alert the reader that the text is undecipherable. A record of emendations, textual notes, and physical details of the letters necessary for reconstruction of the text is in the Textual Apparatus. A text is emended only in such specific details as obvious typographical mistakes or passages incomprehensible to the reader. In two letters to Cora, for example, William Howe Crane practiced typing on his newly acquired typewriter. The errors were typically the result of inadvertently hitting an adjacent key on the keyboard, so that "your hint," for example, was typed as "ypur hint." Errors in letters that exist only as typed transcriptions or printed versions are preserved with only one or two exceptions—for example, "Iv'e" emended to read "I've"—because it is unknown whether the writer, transcriber, or compositor committed the error. In these typed or printed versions, editorial comment and such descriptive devices as *sic* are those of the transcriber or the person quoting the letter in an article or book. Few of the emendations appear in Crane's letters, and only his habit of not crossing a *t* is silently corrected. With the exception of emendations, the editors have attempted to insure that the text in this edition accurately reflects what the writer composed, including mistakes.

Establishment of copy-text, the document on which each letter or inscription is based, has generally not been difficult because the document itself, in whatever state it survives, has sole authority. In three cases, two slightly different versions of the same letter exist. In these instances, one version is chosen as copy-text, with a textual note explaining the rationale for the selection, and emended if appropriate to reflect variants in the other version. All variants between both versions are recorded in the Textual Record. The copy-texts for Crane's letters to John Northern Hilliard are discussed separately in Appendix B. To establish the text, we visited the Library of Congress, New York Public Library, and Newark Public Library; university libraries at Columbia, Connecticut, Dartmouth, Indiana, Lafayette, Minnesota, New York University, Ohio State, Syracuse, and Virginia; and private collections. At each place we examined holographs or whatever form in which the documents exist and requested photocopies. Using these copies, we entered into a word processor the texts of all of the letters and inscriptions and produced a typescript for proofreading. When possible, we returned to a library to proofread the typescript against the original document. In a few cases involving libraries we could not visit again, a librarian confirmed whether or not a mark on the photocopy was punctuation or the result of a piece of dirt on the photocopier.

The letters and inscriptions are preceded by the name of the author, or recipient, or both for letters about Crane, and symbols describing the physical state and location of the documents. A list of descriptive symbols, location symbols, and short titles used throughout editorial commentary appears at the end of this section. The placement of several parts of the letters is regularized according to the following procedure: date, location, complimentary close, and signature are set flush against the right margin; salutation and postscript, flush left. The original paragraphing is preserved, but no attempt is made to reproduce line-division or the exact style of indentation. Square brackets enclose a conjectural address or date inferred from a postmark or internal evidence. A letter that can be dated only by month and year or just year, as in [October 1897] or [1899], is placed at the end of the section for that month or year. A questionable date is recorded with something similar

16   *Editorial Practice*

to one of the following, whichever is appropriate: [5? August 1899], [March? 1894], or [1897?]. The questionable dating precedes the question mark. The following details are not recorded: page numbers on letters, the use of superscript in such abbreviations as Mr. and Wm., such insignificant marks as random lines drawn in a margin, horizontal bars drawn above and below roman numerals, and such stylistic flourishes as paraphs under signatures. The few occasions in a typed letter in which the correspondent wrote out the complimentary close or postscript in longhand are not recorded. Also ignored are obvious typographical mistakes made by Crane while he practiced typing in 1899. For example, Crane typed "bost" then interlined a second "o" by hand to spell "boost." In another instance he typed "G" at the end of a line; realizing there was no space to complete the word, he started it again on the next line and typed "Gentleman." In a third case, because the platen of the typewriter did not roll, Crane inadvertently typed one line over another. Seeing his mistake, he retyped the lines. These sorts of mistakes prove only that Crane was a poor typist and his machine needed repair.

Double underlining for emphasis is treated as single underlining, and quotation marks appear inside or outside punctuation depending on what the writer did. If a hyphen is typed following a colon in a salutation (e.g., "Dear Mr. Crane:-"), the hyphen is treated as a one-em dash, which the writer intended. The use of letterhead stationery is recorded but not reproduced in type facsimile. If the letterhead contains information unessential to the study of Crane—e.g., a statement about the facilities at a hotel—an ellipsis replaces the information; enough of the letterhead is quoted to give the reader its source. If the first three numbers in the date of the year—i.e., "189"—are preprinted on stationery, this fact is not recorded. In the complimentary close, such abbreviations as "vy" for "very" and "yrs" for "yours" are maintained to preserve the flavor of the original document. If the close is illegible, it is written out and spelled correctly. For inscriptions, line divisions are preserved, and the date and location, which commemorate rather than simply identify a time and place, appear where they were written, typically at the end.

Descriptive Symbols

AC	autograph card, unsigned
ACS	autograph card, signed
AL	autograph letter
ALfr	autograph letter, fragment
ALfrS	autograph letter, fragment, signed
ALS	autograph letter, signed with name or initial(s)
AMs	autograph manuscript
AMsFr	autograph manuscript, fragment
MsC	manuscript copy
MsFr	manuscript fragment
MSL	manuscript stenographic letter
MSLS	manuscript stenographic letter, signed
TL	typed letter
TLfr	typed letter, fragment
TLS	typed letter, signed with name or initial(s)
TSLS	typed stenographic letter, signed
TT	typed transcription, holograph not located
TTfr	typed transcription, fragment, holograph not located

Location Symbols

CCamarSJ	St. John's Seminary, Camarillo, California
CLSU	University of Southern California, Los Angeles
CSmH	Henry E. Huntington Library, San Marino, California
CtU	University of Connecticut, Storrs
CtY	Yale University, New Haven, Connecticut
DLC	Library of Congress
DNA	United States National Archives Library
IGK	Knox College, Galesburg, Illinois
InU	Indiana University, Bloomington
IU	University of Illinois, Urbana
KU	University of Kansas, Lawrence
MB	Boston Public Library, Massachusetts
MH	Harvard University, Cambridge, Massachusetts
MiU	University of Michigan, Ann Arbor
MnU	University of Minnesota, Minneapolis
NCaS	St. Lawrence University, Canton, New York

NhD	Dartmouth College, Hanover, New Hampshire
NN	New York Public Library
NNC	Columbia University, New York City
NNU	New York University
NSyU	Syracuse University, New York
OU	Ohio State University, Columbus
PEL	Lafayette College, Easton, Pennsylvania
PHi	Historical Society of Pennsylvania, Philadelphia
RPB	Brown University, Providence, Rhode Island
TxU	University of Texas, Austin
UPB	Brigham Young University, Provo, Utah
ViU	University of Virginia, Charlottesville
VtMiM	Middlebury College, Middlebury, Vermont

Short Titles

Allen	Frederick Lewis Allen, *Paul Revere Reynolds* (New York: privately printed, 1944)
Beer	Thomas Beer, *Stephen Crane: A Study in American Letters* (New York: Knopf, 1923)
Berryman	John Berryman, *Stephen Crane* (1950; rpt. Cleveland: World-Meridian, 1962)
Gilkes	Lillian Gilkes, *Cora Crane: A Biography of Mrs. Stephen Crane* (Bloomington: Indiana Univ. Press, 1960)
Letters	R. W. Stallman and Lillian Gilkes, eds., *Stephen Crane: Letters* (New York: New York University Press, 1960)
Linson	Corwin K. Linson, *My Stephen Crane*, ed. Edwin H. Cady (Syracuse: Syracuse University Press, 1958)
SCrN	Stephen Crane Newsletter
Stallman BIBL	R. W. Stallman, *Stephen Crane: A Critical Bibliography* (Ames: Iowa State University Press, 1972)
Stallman BIO	R. W. Stallman, *Stephen Crane: A Biography*, rev. ed. (New York: Braziller, 1973)
Work	Wilson Follett, ed., *The Work of Stephen Crane*, 12 vols. (New York: Knopf, 1925-27)
Works	Fredson Bowers, ed., *The Works of Stephen Crane*, 10 vols. (Charlottesville: The University Press of Virginia, 1969-76)

Editorial Practice 19

Chronology

1871   Stephen Crane born 1 November in Newark, New Jersey, fourteenth and last child of Jonathan Townley Crane, presiding elder of Methodist churches in the Newark district, and Mary Helen (Peck) Crane, daughter of a clergyman and niece of Methodist Bishop Jesse T. Peck. Only eight of the thirteen Crane children who preceded Stephen were living at the time of his birth. His Revolutionary War namesake (1709-80) had been President of the Colonial Assemblies and delegate from New Jersey to the Continental Congress in Philadelphia. He returned home shortly before the Declaration of Independence was signed.

1874-80   Jonathan Townley Crane serves as minister of Methodist churches in Bloomington and then Paterson, New Jersey. Mrs. Crane active in the Women's Christian Temperance Union. Family moves in April 1878 to Port Jervis, New York, on the Delaware River, where father becomes pastor of the Drew Methodist Church, a post he holds until his death on 16 February 1880.

1883   Mother and younger children move to Asbury Park, a resort town on the New Jersey coast. Stephen's brother, Townley, operates a summer news-reporting agency for the *New York Tribune*. Another brother, William Howe Crane, remains in Port Jervis, where he practices law and becomes a founding member of the Hartwood Club, an exclusive hunting and fishing preserve in nearby Sullivan County.

1884 Agnes Elizabeth, a sister who encouraged Stephen's first writings and was his closest companion, dies in May at the age of twenty-eight.

1885-87 Stephen attends Pennington Seminary (New Jersey), a Methodist boarding school where his father had been principal, 1849-58.

1888 In January Crane enrolls in Claverack College and Hudson River Institute, a co-educational, semi-military high school and junior college in Columbia County, New York. In summer months from 1888 through 1892 he assists Townley in gathering shore news at Asbury Park.

1890 Publishes first sketch, "Henry M. Stanley," in the February issue of the Claverack College *Vidette*. Is first lieutenant in the school's military regiment and adjutant to its commander, Colonel A. H. Flack. Writes the "Battalion Notes" column in the June issue of the *Vidette*, in which he is gazetted captain. Leaves Claverack, having completed only two-and-a-half years of the four-year curriculum and in the fall enters Lafayette College (Easton, Pennsylvania) as a mining-engineering student. Joins Delta Upsilon fraternity. Withdraws from the college in the first month of the second semester, "without censure," according to minutes of the faculty.

1891 Transfers to Syracuse University in January. Plays catcher and shortstop on the varsity baseball team. Becomes Syracuse stringer for the *New York Tribune*. First short story, "The King's Favor," appears in the *University Herald* in May. Also publishes a literary hoax, "Great Bugs in Onondaga," in the 1 June *Tribune*. In August Crane meets Hamlin Garland, who was presenting a lecture series on American literature at Avon-by-the-Sea. Reports Garland's lecture on William

Dean Howells in the 18 August issue of the *Tribune*. Becomes familiar with Garland's "veritism" and Howells' theories of literary realism. In mid-June Crane goes on a camping trip in Sullivan County, New York, near Port Jervis, with Syracuse Delta Upsilon fraternity brother, Frederic M. Lawrence, and two other friends, Louis E. Carr, Jr., and Louis C. Senger, Jr. This experience contributes to the background of his Sullivan County writings. Fails to return to college in the fall. Begins to explore the slums of lower Manhattan while living with his brother, Edmund, in Lake View, New Jersey. Mother dies on 7 December.

1892　A number of the Sullivan County tales and sketches appear in the *Tribune*. Also a New York City sketch, "The Broken-Down Van" (10 July), which anticipates *Maggie*. The *Tribune*'s columns are closed to Crane shortly after his article, "Parades and Entertainments" (21 August), offends both the Junior Order of United American Mechanics and *Tribune* publisher Whitelaw Reid, Republican candidate for Vice President. In October Crane moves into "The Pendennis Club," a rooming house at 1064 Avenue A in Manhattan inhabited by a group of medical students. Shares a room with Frederic M. Lawrence overlooking the East River and Blackwell's Island. Revises *Maggie*.

1893　*Maggie: A Girl of the Streets* privately printed in March under the pseudonym of Johnston Smith. Crane is introduced to Howells by Garland. Begins composition of *The Red Badge of Courage*, probably in late March or April. Shares a loft in the old Needham building on East 23rd Street, recently abandoned by the Art Students' League, with artist and illustrator friends and lives in poverty in various New York City tenements.

1894　Writes social studies such as "An Experiment in Misery" and "In the Depths of a Coal Mine." Begins *George's Mother* in May and completes the novel in November. Takes some of his poems and the manuscript of *The Red Badge of Courage* to

Garland in the spring. In August Crane camps with Lawrence, Carr, and Senger in Milford, Pike County, Pennsylvania. The *Pike County Puzzle*, largely written by Crane, is a burlesque account of this experience. Negotiates with the Boston publisher Copeland and Day over *The Black Riders*. Retrieves the manuscript of *The Red Badge* from S. S. McClure, who had held it from May until October, and sells it to the Bacheller, Johnson and Bacheller newspaper syndicate. A truncated version of the war novel appears in the *Philadelphia Press,* the *New York Press,* and an undetermined number of other newspapers in December.

1895   Crane journeys to the West and Mexico as a feature writer for the Bacheller syndicate. Meets Willa Cather in the office of the *Nebraska State Journal* in February. His first Western sketch, "Nebraska's Bitter Fight for Life," describing drought and blizzard conditions in the state, is widely syndicated on Sunday, 24 February. Sends final revision of *The Red Badge* to D. Appleton and Company in early March. *The Black Riders* is published in May. Crane becomes a member of the Lantern Club on William Street in Manhattan, founded by a group of young journalists. Spends summer at the home of his brother Edmund in Hartwood, New York, where he writes *The Third Violet*. Publication of *The Red Badge of Courage* in autumn projects Crane to fame in the United States and England.

1896   *George's Mother*, an expurgated version of *Maggie*, and *The Little Regiment* are published. *The Third Violet* is serialized by the McClure syndicate. Crane visits Washington in March to gather material for a political novel. Joins Author's Club. Becomes member of the Sons of the American Revolution in May. In September he becomes *persona non grata* with the New York City police by appearing in court to defend Dora Clark, a known prostitute who had falsely been arrested for soliciting while in his company on the night of 16 September. Leaves for Jacksonville, Florida, at the end of November on his way to report the Cuban insurrection for the Bacheller syndicate. Meets Cora Taylor at her "nightclub," the Hotel de Dream.

1897   The *Commodore*, carrying men and munitions to the Cuban rebels, sinks off the coast of Florida on the morning of 2 January. Crane and three others, the ship's captain, the steward, and an oiler, spend thirty hours on the sea in a ten-foot dinghy. Incident is the source for "Stephen Crane's Own Story" (*New York Press*, 7 January) and "The Open Boat." Crane goes to Greece to cover the Greco-Turkish War for the *New York Journal* and the *Westminster Gazette*. Cora, who accompanies him, sends back dispatches under the pseudonym Imogene Carter. *The Third Violet* published in May. Stephen and Cora settle in England at Ravensbrook, Oxted, Surrey, as Mr. and Mrs. Stephen Crane. In September they visit Ireland with Harold Frederic and Kate Lyon. Sidney Pawling, editor and partner in the firm of William Heinemann, Crane's English publisher, introduces him to Joseph Conrad in October. They become close friends. Also meets Ford Hueffer (later Ford Madox Ford). "The Monster," "Death and the Child," and "The Bride Comes to Yellow Sky" are written this autumn.

1898   "The Blue Hotel" is completed in the first week of February. The sinking of *The Maine* impels Crane to return to New York. He attempts to enlist in the United States Navy but fails the physical examination. *The Open Boat and Other Tales of Adventure* appears in April. Crane goes to Cuba as a correspondent for the *New York World*. Reports the landings at Guantánamo, the advance on Las Guásimas, and the Battle of San Juan Hill. When he is discharged from the *World* in July, he contracts with Hearst's *New York Journal* to cover the Puerto Rican campaign. After the Protocol of Peace is signed in August, he enters Havana and leads a semi-underground existence for three months, communicating infrequently with Cora and his family. Returns to New York at the end of December and sails for England on the 31st.

1899	In February the Cranes move to Brede Place, Sussex, rented by Cora from Moreton Frewen, whose wife, Clara, is a sister of Lady Randolph Churchill. They form friendships with Henry James, H. G. Wells, and Edward Garnett. Crane's second book of poems, *War Is Kind*, appears in May. Completes *Active Service*, which is published in October. Writes a series of stories about children set in the Whilomville (Port Jervis) setting of "The Monster." *The Monster and Other Stories* published by Harper in December. Finishes Cuban War stories and sketches of *Wounds in the Rain*. Increasingly forced into hackwork to repay enormous debts incurred through his and Cora's extravagance. Suffers tubercular hemorrhage at the conclusion of an elaborate three-day house party at Brede Place.
1900	Continues struggle to control debts and meet deadlines. *Whilomville Stories* and *Wounds in the Rain* published. Suffers new hemorrhages at the beginning of April. Travels to Germany's Black Forest in May, although little hope is held for his recovery. Dies on 5 June of tuberculosis in a sanitarium at Badenweiler. Body is returned to the United States for burial at Evergreen Cemetery in Elizabeth (now Hillside), New Jersey.
1901	*Great Battles of the World* appears. Researched and in part written by Kate Frederic.
1902	*Last Words*, an anthology compiled by Cora, published in England only. Contains a number of early pieces and eight new stories and sketches, two of which were completed by Cora.
1903	*The O'Ruddy* appears after delays caused by the reluctance of other writers to finish the novel, which was finally completed by Robert Barr, whom Crane had originally designated for the task.

The Correspondence of
Stephen Crane

School and College

Like his senior contemporaries in the creation of American fiction, Mark Twain and Henry James, Stephen Crane never completed the course of study in any educational institution. Delicate health prevented regular school attendance until he was eight years old, and this was interrupted when his father died in February 1880. Mary Helen Crane moved her brood from the Methodist parsonage in Port Jervis, New York, to a boarding house in Roseville near Newark and back to Port Jervis for a time when Stephen developed scarlet fever. From Roseville the Cranes went to Asbury Park on the New Jersey shore, where Stephen presumably attended school from 1883 until the fall of 1885, when he entered Pennington Seminary, a coeducational boarding school of which Jonathan Townley Crane had been principal from 1849 to 1858. Stephen's transfer to Claverack College and Hudson River Institute in January 1888 at the age of sixteen was motivated primarily by his interest in Claverack's military training program. "He loved to play at soldiers from his earliest childhood," his sister-in-law, Mrs. George Crane, recalled. "Most of his playthings were in the form of toy soldiers, guns and the like," and "his fondness for everything military induced his mother to send him to the Claverack Military Academy."

The Claverack experience was idyllic for Crane. He would later characterize it as the happiest period in his life. He had his most intense period of exposure to nineteenth-century English and American literature and the classics, although he never read deeply or widely; contributed his first signed article, a two-column sketch on the exploits of Henry M. Stanley, to the school's magazine, *Vidette*, and fell in love with two redheads, Harriet Mattison and Jennie Pierce. Summers were spent helping his brother Townley collect society gossip along the New Jersey shore for his Asbury Park news agency. Crane's studies were eclectic. Students of the three-year Classical or Academic programs at Claverack were prepared to enter the third year of college. There was also a Commercial Department for boys and girls. The *Thirty Fourth Catalogue of Claverack College and Hudson River Institute* (1888) lists Crane among the Classical students, although he later apparently switched to the Academic curriculum. It is unlikely he adhered to the requirements of either very closely, for when he entered Lafayette College in the fall of 1890, having completed two and a half years at Claverack, he was still only a freshman.

Crane was able to indulge his love of military panoply to the full at Claverack, and he rose rapidly in the ranks of the student battalion, being gazetted captain in the June 1890 issue of *Vidette*. His "perfectly hen-like attitude toward the rank and file" during a prize drill was sardonically described by a classmate, Harvey Wickham. Crane was preparing himself for West Point and a career as a professional soldier, but his older brother William, who had often entertained him with knowledgeable accounts of the Battles of Chancellorsville and Gettysburg, was convinced that there would be no war in Stephen's lifetime and that consequently he would not prosper as an army officer. Crane, therefore, sought a more practical outlet for his ambitions in the mining-engineering course at Lafayette College, but he departed from Claverack with deep regret. Later he would write ambivalently on the reverse of a photo of the school (NSyU) that it was "A place around which tender (?) memories cling."

At Lafayette, Crane joined Delta Upsilon fraternity, played intramural baseball, and roomed by himself in the rear of East Hall, where, according to Ernest G. Smith of the class of 1894, he terrified a group of hazing sophomores who broke down his door by confronting them with a revolver. Apart from his fraternity activities, it is unlikely that Crane enjoyed much social life in his few months as a Lafayette student. The 1894 issue of *Melange*, the yearbook of the junior class published in 1893, contains an article entitled "Our Departed" in which Crane is contrasted with a classmate who had the same surname:

> Funny fowls were these two Cranes,
> Steve had wit and Dwight had brains,

> Dwight was short and Steve was tall,
> One had grit, the other gall.

The writer may well have had confused memories of the two Cranes. Stephen was considered sententious and withdrawn rather than witty by his fraternity brothers at Syracuse. Clarence Peaslee correctly describes him as "under the average height" (Crane was approximately 5'7") and "very gritty."

Crane received grades in four courses for the term ending in December: 60 in algebra, 88 in French, 92 in elocution and 0 in theme writing. (The "themes" would have had to be on his technical area of specialization and not general subjects.) His excessive absences probably prevented his being graded in other courses. After the Christmas holidays he returned briefly to Lafayette, although the semester was over. Despite his academic deficiencies, he was not, as is often stated, asked to leave the college. He transferred at the insistence of his mother, who believed that as the grand nephew of Bishop Jesse Truesdell Peck, one of the founders of Syracuse University, Stephen was entitled to a scholarship at the Methodist institution.

Stephen stayed briefly with the Bishop's widow before moving into the Delta Upsilon house at Syracuse. He registered as a science major. Anna E. Wells of Port Jervis remembered him at this time as "slender and pale" with "the look of a student," but according to his teammate, Mansfield J. French, he devoted most of his energies to baseball and won local acclaim as catcher and sometimes shortstop of the Syracuse varsity team. The legend that he was offered a position on a major baseball team originated with Thomas Beer and is unsubstantiated and improbable.

At the end of the semester, Crane had earned only a single grade, an "A" in English literature. Much of the time had been spent interviewing criminals and prostitutes in the Putnam police court and exploring the shabby entertainment district of the city as correspondent for the *New York Tribune*, but his greatest journalistic success of this period was not a piece of literary realism but a hoax, "Great Bugs in Onondaga," which appeared in the *Tribune* on 1 June 1891. Crane reported that a locomotive hauling stones from limestone quarries located between Jamesville and Syracuse was halted by huge bugs with armor-like shells that swarmed along the tracks and died with explosive crackling sounds as they were crushed under the wheels. In a May 1891 issue of the

University Herald, he published a humorous sketch, "The King's Favor," based on an interview with the prominent tenor Albert G. Thies at Claverack the previous spring. He followed this up with a Sullivan County sketch, "The Cry of a Huckleberry Pudding," which appeared in the 23 December 1892 issue of the *Herald*, long after Crane had left the campus. As at Lafayette, Crane's departure from Syracuse University seems to have been entirely voluntary rather than at the suggestion of the administration. By the spring of 1891, he had determined that his future was in writing and that continued attendance at college would not advance his career.

Legend has it that a draft of *Maggie* was written in the Delta Upsilon house at Syracuse. Clarence L. Peaslee remembered Crane's discussing the story with his fraternity brothers, and Frank Noxon recalled manuscript sheets of *Maggie* lying about the room Crane shared with Clarence N. Goodwin. But Goodwin himself and another fraternity brother, Frederic M. Lawrence, relegate the composition of the novelette to the autumn of 1892, when Crane roomed with Lawrence in the boarding house on Avenue A in Manhattan he named the Pendennis Club. Crane may have sketched out a story about a prostitute in his final semester of college, but the satires and burlesques he was writing at this time in what he later called his "clever, Rudyard Kipling style"—"The King's Favor," "A Foreign Policy in Three Glimpses," and "The Camel"—lack the impressionistic realism and illusion-shattering irony of the Bowery novelette. If there was a Syracuse version of *Maggie*, it must have been very different from the book Crane published two years later. Although Crane's experiences on the drill fields of Claverack and as an athlete and fledgling newspaper correspondent in his single year of college contributed significantly to his development as a writer, he had yet, as he later expressed it, to acquire his artistic education on the Bowery.

1888-1893

1. TO E. L. GRAY, JR.[1]
Inscribed on a leaf from a lost autograph album, ViU.

Whist

Very Sincerely
Your F'riend
S. T.[2] Crane
New York City

C.C.&H.R.I.   March 27, 1888

[1]A classmate at Claverack College and Hudson River Institute (C.C.&H.R.I.).
[2]Stephen was alone among the fourteen Crane children in having no middle name; his namesake, the Revolutionary War Stephen Crane, a New Jersey delegate to the Continental Congress, did not have one. Nevertheless, at Claverack he occasionally used the middle initial "T." As Cora Crane explained in her Note Book (NNC), written shortly after Stephen's death, "When at Claverick [sic] he was ashamed of being only boy without middle name so called himself Stephen *D*. Crane." Despite the emphasis Cora gives the letter, "D" undoubtedly represents her faulty recollection of the "T" Crane told her he had used at Claverack, a likely choice because Townley was the middle name of his father as well as of his brother and sister, Jonathan and Elizabeth.

2. TO ODELL HATHAWAY[1]
Letters, p. 6.

Asbury Park
Xmas morning [1888 or 1889]

Hello central:
hello:

Give me tough Hathaway, Middletown Well, old man, I hope you are having a merry, merry X'mas. I expect to stop up and see you as I promised but cant tell for sure yet. Johnnie wrote me that he was afraid he couldn't show up, but would try. I expect to go to P.J. in a few days and on my way back will stop and see you I heard from Puzey and I also heard a voice from Mich.[2] say he had not left my overcoat on the route. Write me here at A.P. Merry Xmas to you and all your friends.

Yours sincerely
Stephen Crane

[1] A Schoolmate of Crane at Claverack. Hathaway was a resident of Middletown, New York. Transcriptions of Crane's letters to him were made available to R. W. Stallman by Odell Hathaway, Jr. The holographs were apparently retained by the family, with the exception of No. 8, which was donated to the Syracuse University chapter of Delta Upsilon fraternity.

[2] Probably a schoolmate from Michigan to whom Crane lent his coat and who had written Crane assuring him that he had not lost it en route home for the Christmas holidays.

3. TO ARMISTEAD BORLAND[1]
Inscribed in an autograph album, NSyU.

You little Annex[2]—
That *would be* on a level
With desperados and the like
F'our to one

Isn't much fun
For the fellow the kids go to fight
Very sincerely
Your friend
Stephen T. Crane
N.Y.C.

C.C.&H.R.I.
April 4, 1889

[1] Armistead ("Tommie") Borland, a Claverack schoolmate from Norfolk, Virginia. In his unpublished biography, "Flagon of Despair: Stephen Crane" (NSyU), Melvin H. Schoberlin quotes passages that Borland apparently wrote to him: " 'I was only a kid of fourteen and "Steve" was my hero and ideal. I must have been somewhat of a nuisance to him always hanging around—sometimes when I was not wanted. I tried to copy him in every way and learned many things, not all for the good of my immortal soul—the rudiments of the great American game of poker and something more than the rudiments of the ways of a man with a maid' " (p. V-17).

Borland felt that Crane was "a congenital introvert, and his intimacy with other men was out of character and went only so far as was necessary to give the appearance of normal behavior. . . . He had no intimates and was not *popular* and didn't want to be; he would have scorned the idea of popularity. . . . He was extremely irregular in his habits—a law unto himself, indifferent [!] to the opinions of others who might be critical of him, reserved and more or less difficult to approach. He was slow to anger but became viciously ungovernable when aroused" (p. V-9).

[2] Harvey Wickham, another schoolmate, in "Stephen Crane at College," *American Mercury*, 7 (March 1926), 291, reports that by the time Crane arrived at Claverack College, the reputation of the school had declined: "The college, in fact, had become all absorbed in the Hudson River Institute—a mere boarding school. . . . and the Institute itself was being eaten into by an annex, which was not up to the level of even a high school. Old Claverack was dead."

4. TO ARMISTEAD BORLAND
Inscribed in an autograph album, NSyU.

Ah! Tommie! when you
get back to Dixie, remember
how often you used to
be fired out of #117[1] and

how you always came
directly in again.
Your sincere friend
Stephen Crane

C.C.&H.R.I.
March 10, 1890

[1] In "Flagon of Despair: Stephen Crane," p. V-5, Schoberlin writes that Crane was assigned at Claverack "to cubicle 117 'Flack Alley,' as the third-floor corridor of the boys' dormitory was commonly called." The corridor was named after the Reverend Arthur H. Flack, who succeeded his father as president of the school.

5. TO ODELL HATHAWAY
Letters, pp. 6-7.

Asbury Park
Sunday, June 15, 1890

My dear "Tough"

I thought I would enjoy writing to you today, as I am home with lots of friends, yet, longing for some of my old companions at Old Claverack. I am smoking a cigar after a 10.00 AM breakfast of roast pigeon and gooseberries yet I wish to God I was puffing on a cigarette butt after a 7.00 AM breakfast of dried-beef and oat meal at H.R.I. If you see Tuttle[1] give him my kindest regards and tell him to write. Goodbye, old man, write to me. I dont forget my friends and you will always have my best wishes.

Yours ever
Stephen Crane

[1] Hiram B. Tuthill.

6. TO ODELL HATHAWAY
Letters, p. 7.

[Lafayette College, September or October 1890]

Dear Boys,

I send you a piece of the banner we took away from the Sophemores [*sic*] last week. It dont look like much does it? Only an old rag, ain't it? But just remember I got a *black and blue nose,* a barked shin, skin off my hands and a lame shoulder, in the row you can appreciate it. So, keep it, and when you look at it think of me scraping [*sic*] about twice a week over some old rag that says "Fresh '94" on it.[1]

Stephen Crane

[1] Crane's college letters belie the legend perpetuated in Thomas Beer's biography of the young American artist, scorned and isolated in a Philistine society. Crane joined a fraternity, played baseball, flirted with girls, and participated enthusiastically in the annual freshman-sophomore tug of war at Lafayette College. He did everything expected of him except study.

7. TO A CLAVERACK COLLEGE SCHOOLMATE
ALS, NSyU.

#170 East Hall Lafayette College.
[November? 1890]

My dear boy,

Your letter gladly recd. So you are not having a hell of a time at C.C., eh? Well, you had better have it now because, mark my words, you will always regret the day you leave old C.C. The fellows here raise more hell than any college in the country, yet I have still left a big slice of my heart up among the pumpkin seeds and farmers of Columbia Co. You asked me if I thought as much of Pete[1] as ever. Well, I should think so, and a great deal more besides, and don't you forget it. We both may possibly come up on Thanksgiving and you fellows whom I still love as of old, must give us a jolly time. So long, old man, don't forget me even if I can't be at C.C.

> Yours, as ever
> Stephen Crane

[1] Phebe English, Crane's Claverack College schoolmate.

8. TO ODELL HATHAWAY
TT,[1] NSyU.

> Delta Upsilon Chapter House
> Syracuse N.Y.
> Jan 9th. 1891.

My dear Hathaway,

Those pictures have not come yet and neither has any letters from the little crowd of tough devils who hang out in Sioux's[2] room. I ate like a fiend as soon as I got away from Claverack and am eating like a devil, now, every chance I get. What has Harry had to say to you since I have been gone? Has he jumped on the mob any more? If he has, damn him. The ΔY Chapter here has got a dandy house valued at $20,000.00, situated on a high hill overlooking the entire city. I hope you may all come here sometime, although the fellows here *are* somewhat slow. Yet, . . . [portion of letter missing]. . . . As I said before to Sioux, there are certainly some dam pretty girls here, praised be to God.[3] Not as nice as they as [sic] are in Newburgh, however. There is where the dandy girls are found. Gene has got an awful big belly on him, but he is the same old Gene as of old, good-natured, jolly and sociable. Travis[4] still keeps his same military step that he once used with such success in H.R.I. Brusie[5] is just such a chap that he was; hard, dry, cold and calculating. . . . [portion of letter missing] . . . [This is a] dandy city at least and I expect to see some fun here.

Well here is where I must stop. Give my love to everyone in the old crowd and don't forget this poor devil.

Yours always
Stephen Crane

---

[1] In recent successive moves of the Syracuse chapter of Delta Upsilon from one fraternity house to another, the holograph has been lost.

[2] Sioux was Earl T. Reeve, also nicknamed the Rushville Indian by Crane because he came from Rushville, Indiana.

[3] In "Flagon," Schoberlin quotes Armistead Borland as saying that Crane " 'never ran after any girl. He had a personality and physical appearance—for he was indeed physically attractive without being handsome—that made them curious about him. The mystery and reserve that seemed a part of him accentuated his attraction for the sex. . . . He had, as a boy, a very high inception of personal honor, but I do not think it was proof against favors thrown at him by women to whom he was attracted' " (p. V-22).

[4] Abram Lincoln Travis taught at Claverack for a year after his graduation from Syracuse University and established the Travis Classical School in Syracuse.

[5] Sanford Brusie, like many of Crane's D.U. brothers in the Syracuse University chapter, became a Methodist clergyman.

New York City

The newspaper world of New York City in the Mauve Decade clustered along a triangle of land formed by the junction of Park Row, Spruce, and Nassau Streets, where the offices of the *Tribune, Times, Sun,* and *World* shared the neighborhood with cheap eating houses and disreputable saloons harboring "peter players" who administered knockout drops to potential robbery victims. Close by was the Bowery, the rowdy, glittering Broadway of the lower East Side with its show palaces, brothels, flop houses, and disorderly dance halls. In the autumn of 1891, from the sanctuary of his brother Edmund's home in Lake View, then a suburb of Paterson and now incorporated into that city, Crane made excursions into the slums of lower Manhattan. He was writing Sullivan County sketches, the first of which appeared in the *Tribune* in February 1892; but with the encouragement of experienced journalists who recognized his talent, like Willis F. Johnson, the *Tribune*'s day editor, he was also learning to evoke the Bowery ambience in graphically realistic pen portraits. Crane's earliest New York City sketch, "Travels in New York: The Broken-Down Van" (*Tribune*, 10 July 1892), presents an impressionistic montage of a downtown street blocked by a huge furniture van with a broken wheel. A young girl stepping over the platform of a horse car stalled behind the van anticipates Maggie: "a sixteen-year-old girl without any hat and with a roll of half-finished vests under her arm crossed the front platform of the green car. As she stepped up on to the sidewalk a barber from a ten-cent shop said 'Ah! there!' and she answered 'smarty!' with withering scorn and went down a side street. A few drops of warm summer rain began to fall."

Johnson remembers that when he accepted two Sullivan County sketches for the *Tribune* in the summer of 1891, Crane also showed him a manuscript of *Maggie*, but it is probable that Johnson's 1891 is an error or misprint for 1892. In Hamlin Garland's contradictory reminiscences of Crane, he recalls reading *Maggie* only in book form; yet in an undated note to Richard Watson Gilder, editor of the *Century Magazine*, he enthusiastically recommends to him a draft of the novellete that he most likely saw when he met Crane for the second time in Asbury Park in the summer of 1892. Post Wheeler remembers Crane's telling him that Garland sent the manuscript of *Maggie* to Gilder, but Crane rewrote *Maggie* in the house on Avenue A near 57th Street, where he roomed with Frederic M. Lawrence, and brought it to the *Century* editor sometime in the winter of 1892-93.

Even without Garland's endorsement, Crane would almost inevitably have come to Gilder with *Maggie*. Gilder, also the son of a Methodist minister from New Jersey, had visited the Cranes occasionally during Stephen's childhood and previous to that had founded a short-lived newspaper, the *Newark Morning Register*, with his uncle, R. Newton Crane. Gilder took an active part in tenement reform and opened the pages of the *Century* to moralistic essays deploring the squalor of the New York slums. But the Crane-Gilder interview would have gone very much the way Thomas Beer describes it. Despite his social concerns, Gilder was essentially a conservative and was shocked by the blasphemy and profanity in *Maggie*. He believed that fiction should be elevating, and *Maggie* was, as Crane put it, "too honest" for the genteel readers of the *Century*.

There is little evidence that Crane attempted to interest other publishers in *Maggie*. Johnson, writing almost thirty-five years after the ostensible event, asserts that Ripley Hitchcock, the literary advisor to D. Appleton & Co. and later editor of *The Red Badge of Courage*, "appreciated the merits" of *Maggie*, "but hesitated to recommend its acceptance." In his preface to the memorial edition of *The Red Badge* (1900), however, written three days after Crane's death, Hitchcock narrates that Crane walked into the Appleton office in December 1894 "bringing two short stories as examples of the work which he was then doing for the newspapers" and "was asked if he had a story long enough for publication in book form." Crane responded "hesitatingly that he had written one rather long story," *The Red Badge*, which was then being syndicated in newspapers. Appleton's did publish a stylistically improved and somewhat expurgated version of *Maggie* in 1896 under Hitchcock's editorship, and it is unlikely that he originally rejected the slum novelette. In any event, Crane had it printed at his own expense. Lawrence comments that "he went to a little printing shop on lower Sixth Avenue whose sign we had often noticed. They set a price and it was agreed to without demur." According to Thomas Beer, Crane complained he had paid an exorbitant bill of $869 for 1,100 copies. "A firm of religious and medical printers did me the dirt," he lamented. Reginald W. Kauffman seems to have originated the legend that Crane helped with the typesetting. Crane's contemporaries also disagree about the source of the money required for the paperback edition. R. G. Vosburgh believed that it came from his father's estate, but Lawrence maintains that it was inherited from his mother, who died in December 1891. Johnson says that Crane borrowed the money, and this is amplified by Beer, who states that Crane's brother William lent him $1,000. According to Helen R. Crane, *Maggie* was financed through the sale of some coal mining stock Stephen inherited from his father with the addition of a small loan from William. The origin of the *nom de plume* under which the book appeared is also in dispute. Post Wheeler recalls proposing it to Crane as a joke. Lawrence reports that Crane wished to disguise the authorship of a book that would offend his prudish relatives, and the jest consisted in elevating the plebian "Johnson Smith" into a more aristocratic pseudonym. According to Johnson, Crane chose the two most common surnames in the New York City directory and whimsically added a "t" to the first. Crane told Corwin K. Linson that "the alias was a mere chance. 'Commonest name I could think of. I had an editor friend named Johnson, and put in the "t," and no one could find me in the mob of Smiths.' "

Crane met Linson, a painter and magazine illustrator who had studied in Paris, shortly before the publication of *Maggie*. It was on a divan in Linson's studio at West 30th Street and Broadway in the spring of 1893 that he leafed through old copies of the *Century Magazine* containing the series "Battles and Leaders of the Civil War," which provided much of the military background for *The Red Badge of Courage*. He spent most of the summer at his brother Edmund's home in Lake View, hard at work on the war novel. When he returned to the City in October, he moved into one of the large studios of the old Needham building on East

23rd Street with several young artists and illustrators, among them Frederic Gordon, Nelson Greene, David Ericson, and R. G. Vosburgh, who had remained in the rambling, gloomy structure after the Art Students' League secured new quarters on 57th Street. Here and in other studios and lofts where he found temporary shelter, Crane completed *The Red Badge* and wrote much of the poetry of *The Black Riders*. He described his bohemian life among these "Indians," as he called them in *The Third Violet* and in two sketches, "Stories Told by an Artist" and "The Silver Pageant." It was a poverty-stricken, but essentially carefree, existence. Crane told Hamlin Garland that "they all slept on the floor, dined off buns and sardines, and painted on towels or wrapping paper for lack of canvas." Frequently, Crane's poverty would make it necessary for him to retreat to Hartwood, a tiny village in Sullivan County where his brother Edmund had bought a house in the spring of 1894. It was the closest thing to a home Crane would have during his adult years in America.

Not as a stranger, therefore, did Crane write about the city's poor, for he often shared their condition. His empathy with social outcasts is evident in his depictions of experiences he shared with them on a charity bread line and on a blizzardy night in February 1894 when he and an illustrator friend spent the night in a Bowery flophouse. In "The Men in the Storm" and "An Experiment in Misery," Crane exposes the horrors endured not only by incorrigible tramps but by thousands of young drifters who came to the City seeking their fortunes and, unable to adapt to the grinding competitiveness, were relegated to the world of bread lines, missions, and lodging houses. But unlike his mentor, Hamlin Garland, or William Dean Howells, who favored *Maggie* above all his writings, Crane never formulated convictions about the causes of social injustice. His aesthetic aim was to set forth reality as objectively as possible, and he considered preaching "fatal to art in literature."

When Crane finished *The Red Badge of Courage* early in 1894, he attempted to place it in one of the popular magazines. For a time he believed that the novel had been accepted by McClure's syndicate and magazine, which later in the year sponsored his muckraking article, "In the Depths of a Coal Mine." But McClure, made cautious by the prevailing financial crisis, hesitated to commit himself to an unknown author and stalled until Crane was "near mad," as he wrote Garland,

and took *The Red Badge* to the rival syndicate of Bacheller, Johnson and Bacheller, who published a condensed and truncated version in December in a number of newspapers throughout the United States. In January 1895 Crane set off on an extensive trip through the West and Mexico to write feature articles for the Bacheller syndicate. Following his return in May, he spent most of the summer idling about New York City, Hartwood, and Twin Lakes in Pike County, Pennsylvania, until the book publication of *The Red Badge* by D. Appleton in New York and William Heinemann in London in the autumn of 1895 projected him into fame.

9. TO ODELL HATHAWAY
Letters, pp. 10-11.

> Lake View, N.J.
> Feb. 10, 92

Dear old man: Are you dead? Why dont you write to a fellow? I think you owe me a letter, you terrier. I received a letter from the Rushville Indian.[1] He is well, and evidently happy. He says he is "going to be married to a girl whom" he "really loves." See?

I often think of you, old man, and wonder what has become of you and if you ever think of the old times at C.C. and remember your old friends.

Write to me, now, damn you.

> Yours always truly
> Stephen Crane

[1] Earl T. Reeve.

10. TO ARMISTEAD BORLAND
ALS, NSyU.

>Port Jervis N Y
>F'eb 16, 92

My dear Tommie:—

I was delighted to hear from you. So poor Tommie is in hell is he? Never mind, my boy, I remember when you used to cuss at Claverack and swear it was the damndest hole on earth. I really suppose you would rail at your lot if you were placed on the right-hand side of God almighty in Heaven with nine angels to fan you and a caravan heavily loaded with mint-julips, in the immediate fore-ground. Go to, Thomas, thou art a bird, a regular damned bird.

So you lack females of the white persuasion, do you? How unfortunate! And how extraordinary! I never thought that the world could come to such a pass that you would lack females, Thomas! You indeed must be in a God forsaken country.

Just read these next few lines in a whisper:—I—I think black is quite good—if—if its yellow and young.

I will proceed directly to write to Jones, P. He was a nice boy. He and Tommie were the only two kids I ever cared much about.

Perhaps, you have noticed this pen is damnably bad and that I am writing this letter with great difficulty. You are very right in that case. Therefore appreciate this more.

Pete[1] said she would like to hear from you. Why don't you write to her? "#75 Sip Ave, Jersey City Heights."

I heard from Johns[2] by the same mail that brought your letter. He is hanging out in Ypsilanti Michigan, wherever in hell that may be. Send me Red F'oster's address[3] if you have it.

Take care of yourself, always assure yourself of my distinguished consideration and you will be very happy. Good-bye and Good luck and nice girls to you, my dear Tommie

>Always yours affectionately
>S. C.

—Write often—

[1] Phebe English.
[2] H. B. Johns, nicknamed "Red Sioux" because he came from Sioux City, Iowa.
[3] F. H. Foster of New York City.

11. TO *THE DELTA UPSILON QUARTERLY*
The Delta Upsilon Quarterly, 10 (May 1892), 264.

Asbury Park, N.J.
[spring 1892]

I have no intention of allowing my interest in the Fraternity to wane, and of course would be delighted to subscribe again for the *Quarterly*.

12. TO THE MANAGER OF THE AMERICAN PRESS ASSOCIATION
Letterhead: "Memorandum/ The/ New Jersey Coast News Bureau/ J. Townley Crane, Manager,/ Stephen Crane, Secretary,/ Edgar C. Snyder, Treasurer."
ALS, CSmH.

To Manager
The American Press Asso.
NY

Asbury Park, N.J., August 25 1892

My dear sir:

I am going south and, also, west this fall[1] and would like to know I could open up a special article trade with you. I have written special articles for some years for the Tribune and other papers. Much of my work has been used by the various press associations; and I would like to deal directly with you if possible. Kindly let me know if it would be worth my while to send you copy for consideration.

Yours very truly
Stephen Crane.

[1]Crane preferred travel and war correspondence to metropolitan newspaper reporting. As this letter reveals, he projected a journey to the South and West two and a half years before he obtained a commission to tour these areas for the Bacheller-Johnson Newspaper Syndicate.

13. TO LUCIUS L. BUTTON[1]
Letterhead: "Pendennis Club./ 1064 Eastern Boulevard."
ALS, NSyU.

Lake View, N.J.
Wednesday. [14 December 1892]

My dear Button:

I was glad to be made aware by your genial pen that the dragon is sad because I have escaped her. But if she be vindictive, I will have my revenge. I have had a dog given me. And I am seriously thinking of inflicting it on our admirable land-lady after Christmas. It is a mere little fox-terrier with a nose like a black bead and a pedigree as long as your arm. It evinces a profound tendency to raise the devil on all occasions, which it does, mostly, by tearing up gloves, and wading around in any butter plate, mince-pie, or cake which it may percieve at large. It also has a violent antipathy to larger dogs, cats, and all fowls of the air. Withal, it is a meek little thing when in human presence and keeps it's black, white and tan coat spotlessly clean. If I can prevail upon our dear, domestic tyrant to let me pay it's board, I shall certainly bring it down after Christmas. I adore dogs. I think I shall be again at the Pendennis Club tomorrow night to see you fellows before you all hie away for Christmastide.

I am gratified that you remembered me by your note of this evening and, meanwhile, I remain, my dear boy,

Yours always,
Stephen Crane.

[1]Lucius Lucine Button was one of the medical students who shared lodgings with Crane during the fall and winter of 1892-93 in the boarding house on Avenue A that they referred to as "The Pendennis Club." Button received one of the first of the

privately printed copies of *Maggie* inscribed by Crane, and it was he who took Crane to the tea on 34th Street at which he met Nellie Crouse.

14. TO THE LIBRARIAN OF CONGRESS
ALS on stationery of the Pendennis Club, DLC.

1064 Eastern Boulevard
N.Y.
[about 18 January 1893]

Librarian of Congress:

Enclosed find a printed copy of the title page of a book written by me,[1] and one dollar, for which please send a copy of the record of the copyright which is applied for. to

Stephen Crane

[1] Received by the Library of Congress on 19 January 1893. The typewritten title page read simply: "A Girl of the Streets,/ A Story of New York./ —By—/ Stephen Crane." The name "Maggie" was added later, perhaps at the suggestion of Crane's brother William.

15. TO FRANK VER BECK[1]
"A Night in Bohemia," *The Saturday Evening Post*, 6 February 1904, p. 17.[2]

[January-March 1893]

Dear Verby: Your tiger-skin got loose last night and did great damage along Broadway. Finally captured and taken to the Tenderloin station.

Steve May.
Phil Crane.

[1] William Francis ("Frank") Ver Beck (1858-1933) was an illustrator living in New York City.

[2] This article recounts the only known connection among Ver Beck, Crane, and Phil May (1864-1903). May was a popular British artist and illustrator of books and magazines, especially *Punch*, who came to America for *The Daily Graphic* (England) during the 1893 Chicago World's Fair. Crane and May borrowed Ver Beck's tiger skin to keep warm one night while they strolled up Broadway. When a policeman discovered them at 3:30 A.M., he took them to the station and eventually freed them but kept the skin. The next morning Ver Beck received this note. Crane playfully exchanged the names "Steve" and "Phil."

16. TO BRANDER MATTHEWS[1]
ALS, NNC.

#1064 Ave A. N.Y.C.
March 21st, 93

Mr Brander Matthews

My dear sir: By same mail I send you a very small book which Mr Hamlin Garland thinks will interest you. If you write me what you think of it, you would confer a great favor.

Faithfully yours
Stephen Crane.

[1] Professor of English at Columbia University and a dramatist, critic, and novelist noted for his precise, fastidious style. Matthews might seem a curious choice as a recipient of *Maggie*, but his willingness to accept new directions in literature and his interest in tenement life as "local color" probably motivated Garland to suggest that Crane send him a copy. Matthews' article about his adventures in the slums appeared more than a year later ("In Search of Local Color," *Harper's New Monthly Magazine*, 89 [June 1894], 33-40). Unfortunately, his reaction to *Maggie*, if any, is not preserved.

17. TO JULIUS CHAMBERS[1]
ALS, PHi.

#1064 Ave A. New York City
March 22, 93

Mr Julius Chambers

My dear sir: By same mail I send you a small book which our friend Mr Hamlin Garland thinks you will be pleased with. If you are, you would confer a great favor upon me, the author, if you would write to me of it.

Faithfully, yours
Stephen Crane

[1] James Julius Chambers (1850-1920) was managing editor of Pulitzer's *New York World* until 1891. He was a prolific writer who published travel literature, newspaper correspondence, some two hundred short stories, and several volumes of fiction. Two of his plays were produced in New York.

18. FROM JOHN D. BARRY[1]
Letterhead: "The Forum, Union Square, New York./ Editor's Room."
ALS, NSyU.

March 22, 1893.

My dear Mr. Crane:

Thank you very much for sending me your book. It reached me on my return after an absence of several days from the city. Otherwise, I should have acknowledged it sooner. I have read it with the deepest interest. It is pitilessly real and it produced its effect upon me—the effect, I presume, that you wished to produce, a kind of horror. To be frank with you, I doubt if such literature is good: it closely approaches the morbid and the morbid is always dangerous. Such a theme as yours, in my judgment, ought not to be treated so brutally—pardon the word—as you have treated it: you have painted too black a picture, with no light whatever to your shade. I know one might say that the truth was black and that you tried to describe it just as it was; but, one ought always to bear in mind that literature is an art, that effect, the effect upon the reader, must always be kept in view by the artist and as soon as that effect approaches the morbid, the unhealthful, the art becomes diseased. It is the taint in the peach. I really believe that the lesson of your story is good, but I believe, too, that you have driven that lesson too hard. There must be moderation even in well-doing; excess of enthusiasm in reform is apt to be dangerous. The mere brooding upon evil conditions, especially those concerned with the relation of the sexes, is the most dangerous and the most sentimental of all brooding, and I don't think that it often moves to action, to actual reform work. This, it seems to me, is just the kind of brooding your book inspires. I presume you want to make people think about the horrible things you describe. But of what avail is their thought unless it leads them to work? It would be better for them not to think about these things at all—if thinking ends as it began, for in itself it is unpleasant and in its tendency unhealthful.

Then, too, you give too complete a picture of the vulgar and profane talk of your characters; much less of this would be more effective and less offensive. The finest art in the writing of fiction is in suggestion. It seems to me, for example, that you have over-worked the expression, "What deh Hell?" I find it hard to believe that it would be used at all in several of the situations in which your characters have used it. But, of course, I may be all wrong about this.

But, after all my strictures (I know you will pardon them for I offer them in sincerity), I must acknowledge that there is horror in your book. I believe you have real ability and I hope you will try something else. I would endeavor, if I were you, to study the thoughts as well as the acts of characters. You seem to me to have observed from the outside only. I have little idea of Maggie's personality; she is not much more than a mere figure to me. You have been most successful in drawing her mother, I think.

I offer you these thoughts about your book—not because I think they are worth much—but because you have been so kind as to send it to me and to ask me for my opinion. I should like to talk it over further with you and should be most happy to meet you. Won't you call here some day this week?

Very truly yours,
John D. Barry

[1] Assistant editor of the *Forum* since 1890. Barry's letter is among the earliest critical responses to *Maggie* and exemplifies the unpreparedness of the American literary establishment in the late nineteenth century to accept fictional presentations of the wretched living conditions of the urban poor unadulterated by sentimental pleas for reform. Barry was much more receptive to the experimental poems of *The Black Riders* and read a selection of them to the Uncut Leaves Society in Manhattan on Saturday evening 14 April 1894 because Crane said that "he would rather die than do it." Most likely Barry put Crane in touch with Copeland and Day, the publishers of *The Black Riders*.

19. TO WILLIAM DEAN HOWELLS
ALS, MH.

#1064 Ave A.
March 28, 93

My dear Mr Howells: I sent you a small book some weeks ago. Mr. Garland had, I believe, spoken to you of it. Having recieved no reply I must decide then that you think it a wretched thing?

Yours faithfully
Stephen Crane.

20. FROM WILLIAM DEAN HOWELLS
ALS, NNC.

40 West 59th st.,
March 2e [28 or 29], 1893.

Dear Mr. Crane:

I have not yet had a moment to read the book you so kindly sent me. From the glance I was able to give it, I thought you were working in the right way. When I have read it, I will write you again.

Yours sincerely,
W. D. Howells.

21. TO LUCIUS L. BUTTON
Inscribed on a copy of *Maggie*,[1] Collection of Daniel G. Siegel, Weston, Massachusetts.

[March? 1893]

Stephen Crane
to Budgon.

It is inevitable that you be great{ly}
shocked by this book but continue, plea{se,}
with all possible courage, to the end. For, {it}
tries to show that environment is a tremend{ous}
thing in the world and frequently shapes liv{es}
regardless. If one proves that theory, one makes room {in}
Heaven for all sorts of souls, notably an occasional
street girl, who are not confidently expected to be
there by many excellent people.

It is probable that the reader of this small thi{ng}
may consider the author to be a bad man, bu{t,}
obviously, that is a matter of small consequence to

The Au{thor}

52

¹Crane sent copies of *Maggie* with almost identical inscriptions to a number of his friends and to a few crusading reformers who ignored the book.

22. TO HAMLIN GARLAND
Inscribed on a copy of *Maggie*, InU.

[March? 1893]

It is inevitable that you be gre{atly}
shocked by this book but continue, ple{ase,}
with all possible courage to the end. F'or {it}
tries to show that environment is a tremend{ous}
thing in the world and frequently shapes live{s}
regardless. If one proves that theory, one make{s}
room in Heaven for all sorts of souls (notabl{y}
an occasional street girl) who are not confiden{tly}
expected to be there by many excellent people.

It is probable that the reader of this small thing ma{y}
consider The Author to be a bad man, but, obviously, th{is}
is a matter of small consequence to

The *Auth*{or}

23. TO WILLIAM DEAN HOWELLS
ALS, MH.

1064 Ave A. New York
April 8, 93

Dear Mr Howells:

I write to find if you could write me a letter to Mr. Godkin of the *Evening Post*.¹ I am about to apply to him for work. I would like to get it without badgering people for recommendations, but I know I cant.

However, I have humiliating misgivings that you never do such things. If so, please forget that I have asked you.

Sincerely Yours
Stephen Crane.

[1] Edwin Laurence Godkin (1831-1902) edited the *New York Evening Post* and was founder and editor of the *Nation*.

24. FROM WILLIAM DEAN HOWELLS
ALS, NNC.

40 West 59th st.,
April 8, 1893.

Dear Mr. Crane:

I write you instead of Mr. Godkin, and you can show him my letter, if you like, which I wrote you about your book. You know how well I think you handled that subject, and if I could not agree with you on all points of theory, I thoroughly respected your literary conscience, and admired your literary skill.

Personally I know nothing of you except what you told me in our pleasant interview.[1] But I suppose you can readily establish your respectability to Mr. Godkin.

Yours sincerely,
W. D. Howells.

[1] Wearing a suit borrowed from his journalist friend John Northern Hilliard, Crane had tea or dinner with Howells in his home on what is now Central Park South one evening in the first week of April 1893. Howells read Crane some of Emily Dickinson's verses at this time, and her terse, cryptic lines may have influenced the style of *The Black Riders*.

25. TO LILY BRANDON MUNROE[1]
AL, ViU.

>1064 Ave A. NYC
>[April 1893]

Dearest L. B.

I am sure that you have not concluded that I have ceased to remember. The three months which have passed have been months of very hard work to S. Crane. I was trying to see if I was worthy to have you think of me. And I have waited to find out.

Well, at least, I've done something. I wrote a book. Up to the present time, I think I can say I am glad I did it. Hamlin Garland was the first to over-whelm me with all manner of extraordinary language. The book has made me a powerful friend in W. D. Howells. B. O. Flower of the "*Arena*"[2] has practically offered me the benefits of his publishing company for all that I may in future write. Albert Shaw of the "Review of Reviews" wrote me congratulations this morning and to-morrow I dine with the editor of the "Forum."

So I think I can say that if I "watch out", I'm almost a success. And "such a boy, too", they say.

I do not think, however, that I will get enough applause to turn my head. I don't see why I should. I merely did what I could, in a simple way, and recognition from such men as Howells, Garland, Flower and Shaw, has shown me that, I was not altogether reprehensible.

Any particular vanity in my work is not possible to me. I merely write you these things, to let you know why I was silent for so long.

I thought if I could measure myself by the side of some of the great men I could find if I was of enough value to think of you, L. B.

They tell me I did a horrible thing, but, they say, "its great."

"And it's style," said Garland to Howells, "Egad, it has no style! Absolutely transparent! Wonderful—wonderful."

And I? I have merely thought of you and wondered if you cared that they said these things. Or wether you have forgotten?

---

[1]Crane met Lily Brandon Munroe, then unhappily married to a geologist, at Asbury Park in the summer of 1892. She and Crane were very much in love, as she later told

Ames W. Williams, but she was too mature and practical to elope with an impetuous and impecunious young man some years her junior, and both their families were opposed to a union between them. Lily remembered that Crane was then writing *Maggie*—further testimony that a version of the slum novelette existed in 1892. Sometime after the date of this letter, Crane gave her the manuscript of *Maggie*, which her husband destroyed. Lilly subsequently obtained a divorce and married Frederick Smillie. She and Crane met again on several occasions between 1895 and 1898, but his repeated attempts to induce her to leave her husband for him failed.

[2] Benjamin Orange Flower, editor of the *Arena*, a crusading journal devoted to social amelioration in which many of Hamlin Garland's articles and stories appeared. In the *Arena* Crane was to publish "An Ominous Baby" (May 1894), a story about the Tommie of *Maggie*, who dies in infancy but here is seen as a threat to the children of the rich, and "The Men in the Storm" (October 1894), a brilliant impressionistic sketch of a crowd of outcasts waiting in a blizzard for the door of a charity lodging house to open.

26. TO CORWIN KNAPP LINSON
Photocopy of ALS, ViU.

Thursday. [summer 1893]
136 West 15th St

My dear C. K.: Fortunately, Senger[1] wrote me simaltaneously and enabled me to get your address, that I, might reply to your postal card.

Mr Barry is still out of town and in his absence it is impossible to get the stories you mention.

Have you finished the "Ominous Baby" story yet?[2] At the present time—during these labor troubles—is the best possible time to dispose of it. I am anxious to recieve it from you. Could not you send it to me shortly?

I hope you are having a jolly time in the wilderness.

Yours sincerely
Stephen Crane

[1] Louis C. Senger, Jr., an artist friend of Crane from Port Jervis, served as the model for the Tall Man of the Sullivan County sketches. Senger introduced Crane to Linson, his cousin, in January or February 1893.

[2] Linson illustrated "An Ominous Baby" and other Crane newspaper and magazine stories and reports, notably "In the Depths of a Coal Mine," which was syndicated

under various titles by S. S. McClure in a number of newspapers on Sunday, 22 July 1894, and appeared with Linson's illustrations in *McClure's Magazine*, 3 (August 1894), 195-209.

27. TO LILY BRANDON MUNROE
ALS, ViU.

c/o R. G. Vosburgh
143 E 23*d*
NY
[winter 1893-94?]

Dearest: Although I do not now know what I am to you, I can not keep from addressing you as you still are to me—dearest, the one of all. Many months—or a thousand years: I hardly know—have passed since we met and were comrades; I can readily see that, in that time, I have, perhaps, become a memory to you, a mere figure in a landscape of the past. And it is well for you if it so, and for it I must be glad. Yet you to me, are still a daily vision, a dream that is part of my life, blending itself with my occupations each day. Your face is a torturing thing, appearing to me always, with the lines and the smile that I love,—before me always this indelible picture of you with it's fragrance of past joys and it's persistent utterance of the present griefs which are to me tragic, because they say they are engraven for life. It is beyond me to free myself from the thrall of my love for you; it comes always between me and what I would enjoy in life—always—like an ominous sentence—the words of the parrot on the death-ship: "We are all damned."

And yet, would I escape from it? Not I. It is the better part. Many men have been thus; it is not for me to object to a pain that many have carried, with smiles. Besides, it is supremely true that I concieve those days with you well spent if they cost me years of discontent. It is better to have known you and suffered, than never to have known you. I would not exchange one little detail of memory of you; I would not give up one small remembrance of our companionship. Yet, with it, I suffer and I wished you to know it because you are a woman and though may value me as a straw, you will comprehend why I felt that I must tell you of it. For, surely, it is a small thing. I ask nothing of you in return. Merely that I may tell you I adore you; that you are the shadow and the light of my life;—the whole of it.

I go to Europe in about two weeks—a very short trip.[1] If you would write me before then I could take the memory of it with me. My address is: "Care of R. G. Vosburgh, No 143 East 23*d* St." Do this for me, dearest, for, though it is a weakness in me, I can hardly go without it. Even though you can only consistently be cold, do me this grace.

I have been in town long. I have had a strange life. I have recently heard that Tounley[2] is married. For that, I owe Dottie[3] a necklet. I am delighted to think I am in debt to her. I shall wait and get it in Paris.

The *Arena Co* brings out a book of mine this winter.[4] I wish you to get it, for it will show you how much I have changed. The Boston critics and Mr Howells think it quite extraordinary. I could prattle on here of the men who are now my friends and of the things I now hear—I am foolish enough to desire to tell you, for I wish you to think well of the man you have made.—still.—

Write me, dearest, for I need it. I may leave sooner for Europe than is now my plan. And in my infinitely lonely life it is better that I should have all the benefits you can say to me

Ever yours.
S. C.

[1] Crane did not go to Europe until March 1897, when he was engaged to report the Greco-Turkish War for Hearst's *New York Journal* and the London *Westminster Gazette*.

[2] Stephen's scapegrace brother, Jonathan Townley Crane, Jr., was familiarly referred to as "Tounley" or "Twonley." The diphthong "ow" in "Townley" was informally pronounced as "oo," as in "tooth," hence the phonetic spelling. See Nos. 285, 332, and 585.

[3] Dorothy Brandon, younger sister of Lily Brandon Munroe.

[4] Apparently, Crane negotiated with the Arena Company for a reissue of *Maggie*, but the book was first published commercially under Crane's name by D. Appleton and Company in June 1896.

28. TO ARTHUR D. FERGUSON

Inscribed on an 1893 copy of *Maggie*. Facsimile reproduction of item 129, Catalogue 4296 (28-29 January 1937), American Art Association Anderson Galleries.[1]

[1893]

S. C.

To my dear friend
Arthur D. F'erguson
who does not
hesitate to comprehend that
an occasional conscience may
appear in very strange places
By—The Maker—

[1] According to the catalogue of the sale, Ferguson, a resident of the Pendennis Club, "auctioned off a number of copies of *Maggie* to members of the club, the purpose of the auction being to help Crane, who was badly in need of money. Mr. Ferguson suggested this method of helping Crane, and the latter, to show his appreciation, presented Mr. Ferguson with the present copy."

1894

29. TO LUCIUS L. BUTTON
TT, NSyU.

PRINTERS' CASES

WOOD TYPE

HEBER WELLS,
Successor to
VANDERBURGH, WELLS & CO.,
8 Spruce St., near Nassau St.,
New York, Feb 20th 1894

My dear Budgon:

I write to save you the trouble of calling down this week as I shall be away until a week from Wednesday. I cant have the joy of meeting you at Koster and Bials either. Nevertheless, when I get all my damned books and things straightened out, we shall meet again.

Yours as ever
Stephen Crane

143 East 23d

30. FROM WILLIAM DEAN HOWELLS
ALS, NNC.

40 W 59, March 18, 1894.

Dear Mr. Crane:

I could not persuade Mr. Alden[1] to be of my thinking about your poems. I wish you had given them more form, for these things so striking would have found a public ready made for them; as it is they will have to make one.

Yours sincerely,
W. D. Howells.

Could you tell me where I could find a copy of *Maggie*?

---

[1]Henry Miller Alden, editor of *Harper's Magazine*. Despite Howells' advocacy of realism in fiction and experiments with prose style as represented by *Maggie*, he disapproved of free verse. Emily Dickinson's modernistic techniques, which he admired, extended the boundaries of nineteenth-century conventions of versification but did not abandon them.

31. TO LILY BRANDON MUNROE
AL, ViU.

143 East 23*d* St, N.Y.
Care, Vosburg
[March-April 1894]

Dearest: Truly, I feel that I have decieved you by not starting for Europe today or to-morrow but as a matter of fact, I had postponed it for two reasons. One was because my literary fathers—Howells and Garland—objected to it, and the other was because you had not answered my letter. I did not intend starting for Europe or anywheres else until I had given you sufficent opportunity to reply. It would have been a lonely business—to go so far without a word from you.

To speak, to tell you of my success, dear, is rather more difficult. My career has been more of a battle than a journey. You know, when I left you, I renounced the clever school in literature. It seemed to me that there must be something more in life than to sit and cudgel one's brains for clever and witty expedients.[1] So I developed all alone a little creed of art which I thought was a good one. Later I discovered that my creed was identical with the one of Howells and Garland and in this way I became involved in the beautiful war between those who say that art is man's substitute for nature and we are the most successful in art when we approach the nearest to nature and truth, and those who say—well, I don't know what they say. They don't, they can't say much but they fight villianously and keep Garland and I out of the big magazines. Howells, of course, is too powerful for them.

If I had kept to my clever Rudyard-Kipling style, the road might have been shorter but, ah, it wouldn't be the true road. The two years of fighting have been well-spent. And now I am almost at the end of it. This winter fixes me firmly. We have proved too formidable for them, confound them. They used to call me "that terrible, young radical", but now they are beginning to hem and haw and smile—those very old coons who used to adopt a condescending air toward me. There is an irony in the present situation, that I enjoy, devil take them for a parcel of old, cringing, conventionalized hens. In one magazine office, once, the editor kept me waiting for a good long hour and then made a cool apology in a careless manner that I wouldnt have used upon a dog. I stopped in at that office the other day to see the manager and the editor caught sight of me through the door of his office. "Ah, Crane, my dear boy," he said, "come in and have a cigar and a chat. I'm always glad to see you." And he made haste to be rid of an authoress of some kind who was haggling with him about a story. The bare-faced old grey-headed diplomatist, I wondered if he considered that I had lost my memory. "No—thanks—I'm in a hurry." He seemed really grieved.

I have two books coming out this spring.[2] I will send them to you. One, I think, will make an awful howl. I don't mind it in the least. And as my shorter work will presently begin to appear in the magazines, I will send them to you, also, if you care to have me.

If "Shore Acres" comes to Washington, I wish you would see it played. Young Franklin Garland in the caste is a great friend and Herne himself is a great admirer of my work, they say, so, really he must be a man of the most admirable perceptions,[3] you know. I have accepted his invitation to see the play next Monday night. Those critics whose opinions are valuable say that Herne is the hope of the American stage, so study him.

I think I shall stay in New York until my book can be sent to the publishers and then go to Europe. I was to go this week but waited until I could overcome the objections of those fellows and until I could hear from you. I shall let you know my new plans.

So, the colonel is in Washington? I lost his Brooklyn address but last week in my despair I was going over there to see if I couldn't find him. I had a vague idea of "Kent Ave", and the "Carleton House", and was going to make a search. Give him many assurances of my distinguished consideration and if he ever comes to New York—may th' divil fly away wid me but I'll open the largest bottle on Manhattan Island—no less.

Don't forget me, dear, never, never, never. For you are to me the only woman in life. I am doomed, I suppose, to a lonely existence of futile dreams. It has made me better, it has widened my comprehension of people and my sympathy with whatever they endure. And to it I owe whatever I have achieved and the hope of the future. In truth, this change in my life should prove of some value to me, for, ye gods, I have paid a price for it.

I write to our friend, the ever-loyal Miss Dottie Brandon by this same post—Heaven send her rest. Good-bye, beloved.

[1]Crane occasionally referred to his Sullivan County tales and sketches as "clever" writing.

[2]None of Crane's books appeared in 1894. He is probably referring to the anticipated reissue of *Maggie* by the Arena Company and *The Black Riders*, which was not published by Copeland and Day until May 1895. It is difficult to determine which of the two books Crane believed would "make an awful howl."

[3]James A. Herne's *Shore Acres* began its New York run on 30 October 1893 and transferred to Daly's Theatre on Christmas day, where it ran until late May 1894. Hamlin Garland shared quarters with his younger brother, Franklin, at 107 West 105th, and to this Harlem apartment Crane brought the manuscripts of his poems and *The Red Badge of Courage*.

32. FROM HAMLIN GARLAND
ALS, NNC.

April 17/94.

You'll find me at home any morning at 12. I'd like to know how things are going with you. I am going West on the 25*th*.

Yours sincerely
Hamlin Garland

33. TO HAMLIN GARLAND
ALS, CLSU.

111 West 33d St., City
Wednesday, P.M. [18 April 1894]

Dear Mr Garland: I have not been up to see you because of various strange conditions—notably, my toes are coming through one shoe and I have not been going out into society as much as I might. I hope you have heard about the Uncut Leaves affair. I tried to get tickets up to you but I couldn't succeed. I mail you last Sunday's *Press*.[1] I've moved now—live in a flat. People can come to see me now. They come in shools and say that I am a great writer. Counting five that are sold, four that are unsold, and six that are mapped out, I have fifteen short stories in my head and out of it. They'll make a book. The Press people pied some of Maggie as you will note

Yours sincerely.
Stephen Crane

---

[1] An interview by Edward Marshall with Howells in the 15 April 1894 issue of the *New York Press* quotes Howells' opinion that Crane "is very young, but he promises splendid things" and that *Maggie* is "a remarkable book." An anonymous review of *Maggie* in the same issue questions "if such brutalities are wholly acceptable in literature," but praises Crane above other American writers who had depicted slum life for his realistic and unsentimentalized presentation of its conditions.

34. FROM HAMLIN GARLAND
ALS, NNC.

April 22/94.

Dear Mr Crane:

I saw your study in the *Press* today.[1] It reads amazingly well. If you'll come to the stage door tomorrow night and ask for my brother he will hand you the $15,[2] and also a pass for "Margaret Fleming."

Dont trouble yourself about the borrowing, we all have to do that sometime. You'll soon be able to pay it back and more too. You're going to get on your feet mighty soon.

Yours sincerely
Hamlin Garland

[1] "An Experiment in Misery," *New York Press*, 22 April 1894, Part 3, p. 2.
[2] This loan enabled Crane to redeem the second half of the manuscript of *The Red Badge of Courage* from the typist.

35. TO LUCIUS L. BUTTON
ALS on a postcard advertising the May issue of *The Arena*, PEL.

[April-May 1894]

Dear Button—

Couldn't you drop in for awhile on Saturday night? Sanger,[1] Linson and others will be up.

Thine—
S. C.

[1] In all likelihood, Louis C. Senger, Jr.

36. TO FRANKLIN GARLAND[1]

Inscribed in a copy of *Maggie*, NN.

[April-May? 1894]

To Mr Franklin Garland from his friend.

[1] In a note written in 1930 and loosely inserted into this presentation copy of *Maggie*, Garland recalls: "In the spring of 1894, my brother Franklin and I were living in a furnished apartment on W. 105 St New York City. My brother, then an actor with James A. Herne's *Shore Acres* Co cooked our break-fasts and sometimes our luncheons. Stephen Crane who was living at this time with a group of artists on East 23rd Street, frequently shared our steak and coffee, and it was in token of his gratitude for my brother's food that he signed this copy of *Maggie*."

37. TO ODELL HATHAWAY

Letters, p. 12.

[Hartwood, Sullivan County, N.Y., spring 1894]

Hello, you old devil. I was going through here today on the Ontario & Western and thought I would drop you a line. How's things anyhow. You never answer a mans [sic] letters so thought you might be dead. Write to me at Hartwood Sullivan County, NY, or I'll come down and wipe you off the earth, the same as I used to at H.R.I.

Yours as ever
Stephen Crane

38. FROM HAMLIN GARLAND
ALS, NNC.

474 Elm st.
Chicago. Ill
May 8/94

Dear Mr Crane:

What is the state of things? Did M*c*Clures finally take that war story for serial rights?[1] Write me all the news. I shall be here until June 1*st* probably.

I am nicely located near the Lake and I am writing heavily each day. Keep me posted on New York affairs.

Yours as ever
Hamlin Garland

---

[1] In January or February 1894, Crane offered *The Red Badge* to the S. S. McClure Newspaper Features Syndicate for serialization; but McClure vacillated for months on whether or not to accept the war novel, and in desperation Crane submitted it to the recently formed Bacheller-Johnson Newspaper Syndicate. See No. 52.

39. TO HAMLIN GARLAND
ALS, CLSU.

111 West 33d St.,
May 9, 94.

Dear Mr Garland:—I have not written you because there has been little to tell of late. I am ploding along on the Press in a quiet and effective way. We now eat with charming regularity at least two times per day. I am content and am writing another novel which is a bird.[1] That poem—"The Reformer"—which I showed you in behind Daly's was lost somehow, so I dont think we can ever send it to the *Arena*. I can't remember a line of it.

I saw "*Hannele.*"² It's reason for being is back somewhere in the middle ages but as an irresponsible artistic achievement it's great. I sat and glowed and shivered.

When anything happens I'll keep you informed. I'm getting lots of free advertising. Everything is coming along nicely now. I have got the poetic spout so that I can turn it on or off. I wrote a decoration day thing for the *Press* which aroused them to enthusiasm. They said, in about a minute though, that I was firing over the heads of the soldiers.³ I am going to see your brother soon. Don't forget to return to New York soon for all the struggling talent miss you.

Yours as ever
Stephen Crane

---

¹*George's Mother.*
²Gerhart Hauptmann's dream play, which premiered in New York in 1894.
³It seems unlikely that Crane is referring to the manuscript at NNC entitled "The Gratitude of a Nation," which was not published until 1957 in Daniel Hoffman's *The Red Badge of Courage and Other Stories*. This and its prefatory poem, "A soldier, young in years," omitted by Hoffman, are conventional tributes that would not be characterized as "firing over the heads of the soldiers." More probably, as Thomas A. Gullason maintains ("Additions to the Canon of Stephen Crane," *Nineteenth-Century Fiction*, 12 [September 1957], 157-60), Crane is alluding to the sardonic "Veterans' Ranks Thinner by a Year," which appeared in the *New York Press* on 31 May 1894 in the guise of an eye-witness report of the Decoration Day parade.

---

40. TO L. S. LINSON¹
Inscribed in a copy of *Maggie,* NNC.

With the regards of
Stephen Crane
To L. S. Linson,

May 17th, 1894.

---

¹Brother of Corwin Knapp Linson. Crane and L. S. Linson encountered each other again at the port of Siboney, where American troops disembarked during the last week

of June 1898. Linson was captain of Company D in the 71st Infantry Regiment, New York Volunteers. Writing to his brother about his meeting with Crane, Captain Linson remarked upon "how animated and jolly he appeared, the spirit of the fighter in him. When I met him in your studio he seemed of an entirely different disposition, rather somber" (Linson, p. 106). A few weeks later C. K.'s brother reported, "I met your friend Crane at Santiago. He's going to Manila, he says. He's a hustler, isn't he?" (Corwin Knapp Linson, "Little Stories of 'Steve' Crane,' " *Saturday Evening Post,* 177 [April 1903], 20).

41. FROM E. C. BROSS[1]
Letterhead: "Office of/ The Ridgefield Press,/ Ridgefield, Conn./ E. C. Bross,/ Editor." TLS, NNC.

June 21, 1894.

My Dear Mr. Crane:

I have a few moments to spare now while waiting for the last proofs of the paper, and so I will acknowledge the receipt of your letter and the MSS. I will mail you Garland's Poems[2] in a day or two, after having perused them more fully.

I confess my disappointment that you could not find it possible to run up to Ridgefield during the present month. Had you done so, I should have introduced you to a warm friend of mine, one of the proprietors of the Cedar Rapids Saturday Record, one of the high-class illustrated weeklies of the central country. Now that you are taking your vacation in Port Jervis, I fear that you will find no time in July to come to Ridgefield, but I hope I shall not be disagreeably disappointed.

As regards the MSS. you have perused,[3] I shall be glad to let you examine the remaining chapters as soon as completed, and I feel quite confident that you will agree that my purpose is not ill-advised, for I follow exactly what you surmise. I draw the moral that it is unfair to judge a young woman too harshly for being indescreet through the machinations of some sneaking man devoid of principle. I have the remaining chapters all thought out and am amplifying the matter as rapidly as I can with my other work. Charlotte Carlysle marries the young college student who defies society and he makes her an ornament of the better social world. I use Waymart, restrained as a boy, to find out the life of the so-called ruined girl, and thus the young student is able to bring about certain influences in her favor. Makepeace is shown up eventually as a cur and a sneak, but the end of the story does not assume that the church is responsible for the cowardice, but simply that the church would be greatly purified if it were possible to dig up the noxious weeds such as represented by Makepeace, Rev. Snell, and their ilk. Throughout there is not one line written in the spirit of enmity to absolute right living, but all the sarcastic thrusts are meant to hit hard those despicable traits of character that would blast reputation. I sincerely appreciate your criticism of the chapters you have already seen, and I trust that I will be able to let you examine in a few weeks the entire work, thoroughly revised, in type-written pages, so that you may know that I have altered much of the literary faults and toned down some of the most glaring passages relative to the social sin. The copy you read I assure you was not a revised version; most of it indeed was "first thought," and that was one reason why I hesitated about letting you have it in that form.

I trust that you will meet with great success with your new war story, and I hope we will be able to drive about this beautiful Connecticut country some time in July or in August at the latest. At any time you decide to come here, let me know, and I will provide means and time so that your stay will be as pleasant as possible.

Very fraternally yours,
E. C. Bross

---

[1] Edgar Clifton Bross was editor of the *Ridgefield Press*.
[2] *Prairie Songs* (1893).
[3] Bross' novel, *God's Pay Day* (1898).

42. TO COPELAND AND DAY[1]
ALS, ViU.

Interlaken Camp—
Parker's Glen
Pike Co., Penn.[2]
[about 23 August 1894]

Messrs Copeland and Day:—
Dear sirs:—

I would like to hear from you concerning my poetry. I wish to have my out-bring all under way by early fall and I have not heard from you in some time. I am in the dark in regard to your intentions.

Yours very truly
Stephen Crane

[1]Between 1893 and 1899, at Number 69 Cornhill Street in Boston, Herbert Copeland and Fred Holland Day attempted to produce books in this country in the tradition of fine printing then being revived in England by private presses such as Kelmscott, Ashendene, and Doves. Crane proved to be one of Copeland and Day's more contentious authors, but the format of *The Black Riders* was evolved with his full collaboration. Its stylized floral covers, use of capital letters throughout, and the placement of the poems in the upper portion of each page made the book the object of ridicule for many reviewers, apart from consideration of its contents. In the *Bookman,* Harry Thurston Peck called Crane "The Aubrey Beardsley of poetry." Amy Lowell recalled that "No method more certain to obscure the sincerity of the work could well have been devised." Reviews, however, were mixed, and the controversy made *The Black Riders* one of Copeland and Day's most successful productions. The third printing was exhausted when the firm closed its doors.

[2]Each August from 1894 through 1896, Crane went camping at Twin Lakes near Milford, Pennsylvania, with Frederic M. Lawrence and Louis E. Carr, Jr., whom he depicted as the Pudgy Man and the Little Man in his Sullivan County Sketches. In August 1894, Crane and Louis C. Senger, Jr., the Tall Man of the sketches (Crane was the Quiet Man) published a four-page mock newspaper, the *Pike County Puzzle,* which was probably written by Crane.

43. TO ODELL HATHAWAY
Letters, p. 39.

Hartwood, Sul Co, N.Y.
Sept 7 [1894]

My dear Odell: It was a perfectly shameful thing in me not to have answered your letter sooner but it was a difficult thing to write letters at camp and since my arrival here at Hartwood tonight has been my first real opportunity. I was very glad to hear from you but I felt ashamed too because it recalled to me those days when you used to make weekly demands that I come to Middletown to visit. God always interferes when I try to stop off at Middletown. I have never succeeded in seeing any more of it than can be percieved [sic] from the railroad tracks altho the Powelson used occasionally to ask me after you quit, and one might think that God would not seriously oppose anything that a Powelson was in. I have been wondering what has become of the Sioux Indian and the other stars of the third hall at Claverack. If you have recieved [sic] any letters from them let me know. In the meantime I shall soon make a violent struggle to reach Middletown. And at any rate I remain always grateful to you for your remembrances of the old days at H.R.I.

Yours
Stephen Crane

44. TO COPELAND AND DAY
ALS, ViU.

Hartwood, Sul Co., N.Y.
Sept 9th. [1894]

Messrs Copeland and Day:—

Dear sirs:—We disagree on a multitude of points. In the first place I should absolutely refuse to have my poems printed without many of those which you just as absolutely mark "No." It seems to me that you cut all the ethical sense out of the book. All the anarchy, perhaps. It is the anarchy which I particularly insist upon. From the poems which you keep you could produce what might be termed a "nice little volume of verse by Stephen Crane" but for me there would be no satisfaction. The ones which refer to God, I believe you condemn altogether. I am obliged to have them in when my book is printed. There are some which I believe unworthy of print. These I herewith enclose. As for the others, I cannot give them up—in the book.[1]

In the second matter, you wish I would write a few score more. It is utterly impossible to me. We would be obliged to come to an agreement upon those that are written.

If my position is impossible to you, I would not be offended at the sending of all the retained lines to the enclosed address. I beg to express my indebtedness to you and remain

Yours sincerely
Stephen Crane

[1] See No. 47.

45. TO COPELAND AND DAY
ALS, ViU.

#33 East 22ond St
New York.
[27 September 1894]

Copeland and Day

Dear sirs: I have just returned to the city and recieved your letter this morning. I send herewith the other sheets.

Ten per cent is satisfactory to me. As for the title I am inclined toward: "The Black Riders and other lines," referring to that one beginning "Black riders rode forth,"[1] etc. I don't like an index anyhow, personally, and I think if you agree, we could omit that part. If there is any other matter, my address will be as above until November 20th or about then, when I go west for one of the syndicates. In the meantime, I may come to Boston shortly. I am indebted to you for your tolerance of my literary prejudices.

Yours sincerely
Stephen Crane

[1] An early version of the title poem, "Black riders came from the sea."

46. FROM WILLIAM DEAN HOWELLS
ALS, NNC.

40 W. 59, Oct. 2, 1894.

Dear Mr. Crane:

These things are too orphic for me. It is a pity for you to do them, for you can do things solid and real, so superbly. However, there is room for all kinds,—need if you like!

I do not think a merciful Providence meant the "prose-poem" to last.

Yours sincerely,
W. D. Howells.

47. FROM COPELAND AND DAY
Letterhead: "Copeland and Day/ Publishers Import-/ ers and Vendors of/ Fine Books/ 69 Cornhill Boston." ALS, ViU.

19 Octr 1894

Dear Sir:

We hope you will pardon this delay regarding your verses now with us, and beg to say that we will be glad to publish them if you will agree to omitting those beginning as follows.

   1. A god it is said
Marked a sparrow's fall
   2d. To the maiden
The sea was a laughing meadow
   3d A god came to a man
And spoke in this wise.
   4*th* There was a man with a tongue of wood.
   5*th* The traveller paused in kindness
   6*th* Should you stuff me with flowers
   7*th* One came from the skies.

Should you still object to omitting so many we will rest content to print all but the first three in the above list, though all of them appear to us as *far* better left unprinted.[1]

We are sending by post a couple of drawings either of which might please you to be used by way of fronticepiece for the book; one would be something illustrative, while the other would be symbolic in a wide sense.

As to a title for the book, the one you suggest is acceptable if nothing better occur to you. The omission of titles for separate poems is an idea we most heartily agree with.

We are also sending a blank form to recieve your signature should you decide to entrust the book to our hands: a duplicate will be sent to you upon the return of this copy.

Kindly let us hear from you at as early a date as possible.

greatly obliging
yours vy truly
Copeland and Day

Stephen Crane Esq

---

[1] Despite the intransigence he displayed in No. 44, Crane seems to have agreed to the omission of all the poems Copeland & Day considered objectionable. "To the maiden" and "There was a man with tongue of wood" were published later in *War Is Kind* (1899); "To the maiden," reprinted there from the *Philistine,* 2 (April 1896), 152, and *A Souvenir and a Medley* (May 1896), p. 32. "A god came to a man" and "One came from the skies" remained in manuscript until 1957, and the others are apparently no longer extant.

48. TO COPELAND AND DAY
ALS, ViU.

143 East 23d St
[30 October 1894]

Messrs Copeland and Day

Dear sirs: I enclose copy of title poem.

Sincerely
Stephen Crane

Please note change of address.

49. FROM COPELAND AND DAY
ALS on stationery of Copeland and Day, NSyU.

31 Oct*r* 1894

Dear Sir:

Your letter of yesterday inclosing copy of title lines for your book is recieved, but as yet the drawings have not come to hand: neither new ones or those we forwarded to you. Kindly advise us whether others are being made up.

The form in which we intend to print *The Black Riders* is more severely classic than any book ever yet issued in America, and owing to the scarcity of types it will be quite impossible to set up more than a dozen pages at a time. Of course you wish to see proof for correction, but we would ask whether you wish the punctuation of copy followed implicitly or the recognized authorities on pointing of America or England? All those are at variance more or less severe.

Yours vy truly
Copeland and Day

Stephen Crane Esq.
143 E. 23d St. N.Y.

50. TO LUCIUS L. BUTTON
ALS, PEL. .

143 East 23d St.
Nov. 2 1894

My dear Button: I have been looking you up. Went to 65th St. There they told me 229 East 22d St. Didn't find you. I now try the college. Have had a great run of rotten luck but am now prepared to pay my debts. Meet me if you can in Clark's at 11 o'clock Saturday night.

Yours
Stephen Crane.

51. TO JAMES MOSER[1]
Inscribed in a rebound copy of *Maggie*, NNU.

To Jim Moser from Stephen Crane.
May his smile blossom like
an electric light for many
years. May his genial words
string together like amber
beads for many more years.
And may he not die before
he gets "good and ready."

Gordon's Studio, New York.
Nov 14, 1894

¹James Henry Moser was an artist friend of Crane and Frederic C. Gordon, who created the orchid design adapted by Copeland and Day's artist for the cover of *The Black Riders*.

52. TO HAMLIN GARLAND
ALS, CLSU.

143 East 23d St, NYC
Thursday Nov 15th. [1894]

My dear friend: So much of my row with the world has to be silence and endurance that sometimes I wear the appearance of having forgotten my best friends, those to whom I am indebted for everything. As a matter of fact, I have just crawled out of the fifty-third ditch into which I have been cast and I now feel that I can write you a letter that wont make you ill. McClure was a Beast about the war-novel and that has been the thing that put me in one of the ditches. He kept it for six months until I was near mad. Oh, yes, he was going to use it but—Finally I took it to Bacheller's. They use it in January in a shortened form.[1] I have just completed a New York book that leaves Maggie at the post.[2] It is my best thing. Since you are not here, I am going to see if Mr Howells will not read it. I am still working for the *Press*.

Yours as ever
Stephen Crane

[1] The abridged version of *The Red Badge of Courage* was first serialized by the Bacheller-Johnson syndicate in the *Philadelphia Press*, 3-8 December 1894.
[2] *George's Mother*.

53. TO JOHN HENRY DICK[1]
"Redeeming *The Red Badge*," *Bookman*, 35 (May 1912), 235.

[November 1894]

Dear Dicon: Beg, borrow or steal fifteen dollars. [Bacheller] like the Red Badge and want to make a contract for it. It is in pawn at the typewriter's for fifteen.

Thine,
Steve

[1] A fraternity brother of Crane who borrowed the fifteen dollars from his employer at *Godey's Magazine*. Crane probably needed the money for a revised typescript of *The Red Badge* that Bacheller could cut up for serialization. Characteristically, Crane never repaid Dick for the loan.

54. TO COPELAND AND DAY
ALS, ViU.

#143 East 23d St., N.Y.C.
Dec 10, 94

Messrs Copeland and Day:

Dear sirs: I would like to hear something from you in regard to the poems.

Also, I have grown somewhat frightened at the idea of old English type since some of my recent encounters with it have made me think I was working out a puzzle. Please reassure me on this point and tell me what you can of the day of publication.

Yours sincerely
Stephen Crane.

55. TO COPELAND AND DAY
ALS, ViU.

143 East 23d St. City
15 Dec. 94.

Messrs Copeland and Day

Dear sirs:—There has been no necessity for you to wait impatiently to hear from me for I have answered each of the letters sent to me and, at any rate, you have had opportunities to inform me of it since the 31st Oct. The type, the page, the classic form of the sample suits me. It is however paragraphed wrong. There should be none. As to punctuation, any uniform method will suit me. I am anxious to know the possible date of publication.

Yours sincerely
Stephen Crane

56. TO RIPLEY HITCHCOCK[1]
ALS, NN.

143 East 23d, City
18 Dec 94

Dear Mr Hitchcock: This is the war story in it's syndicate form—that is to say, much smaller and to my mind much worse than its original form.

Sincerely
Stephen Crane

---

[1](James) Ripley Hitchcock (1857-1918), author, editor, and critic, had traveled extensively in the West and Mexico as a special correspondent for the *New York Tribune*. He was literary advisor to D. Appleton and Company, 1890-1902.

57. TO POST WHEELER[1]
TT, NSyU.

143 East 23d St., N.Y.C.
Dec 22d, 94

My dear Wheeler:—I rejoiced tonight in getting your letter down at the Press office. I had not known which quarter of the globe contained you. Of all things I did not expect to find you incarcerated in Newark, where, by the way, I myself was jailed for a certain period—one week, in fact. You apall [sic] me by mentioning a couple of bottles. If I was sure you meant beer no one would reply with more fervent and fraternal joy but I have a damnable suspicion that you mean wine. Know then, my old companion, that I am living upon the glory of literature and not upon it's [sic] pay. Nevertheless we tramped too many leagues of Jersey sand together to let this matter of beer or wine separate us and if during the week that begins 1895 you have time to spare, let me know and I will gladly come to Newark to resume our old acquaintance and, by the same token, we will manage oftener to dine in New York. As far as the literary club [the Lanthorn Club] goes, you will be gladly welcomed, I am sure. My opinion is considered very valuable by my fellow-members since I am usually very chary about giving it.[2] I hope to see you soon as a member of our little clan and I know you will like it. Drop me a line and in the meantime know me to be

Yours very sincerely
Stephen Crane

[1] Post Wheeler (1869-1956), journalist and diplomat, was editor of the *New York Press,* 1869-1900, and later served in American embassies in Tokyo, St. Petersburg, Rome, Stockholm, London, and Rio de Janeiro. Wheeler and Crane were acquainted as children through their mothers, who were active in the W.C.T.U. Wheeler was a charter member of the Lantern Club on William Street in New York, a genial group of newspapermen, editors, and journalists presided over by Irving Bacheller. Crane joined the club shortly after it was founded in May 1895.

[2] This seems to be a reference to the Lantern Club; but according to the Club's perpetual president, Irving Bacheller, Crane did not become a member until his return from Mexico in the spring of 1895 (*From Stores of Memory* [New York: Farrar & Rinehart, 1938], p. 111). In his reminiscences Post Wheeler maintains that he was one of the

founding members of the Lantern Club and intimates that Crane joined later *(Dome of Many-Coloured Glass* [Garden City, N.Y.: Doubleday, 1955], p. 98).

58. TO COPELAND AND DAY

ALS, NSyU.

33 East 22ond St
New York
Sturday [22? December 1894]

Messrs Copeland and Day:

Dear sirs:—It may be that I will be unable to reach Boston before I start for the west and if it so happens,—I should like to hear how the poems are coming on, anyway, and wether there is anything you would care to have my opinion about.

Sincerely yours
Stephen Crane

59. TO CORWIN KNAPP LINSON

Letterhead: "The Continental/ J. E. Kingsley & Co./ Philadelphia." ALS, ViU.

[December 1894]

My dear Linson: I have furnished Mr Bacheller with your address and some time in the near future, he will send for that portrait which you so kindly consented to loan us.[1] He wishes me to express to you our thanks for your charming generosity.

Yours as ever
S. C.

[1]Corwin Knapp Linson's oil portrait of Crane, painted in late 1894 from photographs Linson had previously taken of him, now hangs in the reading room of the Clifton Waller Barrett Collection at the University of Virginia.

60. TO POST WHEELER
TT, NSyU.

Shanley's
1476 & 1478 Broadway, near 42d St.,
1212 Broadway, opposite Daly's,
383 Sixth Avenue, near 23d St.,
New York,..........189 [late 1894]

Dear Post:

Go to hell!

C

61. TO POST WHEELER
TT, NSyU.

Shanley's,
1476 & 1478 Broadway, near 42d St.,
1212 Broadway, opposite Daly's,
383 Sixth Avenue, near 23d St.,
New York,..........189 [late 1894]

Dear Post: Do you want to borrow twenty? Perhaps—me God—you are in need! Your other letter was a fake.

C

62. FROM POST WHEELER
TT, NSyU.

[late 1894]

Dear Stevie

Are you in a hurry for that twenty?

Post W

Good heavens! Forgot all about it! Dont ever mention it!

S.

63. FROM W. McCLURE
ALS, NNC.

Friday A.M. [1894-96?]

Dear Mr. Crane:

Mr. Goddard would like to get a good photo. of you, one of you at work if you have it, if not, a good portrait.

Will you have the kindness to send it to him as early as possible.

Very truly yrs
W. McClure

1895

64. TO COPELAND AND DAY
ALS, NSyU.

143 East 23d St. NYC
Jan 2d, 95

Dear sirs: I return proof sheet instantly. I do not care for a corrected proof. I go west so soon now that the proofs will have to be hurried along or I can get to see but few of them. I wish to know if some manner of announcement card can be printed which I can send to my friends.[1] I think it would benefit matters greatly.

Yours sincerely
Stephen Crane

Copeland and Day.

[1] In response to Crane's request, Copeland and Day published a four-page prospectus for *The Black Riders* that quoted Hamlin Garland's review of *Maggie* in the *Arena,* 8 (June 1893), xi-xii. Garland wrote that "With such a *technique* already at command, with life mainly *before him,* Stephen Crane is to be henceforth reckoned with. . . . a man who impresses the reader with a sense of almost unlimited resource." The prospectus also prints *The Black Riders*, XXVIII, " 'Truth,' said a traveller," for the first time.

65. TO COPELAND AND DAY
ALS, ViU.

143 East 23d St., N.Y.C.
Sunday [6 January 1895]

Dear sirs: I enclose a copy of a recent review in the Philadelphia Press.[1] I have a good many notices but none of them are particular. Most of them call me a prominent youth. Another review that I would like to have used was published in the Arena Magazine some time in '92 I think.[2] It was written by Garland. I suppose it could readily be found at the Arena office. Some parts of it would make good extracts

Sincerely yours
Stephen Crane

[1] Elisha J. Edwards, using his pseudonym of "Holland," reviewed *The Red Badge of Courage* in the *Philadelphia Press* (8 December 1894), the day on which the final installment of Crane's abridged war novel appeared in that newspaper.

[2] A revealing example of Crane's indifference to dates. He had already forgotten that *Maggie* was published in March 1893. He corrects this error in his 10 January letter to Copeland and Day.

66. TO COPELAND AND DAY
ALS, InU.

143 East 23d, NYC
[10 January 1895]

Dear sirs: The notice by Mr Garland is in the June 93 number of the Arena on page 12 of the book notices.

I had no dedication in mind for the volume but on second thoughts I would like to dedicate it to Hamlin Garland in just one line, no more: *To Hamlin Garland*.[1]

My friend, the artist, is very busy but if you will send him here an exact rendering of the words of the cover, he may submit something shortly.[2]

The book I wrote some time ago is difficult to procure but if I can get one I will send it to you.

Sincerely yours
Stephen Crane

[1] Crane did not have Garland's consent to dedicate *The Black Riders* to him. See No. 94.

[2] Frederic C. Gordon sent Copeland and Day a cover design for *The Black Riders* on 4 February, commenting that "The orchid, with its strange habits, extraordinary forms and curious properties, seemed to me the most appropriate floral motive [i. e., "motif"], an idea in which Mr. Crane concurred before he left New York" (ViU). Nevertheless, the publisher asked Gordon to modify the design. When in a letter of 25 February (ViU) Gordon stated that he was too busy to comply with this request, Copeland and Day had their own artist adapt Gordon's drawing of the orchid plant for the first trade edition of *The Black Riders*.

The West and Mexico

"Now that he is dead," Willa Cather wrote in the memoir of her encounters with Crane in the offices of the *Nebraska State Journal*, "it occurs to me that all his life was a preparation for sudden departure." Cather's "When I Knew Stephen Crane," which first appeared in the Pittsburgh weekly, *The Library* (23 June 1900), under her established pseudonym of Henry Nickleman, is the only eyewitness account of the extensive tour of the West and Mexico that Crane undertook for the Bacheller, Johnson and Bacheller newspaper syndicate from late January until mid-May 1895. Like so many other reminiscences about Crane, it is a self-dramatizing and fictionalized delineation of events that Cather misdates as occurring in the spring of 1894 rather than in the first two weeks of the following February. She recalls a conversation with Crane on an "oppressively warm" spring night with "the gurgle of the fountain in the Post Office square across the street and the twang of banjos from the lower verandah of the Hotel Lincoln, where the colored waiters were serving the guests." The blond Crane is described as a dark-haired, emaciated, Poesque youth (a volume of Poe in his jacket pocket) in ill-fitting, disreputable clothing, a portrait of the artist as a young wanderer, impatiently awaiting a check from Bacheller to speed him on his way to Mexico.

Actually, Crane's sojourn in Nebraska was purposeful. He was gathering material for an article on large areas of the state that had suffered a searing drought the previous summer followed by an exceptionally hard winter. He arrived in Lincoln on 1 February, according to notices in the local papers, and went into central Nebraska during the following week. The blizzard so vividly described in "The Blue Hotel" devastated that area on 6 and 7 February, with temperatures from fourteen to eighteen degrees below zero. Crane's article, "Nebraska's Bitter Fight for Life," is the most graphically moving journalistic sketch of his Western trip. Yet, Willa Cather's astonishment at hearing Crane spoken of as "the reporter in fiction" was not misplaced, for, as she put it, "the reportorial faculty of superficial reception and quick transference was what he conspicuously lacked." Crane was master of the impressionistic vignette; effects and sensations interested him far more than names, places, and events. The success of his description of drought and blizzard conditions on the desolated Nebraska prairies depends little upon facts and statistics but upon the controlled expression of his empathy with the will to endure personified in the beleaguered farmers. To the reporter's question "How did you get along?" the grimly understated response is "Don't git along, stranger. Who the hell told you I did get along?" The focus of Crane's attention is not upon the material losses or even the sufferings of the people of central Nebraska but "upon their endurance, their capacity to help each other, and their steadfast and unyielding courage."

Crane left Nebraska on 14 February. He passed through Hot Springs, Arkansas, en route to New Orleans, where Ripley Hitchcock had sent the manuscript of *The Red Badge of Courage* for him to correct. The rigorous process of excision that would impair the structural and thematic unity of the war novel began here. While in New Orleans, Crane wrote a lackluster account of performances by the French Opera Company and a more lively description of the excitement and color of the Mardi Gras. Galveston, Texas, reminded him of a New England town with its cotton steamers, docks, and sailors, but Crane failed to capture the cosmopolitan flavor of the city, a unique quality in nineteenth-century Texas. In his syndicated report headlined "Ancient Capital of Montezuma" in the *Philadelphia Press*, he recounts his entry into Mexico through Laredo and Neuvo Laredo. Here and in his other "City of Mexico" reports, he performs his journalistic duties with more or less stereotyped descriptions of the picturesqueness of America's southern neighbor—the churches, teeming streets of towns and cities with their exotic goods and vendors, drab peasants, and more colorfully dressed stylish residents. Yet, Crane is more deeply concerned with the squalor, ignorance, and apathy of the Mexican lower classes. Three sketches—"The City of Mexico," "The Viga Canal," and "The Mexican Lower Classes"—remained in manuscript and were not published until 1967. The last of these is especially significant in its contrast between the attitudes of the impoverished Indians who accept their economic and social degradation with a passivity that Crane rather perversely interprets as contentment and the potentially dangerous unrest among the rapidly increasing masses of America's urban poor about whom he had written in *Maggie* and his other slum stories:

The people of the slums of our own cities fill a man with awe. That vast army with its countless faces immovably cynical, that vast army that silently confronts eternal defeat, it makes one afraid. One listens for the first thunder of the rebellion, the moment when this silence shall be broken by a roar of war. Meanwhile one fears this class, their numbers, their wickedness, their might—even their laughter. There is a vast national respect for them. They have it in their power to become terrible. And their silence suggests everything. (*Works*, VIII, p. 436.)

Before his trip to the West and Mexico, Crane had recorded his impressions of the growing contrast between wealth and poverty in industrially burgeoning America in sketches and reports such as "An Experiment in Misery," "An Experiment in Luxury," "The Men in the Storm," and "In the Depths of a Coal Mine," but the sharp edge of his irony undercut any strong sense of social commitment. Perhaps his social consciousness solidified during his stay in Mexico City, where he observed the misery of the impoverished from the faded elegance of the Hotel Iturbide, although he avoided any doctrinaire expression of solidarity with them. Nelson Greene, with whom Crane shared a room in the old Art Students' League building on East 23rd Street in the summer of 1895, after he had returned to New York City, recalls that at this time Crane called himself a socialist. Greene felt that Crane had "made a poor fist of his stories—statistics and ordinary matter—which he was doing for the Bacheller Newspaper Syndicate. He didn't think much of them himself." But Crane's travels on the American continent were extremely important to his development as a writer; they inspired the structures and themes of the confrontation Western stories he originated as a genre—"The Blue Hotel," "A Man and Some Others," and "The Five White Mice"—as well as his masterful parody of such situation dramas, "The Bride Comes to Yellow Sky."

67. TO COPELAND AND DAY
ALS, ViU.

143 East 23d St.
Jan 14, 94 [for 1895]

Dear sirs: I start for the west on a very long and circuitous newspaper trip on the last day of this week. I end ultimately in the City of Mexico. I will probably not return before the book is issued. If you can send me more proofs this week, I would like it. I will try to establish a means of cummunication with you. Any answer to a letter of mine will have to be sent very promptly or it will not reach me, as I travel quickly from city to city.

I send you a list of personal friends who would like to get that notice of the poems. I can use many more if you will send them to me in the west. Kindly preserve the list and return it to me when you have finished with it.

Yours sincerely
Stephen Crane

Will you please send, as I requested, the size of the cover, the exact lettering upon it, and, if possible, the probable thickness of the book. The artist needs it.

68. TO COPELAND AND DAY
ALS, ViU.

143 East 23d St.
Friday [18 January 1895]

Dear sirs: The artist wishes to know what you mean by the phrase: "Both sides the same."[1] in relation to the book cover.

My journey to the west is delayed for ten days

Yours sincerely
Stephen Crane

Please dont destroy Ms.

Crane

[1] On the front cover of the first edition of *The Black Riders*, the orchid design rises in the lower left corner and curves upward to the right. On the back cover this design is reversed.

69. TO COPELAND AND DAY
Letterhead: "Cooke's European Hotel . . . St. Louis, Mo.," ALS, MB.

Jan 30 1894 [for 1895]

Dear Sirs: My address for the next ten days will be "Care of Will Owen Jones, The State Journal, Lincoln, Nebraska", and for one month from date it will be—"Care Mr Marrion Baker, The Times-Democrat, New Orleans." Let me hear about the notices.

Yours sincerely
Stephen Crane.

when you lose track of me write in care of Bacheller and Johnson, Tribune Building, New York.

70. TO RIPLEY HITCHCOCK
ALS on Cooke's European Hotel stationery, NN.

[30 January 1895]

Dear Mr Hitchcock: I left New York so suddenly that I was unable to cummunicate with you. My address for the next three weeks will be in care of Mr Will Owen Jones, Editor *State Journal,* Lincoln, Neb. Afterward, I go to New Orleans and letters will reach me there if sent in care of Mr Marrion Baker of the Times-Democrat. Any news of the war story will be grateful to me. If you had not read the story, I would wish you to hear the Philadelphia Press staff speak of it. When I was there some days ago, I was amazed to hear the way in which they talked of it.

I will be glad to hear from you at any time.

Yours sincerely
Stephen Crane

71. TO LOUIS SENGER
ALS on Cooke's European Hotel stationery, NSyU.

[St. Louis, 30 January 1895]

Say, Senger, write to me in care of the State Journal, Lincoln, Nebraska, will you? Any time within ten days. After that, at the New Orleans Times-Democrat office, care Mr Marrion Baker

Crane

72. TO LUCIUS L. BUTTON
ALS, ViU.

> St Louis
> Thurs—[31 January 1895]

Hello, Budge, I am en route to kill Indians. Before I left I called upon you at the place where I thought I was most likely to find you. Write to me at Lincoln in care of Mr Will Owen Jones of the State Journal.
Lincoln, Nebraska, I mean.
My distinguished consideration

> Yours as ever
> Crane

73. TO THE REVEREND THOMAS DIXON
Inscribed on a copy of *Maggie*, as recorded in a review of *The Black Riders* (*Bookman*, 1 [May 1895]), 229, by Harry Thurston Peck.[1]

> [January 1895]

It is inevitable that this book will greatly shock you, but continue, pray, with great courage to the end, for it tries to show that environment is a tremendous thing in this world, and often shapes lives regardlessly. If one could prove that theory, one would make room in Heaven for all sorts of souls (notably an occasional street girl) who are not confidently expected to be there by many excellent people.

[1] Peck refers to this copy of *Maggie*, which "was addressed to the Rev. Thomas Dixon a few months ago, before [Crane] went West on a journalistic trip to Nebraska...." Dixon's copy has been lost.

74. TO RIPLEY HITCHCOCK
Letterhead: "The Lincoln . . . Lincoln, Neb." ALS, NN.

[early February 1895]

Dear Mr Hitchcock: I've just recieved your letter. I would be glad to have Appleton and Co publish the story on those terms.[1] I am going from here to New Orleans. The Ms could be corrected by me there in short order. I shall have to reflect upon the title. I shall not be back to New York for two months.

Yours sincerely
Stephen Crane

[1]Crane signed a contract with D. Appleton and Company on 17 June for the publication of *The Red Badge of Courage*, and the book came out in the first week of October 1895.

75. TO CLARENCE LOOMIS PEASLEE[1]
Quoted in Clarence Loomis Peaslee, "Stephen Crane's College Days," *Monthly Illustrator*, 13 (August 1896), 28.

[Lincoln, Nebraska, 12 February 1895]

As far as myself and my own meagre success are concerned, I began the war with no talent, but an ardent admiration and desire. I had to build up. I always want to be unmistakable. That to my mind is good writing. There is a great deal of labor connected with literature. I think that is the hardest thing about it. There is nothing to respect in art, save one's own opinion of it.[2]

[1]Peaslee was a fraternity brother of Crane at Syracuse University.
[2]The similarity in wording between this letter and No. 78 typifies Crane's habit of repeating himself when he summarized his life and thoughts for reviewers and editors who requested such information. Inscriptions on the cover of *Maggie* show the same tendency.

76. TO CORWIN KNAPP LINSON
ALS, NSyU.

New Orleans
Tuesday [19 February 1895]

Mon ami Linson: Friedweller die schonënberger je suis dans New Orleans. Cracked ice dans Nebraska, terra del fuego dans New Orleans. Table d'hotes sur le balconies just like spring. A la mode whiskers on the citizens en masse, merci, of the vintage de 1712.

Frequented I all the time here again l'etoile de Virginitie sur St Louis Street. Sic semper tyrannis! Mardi gras tres grande but it not does until next Tuesday begin. Spiel! Senger to me one letter wrote filled with abuse. Ce matin I write un article sur le railways du South which were all made in hell.

This boarding-house est le terrible Francais: I have learned to ask for the vinegar at the table but otherwise I shall perhaps to Heaven go through starvation.

Yours ever
Crane.

77. TO RIPLEY HITCHCOCK
Letterhead: "Hotel Royal . . . New Orleans," ALS, NN.

Feb. 20 1895

Dear Mr Hitchcock:

If the manuscript is sent here in care of Mr Baker of the Times-Democrat I shall be able to arrange it before I depart for Mexico.[1] I will not leave here for ten days.

I know it is a most inconvenient arrangement but as I am extremely anxious to have you bring out the book, I am hoping that the obstacles of the situation will not too much vex you.

Yours sincerely
Stephen Crane

c/o Mr Marrion Baker
Times-Democrat
New Orleans

P.S. I shall only be in Mexico one week

[1] A notation at the top of the letter reads, "Ms. sent by express Feb. 25."

78. TO JOHN NORTHERN HILLIARD[1]
Quoted in John Northern Hilliard, "Stephen Crane," *New York Times*, Supplement, 14 July 1900, p. 466.

[February 1895?]

As far as myself and my own meagre success are concerned, I began the battle of life with no talent, no equipment, but with an ardent admiration and desire. I did little work at school, but confined my abilities, such as they were, to the diamond. Not that I disliked books, but the cut-and-dried curriculum of the college did not appeal to me. Humanity was a much more interesting study. When I ought to have been at recitations I was studying faces on the streets, and when I ought to have been studying my next day's lessons I was watching the trains roll in and out of the Central Station. So, you see, I had, first of all, to recover from college. I had to build up, so to speak. And my chiefest desire was to write plainly and unmistakably, so that all men (and some women) might read and understand. That to my mind is good writing. There is a great deal of labor connected with literature. I think that is the hardest thing about it. There is nothing to respect in art save one's own opinion of it.

[1] Journalist, novelist, dramatist, and author of several books on magic, John Northern Hilliard (1872-1935) was at this time contributing editor to *The Union and Advertiser* (Rochester). Simultaneously, he was literary editor of the *Rochester Post Express*. Crane had known Hilliard when they were both reporters in New York City during 1892-93.

79. TO RIPLEY HITCHCOCK
Letterhead: "The Tremont . . . Galveston, Texas," ALS, NN.

March 8 1895

Dear Mr Hitchcock: I sent the Ms from New Orleans. I made a great number of small corrections.[1] As to the name I am unable to see what to do with it unless the word "Red" is cut out perhaps. That would shorten it. I am about to depart into Mexico for three weeks or a month. My address will be Hotel Iturbide, City of Mexico.

Very truly yours
Stephen Crane.

[1] Crane not only made corrections but deleted some 2,000 words from the manuscript.

80. TO COPELAND AND DAY
TTfr (NSyU), item 78, Catalogue 117 (1946), Carnegie Book Shop.

[Galveston, Texas, 9 March 1895]

I liked the circulars. I am about to go into Mexico and will have address for some weeks. . . . I hope you come to an agreement with Gordon in regard to the design. . . .

81. TO LUCIUS L. BUTTON
Letterhead: "Mahncke Hotel . . . San Antonio, Texas," ALS, NhD.

March 12 1895

My dear Button: I am about to venture into Mexico and sever my relations with the United States postal service so it will cost you five cents to answer this note—Hotel Iturbide, City of Mexico—

I would tell you of many strange things I have seen if I was not so bored with writing of them in various articles.[1] This note is merely an attempt to cajole a letter out of you.

There is one thing however,—I met a most intolerable duffer in New Orleans named Butler who let it be known that he was from Akron, O., although I dont see why he should.[2] He told me that he knew your friends there or your friends who have escaped or are about to escape or are planning to escape, or are about to plan to escape from there.

He had fingers like lightning rods and on the street he continually pointed at various citizens with the exclamation: "Look at that fellow"! People in New Orleans dont like that sort of thing, you know. No doubt his ingenuous Akron spirit was amazed at many scenes but for my own part I felt that he should have controlled his emotion.

It is hard to feel kindly toward a man who makes you look like an unprecedented idiot and while I had only a general and humane objection to his making an ass of himself, I felt differently about myself.

He enthusiastically requested me to stop off on my way home in the spring and visit him. I modestly replied that while I appreciated his generosity and his courage, I had to die early in the spring and I feared that I would have to hurry home for the funeral but I had an open date in 1997 and would be happy to see him in hell upon that occasion.

Well, at any rate, I lie, for I was considerate of him, treated him well at times, and was careful of his childish innocence. But there should be a tariff on that kind of an export from Akron, O.

Tell Tommie Parson that this is a straight tip upon the quality of his rivals. I am off for Mexico tonight.

Yours as ever
S. C.

P.S. Be good!

---

[1] Seventeen of Crane's newspaper articles about this trip are collected in Joseph Katz, ed., *Stephen Crane in the West and Mexico* (Kent, Ohio: Kent State University Press, 1970).
[2] Crane is jesting with Button about the provinciality of his hometown, Akron, Ohio. Nellie Crouse, to whom Crane was introduced by Button, also came from Akron.

82. FROM THE BACHELLER & JOHNSON SYNDICATE
Telegram, NNC.

March 25, 1895

Stephen Crane
Hotel Iturbide, Mex

Check mailed friday

Bacheller & Johnson Syndicate

83. TO WICKHAM W. YOUNG[1]
Letters, p. 55.

The American Club
City of Mexico
Hotel Iturbide
City of Mexico
March 30, 1895

My dear Wick: This is to say that I am well and am going to ascend Popocatapetl [sic]. Wether [sic] I will be well afterward is a matter of speculation. Give my adieus in a general manner to Middletown.

Yours Sincerely
Stephen Crane

[1] A cousin of Crane's Claverack College classmate, Harvey Wickham. Young was among those who camped with Crane at Twin Lakes in Pike County, Pennsylvania.

84. FROM COPELAND AND DAY[1]

TTfr in a manuscript of Corwin Knapp Linson's *My Stephen Crane*, p. 194, NSyU.

May 1, 1895

At last The Black Riders are sent to you—three copies

[1] A fragment quoted in Corwin Knapp Linson's manuscript reminiscences of his friendship with Crane but not included in the published version of *My Stephen Crane*. (An earlier draft of the book is at NNC.) Linson adds that Copeland and Day's lack of a permanent address for Crane prevented them from sending more copies. Publication of *The Black Riders* was officially announced in the *Publishers' Weekly* of 11 May 1895.

85. TO CURTIS BROWN[1]

Inscribed in a copy of *The Black Riders*, TxU.

To Curtis Brown—
—not at all reluctantly
but with enthusiasm—
From Stephen Crane

May 26, 1895.

[1] Sunday editor of the *New York Press* and later a literary agent in London.

86. TO COPELAND AND DAY
Letterhead: "The Hartwood Club."[1] ALS, ViU.

Port Jervis, N.Y.
June 8 1895

Messrs Copeland and Day

Dear Sirs: I returned from Mexico some days ago but have come up here for a time because I am not in very good health. I would be glad to learn of the Black Riders. I see they are making some stir. My address will be c/o Lantern Club, 126 Williams St, N.Y.C.[2]

I remember writing you once that I positively had no portrait of myself I forgot the one The Bookman used. At any rate it did not belong to me.

Yours sincerely
Stephen Crane

---

[1] Stephen's brother William Howe Crane was one of the founders of the Hartwood Club, an exclusive hunting and fishing preserve in Sullivan County near the village of Hartwood and only a few miles from Port Jervis. Stephen visited the Club a number of times by himself and with members of his family, and after the success of *The Red Badge* he bought a $500 share in the Hartwood Association. Nevertheless, in a letter written in May 1960, Edith F. Crane, one of Edmund's daughters, told Lillian Gilkes that "he did not like the membership there generally, and said so in the privacy of the family" (OU).

[2] The Lantern or Lanthorne Club was organized by a group of young journalists and writers including Post Wheeler, Edward Marshall, Richard Watson Gilder, Irving Bacheller, and Willis Brooks Hawkins. On Saturday evenings, one of the members read a literary composition and was criticized. Favorable comments were not permitted. The clubhouse was a shanty on the roof of an old house on William Street near the Brooklyn Bridge. It was decorated as a ship's cabin with lanterns, and an old ship's lantern hung outside the door. Prominent visitors included William Dean Howells and Mark Twain. The most notable publication of the club was *The Lanthorn Book* (1898), in which Crane's "The Wise Men" appeared. The book was limited to 125 copies, and all contributions were signed by their authors except for that of Hawkins, whose signature was printed in facsimile.

Elbert Hubbard and the Philistines

Like many events in Crane's life before the publication of *The Red Badge of Courage*, the time and place of his first meeting with the flamboyant Elbert Hubbard, self-styled "General Inspector of the Universe," is difficult to determine. Hubbard, who also affected the title of "Fra Elbertus," was patron of an artsy-craftsy community in the upper New York State village of East Aurora known as the Roycrofters or King's Craftsmen, which produced bland handmade furniture and published books in sincere but lackluster imitation of those printed in England by William Morris' Kelmscott Press. Hubbard sought to emulate Morris' conception of the book as art and introduce it into the American consciousness. Perhaps Hubbard met Crane early in 1894, when he visited New York City to gather material for his *Arena* article, "The Rights of Tramps," which appeared in April, the same month that Crane's short story on a similar theme, "An Experiment in Misery," was featured in the *New York Press*. Hubbard went to England later that spring to do field research for his *Little Journeys*, an immensely popular series of chatty booklets on the careers of writers, artists, musicians, and other prominent figures. Upon his return, he tarried in New York, successfully negotiating with G. P. Putnam's Sons to publish twelve of his *Little Journeys*, one a month for a year. Subsequently, they were issued from East Aurora. Thomas Beer maintains that at this time Hubbard also bought two essays on social themes from Crane for his forthcoming pocket magazine, *The Philistine: A Periodical of Protest*, but lost them on a train. In any event, the letter he wrote to Crane on 11 June 1895, accompanying a copy of the first issue of the *Philistine*, which contained his review of *The Black Riders*, lacks the introductory tone that some biographers have ascribed to it. Most likely, he and Crane were already acquainted.

Satirical and irreverent, the *Philistine* was the most popular and long-lived of the little magazines of the 1890s, easily outstripping such contemporaries as the *Lark*, the *Chap-Book*, and the *Lotus*. It was issued monthly for twenty years from June 1895 through July 1915, when it was discontinued following Hubbard's death in the sinking of the *Lusitania*. Spurred by the impetus given it through Hubbard's most famous preachment, "A Message to Garcia" (*Philistine*, March 1899), it eventually reached a circulation of well over 100,000. The first three issues of the *Philistine* were turned out on a handpress by Henry Persons Taber, a lithograph salesman for Cosak & Company. His name appeared on the masthead as editor from July through December 1895. (In the January 1896 issue he was designated "Datary," a characteristically sardonic Hubbard touch.) Later Taber claimed to have founded the entire Roycroft enterprise, including the *Philistine*, and to have suggested the *Little Journeys* to Hubbard, but from the beginning Hubbard's hand and voice were apparent in these ventures. In February 1896, after a quarrel about the suitability of a Hubbard article for the *Philistine*, Taber severed his connection with the Roycrofters.

Much of the popularity of the *Philistine* must be attributed to Hubbard's sound grasp of business principles and empathy with middle-class American values and perspectives. Before his sudden conversion to literature, he had been General Manager of J. D. Larkin & Co., a leading manufacturer and distributor of soap products. He was a masterful salesman and had a perfect genius for advertising. Hubbard's philistinism was an epithet of contempt for the "Chosen People" who had become arbiters of literary taste, men such as Howells of *Harper's*, Gilder of the *Century*, and McClure of *McClure's Magazine*. Crane's unconventional writing suited Hubbard's aesthetic program. He did not admire Crane's poetry but recognized in it an excellent vehicle for the expression of his own *fin de siècle* iconoclasm. To Lyman Chandler, who became one of his aids in the Roycroft Press enterprises, Hubbard confessed that in his opinion, "Nobody understands Mr. Crane, he only makes us feel creepy which is all according to his creed—that poetry should impart a *feeling* and not teach a truth. All scripture is mystical and affords various interpretations, so prophecy of the highest order is always a bit boozy. Many people all over the U.S. are going after Mr. Crane."

Hubbard's magazines, the *Philistine*, the *Roycroft Quarterly*, and the *Fra*, became the chief periodical outlets for Crane's poetry, the greatest density of this publication taking place between August 1895 and June 1896. Such exposure may not have been entirely to Crane's advantage. As Amy Lowell put it, "It was difficult for the world to believe that a man championed by the arch-poser, Elbert Hubbard, could have merit.... It was a thousand pities that poems such as these should appear under the aegis of the Roycrofters." Furthermore, while the ambience of the *Philistine* was basically satiric, there seems to be an undertone of rancor in such good-natured raillery as the quip in the November 1895 issue: "Why Bliss Carman and Stephen Crane do not write for *Lippincott's* has long been a mystery to me. Some of their verse is bad enough. But the secret is out. They have only two names apiece." Hubbard also published a number of Crane's short stories and sketches. He appreciated these more, especially when they embodied themes of social criticism, *épater les bourgeois*. In the January 1897 *Philistine* he reprinted "The Men in the Storm" from the October 1894 *Arena* and commented, "Can you read the sketch in this issue entitled 'The Men in the Storm' and say that Stephen Crane is not a man of generous sympathies and clear, vivid insights?"

By November 1895 the spirited, critical controversy over *The Black Riders* and nationwide favorable reaction to *The Red Badge of Courage*, despite lagging sales, made Crane an intriguing figure upon whom Hubbard could center his campaign against stodginess in literature while simultaneously promoting the Roycroft endeavors. With his customary ingenuity, he activated the Society of the Philistines, a paper organization that ostensibly published the *Philistine*, in order to tender a dinner honoring America's rising young literary genius. The twenty-four-year-old Crane, whose fame had come too suddenly, failed to recognize the self-aggrandizing motivation behind Hubbard's scheme and was flattered by formal recognition from the Fra and his coterie of hustling journalists. Willis Brooks Hawkins, a fellow member of the Lantern Club and editor of *Brains*, one of the earliest magazines devoted to advertising, who was at this time Crane's closest friend, urged the diffident young writer to accept the invitation and saw to it that he was properly attired for the occasion. Hawkins, like Crane, believed that the Philistine banquet would be a dignified celebration of his young friend's literary success. This is most likely what Hubbard himself anticipated, as he indicated in his epistolary assurances to Crane and the three pamphlets he published to commemorate the occasion.

The first of these was an elaborate eight-page invitation by "The Members of the Society" to meet Crane at dinner in East Aurora on Thursday evening, 19 December 1895. Because of the inconvenient location of that village, the site was changed to Buffalo—first to the Iroquois and then to the Genesee Hotel. A souvenir menu of the occasion entitled *"The Time Has Come," The Walrus Said, "To Talk of Many Things"* displays a full-page cover design caricaturing the title of *The Black Riders*. It publishes for the first time Crane's poem "I have heard the sunset song of the birches" and includes the responses of some three dozen invited guests who declined to attend the banquet. Significantly, prominent writers such as Irving Bacheller, Richard Harding Davis, Hamlin Garland, and Ambrose Bierce sent regrets, probably unwilling to participate in one of Hubbard's publicity stunts. Bierce, who would not leave California to go to Washington for some months, had the legitimate excuse of distance, but even Ripley Hitchcock and Daniel Appleton, the editor and publisher of *The Red Badge*, found it inconvenient to attend. Some of the replies printed in the menu were tributes and others were forthrightly humorous, but a few were tinged with what appear to be sarcastic allusions to Hubbard's exploitation of Crane. Walter Blackburn Harte commented that "The trade of literature contains the best fellows in the world—and some of the damndest rogues," while S. S. McClure expressed his admiration for Crane but also his preference to "admire the valiant Philistines—from a safe distance." The most ambitious of Hubbard's pamphlets, *A Souvenir and a Medley*, the first of three issues of the *Roycroft Quarterly*, reprints Hubbard's essay on Crane from the *Lotos* (March 1896), seven Crane poems and his East Side sketch, "A Great Mistake," from the *Philistine*, and publishes for the first time his cryptic playlet, "A Prologue," and a new poem, "Fast rode the knight."

Considering Hubbard's ambiguous motivations and the ill-assorted group of guests who assembled at the Genesee Hotel ("freaks or near freaks" Crane's Syracuse fraternity brother Frank Noxon called them), it is not surprising that the Philistine banquet degenerated into a fiasco.

Taber, Crane, and the other speakers were heckled and ridiculed, according to Noxon. Claude Bragdon expressed his indignation at the rowdy progress of events and threatened to bolt the room in protest, but his way was blocked by Hawkins, who was determined to preserve Crane's dignity to the extent that this was possible, but later Hawkins admitted that "Stephen was in a blue funk." Crane must have been severely disillusioned by the squalor of what he had anticipated would be a sincere tribute to his literary accomplishments. Hubbard exploited the event to the utmost. The *Buffalo Evening News* of 20 December carried a laudatory account of the banquet entitled "The Philistines at Dinner." As Crane wrote Nellie Crouse, "This is not at all what happened." Hubbard also appended a number of other favorable newspaper reports of the affair in *A Souvenir and a Medley*. Although Crane undoubtedly came to realize he had been used, he put a brave face on the matter, and his friendship with Hubbard remained, to all appearances, undiminished. Throughout Crane's lifetime his poems and sketches, as well as constant commentary about his work, continued to appear in the *Philistine*, and the custom was renewed from 1908 through 1916 in the *Fra*, the last and most staid of Hubbard's periodicals.

87. FROM ELBERT HUBBARD

Letterhead: "The Philistine: A Periodical of/ Protest. Cambridge, Mass./ Office of the Business Manager,/ East Aurora, New York." ALS, NNC.

E Aurora [New York] June 11, 95

Dear Mr Crane:

I mail you a copy of The Philistine, and trust you will not take to heart the little stunt on The Black Riders.[1] We will take it all back in next issue. Can't you send us a bit of ms? You can help us and we will try awfully hard to help you. You are the coming man I believe—it may be slow and it may not. I sincerely wish you well.

With regards, I am,
Respectfully Yours,
Elbert Hubbard

[1] In his review of *The Black Riders* (*Philistine*, 1 [June 1895], 27), Hubbard remarks that "Messrs. Copeland & Day of Boston recently published for Mr. Stephen Crane a book which he called 'The Black Riders.' I don't know why; the riders might have as easily been green or yellow or baby-blue for all the book tells about them, and I think the title 'The Pink Rooters' [i.e., 'The Pink Roosters'] would have been better, but it doesn't matter."

88. FROM WILLIAM DEAN HOWELLS
Letterhead: "Iroquois . . . Buffalo, N.Y." ALS, NNC.

June 13, 1895

Dear Mr. Crane:

I expect to be at home Friday night and if I'm in good repair, I shall be glad to dine with you Saturday. You wont mind my backing out at the last moment?

Yours sincerely
W. D. Howells.

89. TO GORDON PIKE[1]
Inscribed in a copy of *The Black Riders*, ViU.

To Gordon Pike
with the friendship of
Stephen Crane

New York City, June 28, 1895

[1] Pike (1865-1925) was a New York architect.

90. TO COPELAND AND DAY
ALS, InU.

>Lantern Club
>#126 Williams St
>New York City
>[June? 1895]

Messrs Copeland and Day

Dear sirs I cant seem to light on a copy of Maggie.

I have considerable work that is not in the hands of publishers. My favorites are eight little grotesque tales of the woods which I wrote when I was clever.[1] The trouble is that they only sum 10000 words and I can make no more.

If you think you can make one of your swell little volumes out of 10000, the tales would gain considerable lengthy abuse no doubt.

Mr Howells wishes the Black Riders to review in Harper's Weekly.[2] Jordan of Current Literature wishes it for the same reason.[3] If you could send me a few at the Lantern Club, I would like them. I am particularly anxious to see the green ones.[4]

I see they have been pounding the wide margins, the capitals and all that but I think it great.

>Yours sincerely
>Stephen Crane

[1] See No. 31, n. 1.
[2] *Harper's Weekly* did not review *The Black Riders*.
[3] William G. Jordan. The writer of "Stephen Crane, Author of *The Black Riders*," *Current Literature*, 18 (July 1895), 9, which deals primarily with *Maggie*, was either Harry Thurston Peck, who wrote "Stephen Crane, Author of *The Black Riders and Other Lines*," *Bookman*,1 (May 1895), 229-30, or someone who plagiarized Peck's article.
[4] Copeland and Day published *The Black Riders* in a "trade" edition of 500 copies bound in light-gray laid paper over boards. Fifty copies printed in green ink on Japan paper and bound in cream laid paper over boards without design or lettering (except for a label on the spine identifying the title, author, and year of publication) were issued simultaneously. Of these green-ink copies, three examples have been found in white vellum covers stamped in gold both front and back with an orchid design similar to what appears in black on the covers of the regular edition.

91. TO LILY BRANDON MUNROE
ALS, ViU.

> Lantern Club
> #126 William St
> New York
> [first week of July? 1895]

My dear L. B.: Copeland and Day of Boston which to re-print those old Sullivan County tales of mine and there is no one in the world has any copies of them but you. Can you not send them to me?

Are you coming north this summer? Let me know, when you send the stories. I should like to see you again.

> Yours as ever
> S. C.

92. TO AN UNKNOWN RECIPIENT
ALS, Rosenberg Library, Galveston, Texas.

> Bacheller Syndicate
> The Tribune Buildg
> New York City
> July 10 [1895]

My dear Major:[1] I did not recieve your notice of my appointment as honorary member of the Aziola Club until yesterday or a reply would have been in your hands long ago. It is immensely gratifying to me to be thought at all worthy of so particular an honor, and I shall always think of it with extreme pleasure. Some day I hope to be able to in some way return the altogether fine hospitality of the Aziola Club, by meeting you or any of your friends here in New York. And I shall always remain to you, my dear major,

> Yours sincerely
> Stephen Crane

[1] The major, a member of a businessman's club called the Aziola Club in Galveston, Texas, remains unidentified. Jane A. Kenamore, Archivist of the Rosenberg Library in Galveston explains that "Colonel, Captain, and Major were common appelations here after the Civil War, so it could have been any one of a number of people" (undated letter from Kenamore to Sorrentino).

93. FROM WILLIS BROOKS HAWKINS

Letterhead: "Brains/ Devoted to the Art of Advertising,/ Downing Building,/ P. O. Box 572, New York./ Editor's Room." ALS, NNC.

July 10, 1895.

Dear Stephen: This is merely to remind you that the club[1] has accepted Mr. Walker's invitation to lunch and a sail with him on Wednesday, July 17. We leave the Grand Central Station for Irvington at 12:10 o'clock.

Yours,
Willis B. Hawkins, Sec'y

[1] The Lantern Club.

94. TO HAMLIN GARLAND

ALS, CLSU.

Lantern Club
#126 William St.,
New York City
[about 17 July 1895]

Dear Mr Garland: I have lost your address and so for certainty's sake, send this to the Arena. I am just returned from my wanderings in Mexico.[1] Have you seen the *Black Riders*. I dedicated them to you but I am not sure that I should have done it without your permission? Do you care? I am getting along better—a little better—than when I last saw you. I work for the Bachellers.[2]

Yours sincerely
Stephen Crane

[1]The length of Crane's Western trip is uncertain. He left near the end of January, for he was in St. Louis on 30 January, but the evidence regarding his return is contradictory. Linson, p. 89, claimed that the Lantern Club held a dinner for Crane on 7 April, but Joseph Katz, in *Stephen Crane in the West and Mexico* (Kent, Ohio: Kent State University Press, 1970), p. xx, n. 19, has inferred from a hotel bill that Crane was still in Mexico City on 15 May. In *Contacts* (London: Cassell, 1935), p. 223, Curtis Brown stated that Crane inscribed a copy of *The Black Riders* on 26 May 1895 (No. 85), shortly after his return.

[2]The Bacheller, Johnson & Bacheller newspaper syndicate.

95. FROM ELBERT HUBBARD
ALS, NNC.

E Aurora N.Y. July 20, '95

Can't we run a page ad. of your books? No chg.

Dear Mr Crane:

Your valued favor rc'd.[1] The lines you send appeal to me strangely and we will take great pleasure in printing them. Now about pay, are you rich enough in these choice things (and in gold) so you can present us these verses? Of course you see we are not running this little magazine with any hope of a financial return—simply making a plea for liberty in Letters, and so far the press of the country has treated us most generously.

Awaiting your kind reply, I am, with high esteem—

Sincerely Yours
Elbert Hubbard

Frontispiece of the Annual Catalogue of Claverack College and Hudson River Institute, 1887–1888 *(Collection of Stanley and Mary Wertheim)*

Cadet group of officers and noncommissioned officers at Claverack College and Hudson River Institute in 1889. Stephen Crane is third from the right in the middle row. (Newark Museum, Newark, New Jersey)

Stephen Crane seated at right in student group, probably at Syracuse University in the spring of 1891. (Barrett Collection, University of Virginia)

Study for Corwin Knapp Linson's portrait of Stephen Crane, 1894. (Barrett Collection, University of Virginia)

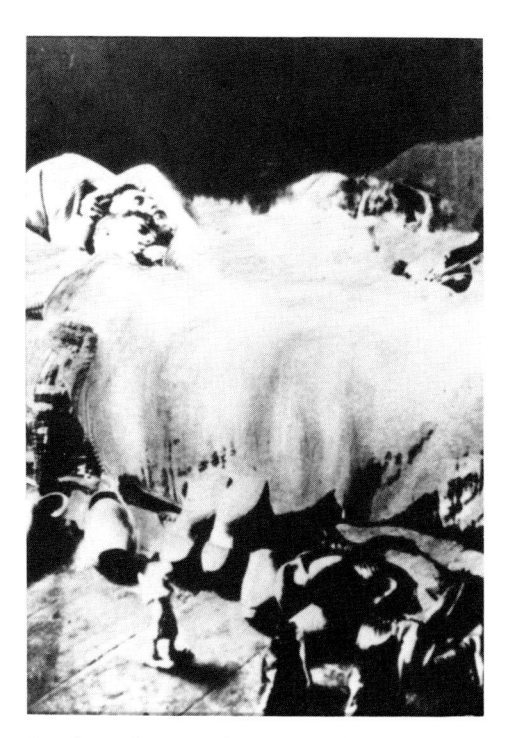

Stephen Crane asleep in bed with another man during bohemian days at the Art Students' League, 1893–1894. As explained by his niece, Edith Crane, in a letter to Thomas Beer (30 December 1933): "A couple of friends finding him and another friend asleep together, had quietly piled up all the shoes they could find around the sleeping pair, adding even wooden shoes and a statuette, and had taken their picture." (Barrett Collection, University of Virginia)

Corwin Knapp Linson's oil portrait of Stephen Crane, 1894. (Barrett Collection, University of Virginia)

Hartwood
Sullivan Co., N.Y.
January 27th.

Dear Mr Heineman:

I have just read Mr George Wyndham's review and I feel glad to be able to write you that I think it a very wonderful thing. Of course it is difficult for me to speak of The Red Badge of Courage as I wrote it when I was between twenty-one and twenty-two years of age and have lost sense of its being of any value. Still I am conscious that Mr Wyndham has reproduced in a large measure my own hopeful thoughts of the book when it was still for the most part in my head. As near as a man can do it, he convinces me that the thing is in some ways an artistic success. As far as I know he is the one writer to arouse in me the joyful hope that perhaps the book is good. I wish you would extend to him a serious expression of my gratitude and appreciation. If it were not my own work that was under discussion I would give you many reasons for my thinking the article in The New Review a very remarkable essay.

Yours sincerely
Stephen Crane

P.S.: If you would care to send me two or three copies of The New Review of January I would be very glad. I trouble you only because being at Hartwood it would be immensely difficult to otherwise get them.

*Nellie Crouse, Akron, Ohio, winter of 1896.
(Syracuse University)*

A letter from Stephen Crane to his English publisher William Heinemann, 27 January [1896]. (Newark Museum, Newark, New Jersey)

Cora Crane at the time of her marriage to Captain Donald William Stewart. (Syracuse University)

A letter from Stephen Crane to his brother, William Howe Crane, from Athens, 10 April [1897]. (Columbia University)

GRAND HOTEL D'ANGLETERRE
ATHENS (GREECE)
ELECTRIC LIGHT THROUGHOUT THE BUILDING

April 10

My dear Will: I arrived in Athens three days ago and am going to the frontier shortly. I expect to get a position on the staff of the Crown Prince. Won't that be great? I am so happy over it I can hardly breathe. I shall try — I shall try like Hayes to get a decoration out of the thing but that depends on good fortune and is between you and I and God. Athens is not much ruins, you know. It is mostly adobe creations like Mexico although the Acropolis sticks up in the air precisely like it does in the pictures. I was in Crete but saw no fighting. However the exhibition of foreign war-ships was great. The reputation of my poor old book has reached a few of the blooming Greeks and that is what has done the Crown Prince business for me. If I get on the staff I shall let you know at once. They say I've got a sure thing. They like Americans very much over here anyhow, or rather they hate all the others and so we have an advantage. It isn't usual so much for a foreigner of standing to get on the staff but then it sounds fine and it really is fine too in a way and I am so happy tonight I can hardly remain silent and write

GRAND HOTEL D'ANGLETERRE
ATHENS (GREECE)
ELECTRIC LIGHT THROUGHOUT THE BUILDING

I hope and pray that you are all well and that I see you all again. Love to everyone
Yours affectionately
S.

Write to me here

Cora Crane in the uniform of a war correspondent in Greece. Inscribed to Stephen Crane with her pen name, "Imogene Carter." (Syracuse University)

[1] Crane's reply to No. 87. Crane had sent two poems: "The chatter of a death-demon from a tree-top," *Philistine*, 1 (August 1895), 93, and "Each small gleam was a voice," *Philistine*, 1 (September 1895), 124.

96. FROM ELBERT HUBBARD
ALS, NNC.

E Aurora. N.Y. [after 20] July 95,

My dear Mr Crane:

I thank you very much for your kind letter just rec'd. I am sure that your verses will do us good, and we will take great pleasure in giving you a full page for an announcement in the Sep. issue.[1] I suggest setting the announcement in caps and placing it at top of page after the manner that you have made distinctive.

I know the Literary Editor of the Rochester Democrat. He is a first rate good fellow who has a column to fill up every day. What will he say when he sees your work in the Philistine? Why he'll congratulate us on having secured so able a contributor.

I do not confess to an unqualified liking for your work. When you hand me the book I am grown suddenly blind. It rather appeals to my nerves than to my reason—it gives me a thrill. Your work is of a kind so charged with electricity that it cannot be handled. It is all live wire. It eludes all ordinary criticism and it escapes before one can apply his Harvard Rhetorical Test. What is left? I'll tell you, we can stand off and hoot—if we have columns to fill we can fill them with plain hoot. Your lines show too much individuality to pass by and so we laugh and work the feeble joke. Thank God for the feeble joke! It fills in many an awkward pause. Those Roman soldiers hailed him "King of the Jews!" It was a great joke and the only thing they could think of to say or do.

With high esteem I am

Sincerely Yours
Elbert Hubbard

[1] Not only did Hubbard pay Crane nothing for his poems, but he also failed to fulfill his promise to advertise the October 1895 publication of *The Red Badge of Courage* in the *Philistine*.

97. FROM WILLIAM HOWE CRANE
ACS, NNC.

Port J., July 29/95.

I see by the paper that you are going to Twin Lake[1] soon. Cornelia and the children went away on Saturday to spend the rest of the summer.

Yours truly,
W*m*. H. Crane.

[1] Twin Lakes, near Milford in Pike County, Pennsylvania, where Crane camped for a few weeks in August with a group of friends.

98. TO RIPLEY HITCHCOCK
ALS, Collection of Stanley and Mary Wertheim, New York City.

Parker's Glen,
Pike County, Penn.
August 3*d* [1895]

Dear Mr Hitchcock: Please send all proof[1] to the above post-office. As a matter of fact I dont care much to see the page proof.

Yours sincerely
Stephen Crane.

[1] Page proof of *The Red Badge of Courage*.

99. TO KARL KNORTZ[1]
ALS, NSyU.

>Parker's Glen,
>Pike Co, Penn.,
>August 3d, 95

Mr Karl Knortz;

Dear sir: I have requested the publishers to forward you at once a copy of The Black Riders and I remain anxious to see your frank opinion of it as expressed in the Leipsic publication.

>Sincerely yours
>Stephen Crane

[1] Head of the German Department in the public schools of Evansville, Indiana. Edwin H. Cady and Lester G. Wells, in their edition of *Stephen Crane's Love Letters to Nellie Crouse* (Syracuse: Syracuse University Press, 1954), p. 79, mention that Knortz had translated Longfellow and Whittier into German. Whether or not he reviewed *The Black Riders* for a Leipzig publication as Crane anticipated is unknown.

100. TO COPELAND AND DAY
ALS, ViU.

>Parker's Glen,
>Pike Co., Penn.
>August 3d. [1895]

Copeland and Day

Dear sirs: Please forward a "Black Riders" to the enclosed gentleman.[1]

>Sincerely
>Stephen Crane

At my charge if necessary.

[1]Crane apparently enclosed Karl Knortz's name and address with this letter.

101. TO WILLIS BROOKS HAWKINS
ALS, ViU.

Parker's Glen
Pike Co., Penn
August 9, '95

My dear Willis: I am cruising around the woods in corduroys and feeling great. I have lots of fun getting healthy. Feel great.

If anything in the way of notices comes out and you see it, send them to me here for I feel out of the world.

There are six girls in camp and it is with the greatest difficulty that I think coherently on any other subject.

Wish you could come up some Sunday. Only—it is with the greatest trouble that any one can reach here. Four deadly miles up the mountain from the Erie's station at Parker's Glen. If you would care to do it let me know and I will tell you how to do it.

My remembrances to Mrs Hawkins and to Florence

Yours, as ever
S. C.

102. TO WILLIS BROOKS HAWKINS
ALS, ViU.

> Parker's Glen
> Pike Co, Penn
> August 18. [1895]

My dear Willis: The Philistine people have written to me about the notice of *The Red Badge of Courage* which they wish to bring out in their September number, What shall I say in it. I dont know how to write those notices. Can you advise me concerning a little notice. (I meant to say *will* you.) I hope you are awfully well. Did you get my last letter. My remembrances to all the lanterns,[1] I am getting mighty anxious to hear the Apache Scalp Dance again. I will down however in about 2 weeks more.

> Yours as always
> S. C.

[1] Members of the Lantern Club.

103. TO RIPLEY HITCHCOCK
ALfr, NN.

> Parker's Glen
> Pike Co. Penn
> August 26 [1895]

Dear Mr Hitchcock: The title page proof is all right.
Will you write an ad. for the Philistine & send it to me here?

119

104. FROM ELBERT HUBBARD
ALS on *Philistine* stationery, NNC.

E Aurora Aug 26 [1895]

My Dear Mr Crane:

I sent you several copies of The Philistine to New York on 1*st* inst but I fear that they missed you. Have just sent more to your present address.[1]

Will use the "Lantern Song" this month—we are putting it in caps on first page.[2]

Your poem in Aug number[3] brought us more notices than all other articles combined. Several very complimentary, but others mystified of course.

With high regard I am
Sincerely Yours
Elbert Hubbard

P.S. Why can't you come up and stay a month with me here at the farm?

---

[1] Parker's Glen, Pike County, Pennsylvania.

[2] Poems in *The Black Riders* were untitled. Hubbard published "Each small gleam was a voice" in the September issue of the *Philistine* under the title "A Lantern Song," but he did not place it on the first page.

[3] "The chatter of a death-demon from a tree-top," *Philistine*, 1 (August 1895), 93.

105. FROM EDWARD E. HALE, JR.[1]
ALS, NNC.

Schenectady, N.Y.
Sept 5th 95

My dear Mr Crane,

Mr Howells tells me that I must apply to you about your story "Maggie." If you would send me a copy I should be glad to send you the proper return.

You may not feel particularly complimented to know that I was led to wish to see it, through an interest in dialect study. Not being, however, an entire stranger to your work, I am sure I shall enjoy it much from other, and perhaps more legitimate, points of view.

Believe me
Yours truly
Edward E. Hale, Jr.,
Union College,
Schenectady,
N.Y.

[1] Son and biographer of the author of *The Man Without a Country*.

106. TO WILLIS BROOKS HAWKINS
ALS, ViU.

Office of The Press.,
Philadelphia, Sept 6. [1895]

Dear Willis: It is dramatic criticism and nuttin else.[1] I've taken it and am to go to work at once. I will however be in New York on Tuesday night for the dinner, and will talk at length to you. I wrote to Mr Howells to-day asking him to come to the dinner.

Yours as ever
S. C.

¹Crane believed he had been engaged to write dramatic criticism for the *Philadelphia Press*, which had published his only effort in this genre, the syndicated "Grand Opera in New Orleans," the preceding March. As No. 107 reveals, the business office of the *Press* did not approve the appointment.

107. TO WILLIS BROOKS HAWKINS
ALS, ViU.

2840 Ridge Ave.
Philadelphia
Tuesday. [10 September 1895]

Dear old man: Things fell ker-plunk. Stranded here in Phila. Dont you care! Nice town. Got lots of friends, though, and 23,842 invitations to dinner of which I have accepted 2.

The Press wanted me bad enough but the business manager suddenly said: "Nit"

Yours as ever
S. C.

108. TO WILLIS BROOKS HAWKINS
ALS, ViU.

#2840 Ridge Ave.,
Philadelphia
Sept 18. [1895]

My dear Willis: I am going to stay down for a few more days. If you see anything for me in New York holler quick. I am with some friends, pretty good time but I am engaged at last on my personal troubles in Mexico.[1]

Yours as ever
S. C.

[1] Crane had been pursued in Mexico by a bandit named Ramon Colorado. He fictionalized this adventure in a syndicated newspaper sketch published as "One Dash—Horses" in the *Philadelphia Press*, 4 and 6 January 1896.

109. TO WILLIS BROOKS HAWKINS
ALS on telegraph blank, ViU.

Answer
165 W 23d
[early October 1895]

My dear Willis: Can you bring over a poker contingent tonight. The place is all torn to shreds—I'm moving to Hartwood[1] but would be glad to welcome a poker party.

S. C.

[1] In a letter written on 11 May 1960 to Lillian B. Gilkes (OU), Edith F. Crane recalled that Crane brought along with him his possessions:

Some of the things are three chairs that are much admired antiques now. There are two wall plaques, round ones of plaster. One is the head of Mozart, the other of Beethoven. Two beautiful large casts of a lion and a lioness have been broken. There was a full set of teacups, and a set of wine, or whiskey glasses. There's a beautiful little Cloisonne teapot. [There] stood in one corner of our living room a bedwarmer tied with a big satin bow. In another was our large tiptop table over which he draped his serape. There are besides two framed engravings that look as though they are illustrations for *The Red Badge*. There was another picture painted in colors. Agnes [Edith's sister] took it when she married and we never got it back.

"Mame," Uncle Stephen said to my mother, "If I don't come back, these things are yours."

110. TO WILLIS BROOKS HAWKINS
ALS, ViU.

165 West 23d
[early October 1895]

My dear Willis: By all means you fellows come here tonight. Looked for you this afternoon in the Downing Build'g. This will be my last game—perhaps. Expect to skip for the country. Dont let the game fall through.

Yours
S Crane

111. TO FREDERIC M. LAWRENCE[1]
Inscribed in a copy of *The Red Badge of Courage*, as recorded in Frederic M. Lawrence, *The Real Stephen Crane*, ed. Joseph Katz (Newark: Newark Public Library, 1980), p. 13.

[early October 1895][2]

Stephen Crane
and
F. Mortimer Lawrence, M.D.
Of a friendship that began when books and
medicine alike were dreams
and ended—
This from one to the other.[3]

¹A fraternity brother of Crane at Syracuse. Crane shared rooms with Lawrence, a medical student, at 1064 Avenue A, the "Pendennis Club," in New York City while he was revising *Maggie* in the autumn of 1892.

²Lawrence, in *The Real Stephen Crane*, p. 14, says that the date was included with the inscription, but he does not cite it.

³Lawrence described the occasion for the signing: "I will never forget the day Crane and I went to Wanamakers and actually purchased our first copy and tenderly carried it around the corner to the old Rathskellar, there to feast our eyes on its pages" (p. 13).

112. TO IRVING BACHELLER
Inscribed in a copy of *The Red Badge of Courage*, ViU.

To Mr Irving Bachellor,
with the esteem and
regards of Stephen Crane.

Oct 14, 1895

113. TO WICKHAM W. YOUNG
Letters, p. 64.

The Hartwood Club
Hartwood Sul Co, N.Y.
Oct 21st, 1895

My dear Wick: My brother William H. is running for Surrogate of Orange County on the Democratic ticket and although I know you fellows dont care so much for politics I am immensely interested in seeing the boy make a creditable record for himself wether [sic] he gets elected or not. The other man is Howell from here and he isn't so nice. Surrogate isn't much of a political office any how, and you can swallow all the rest of the Republican ticket if you like. Be careful, though, about the mechanical part of it. Understand you know that this is merely a broad general hint and I know too that any kind of a man will do just as he damned pleases in the matter, but—you see how it is. Let me hear wether [sic] this makes you made [sic] or not. I am going to gun for W.W.W. and A.A., too.

Yours as ever
Stephen Crane

114. TO WICKHAM W. YOUNG
Letters, p. 64.

Hartwood, N.Y.
Oct 23d, 95

My dear Wick: I am delighted at your good-nature in the election business. Will is a good fellow and very honest and clever. I would like to snare Arly and Bill Woodward but dont quite know how to go about it as I dont feel that I know them as well as I do you and anyhow I hate to monkey about politics. I used to think that distinquished [sic] merit had some weight but it isn't worth a damn, relatively speaking. The man who hustles is the man who gets there and if some honest person is opposing a thief, he wants to be busy or the thief will snow him under, which is, after all, what everybody knows.

I am working pretty well here. Better than in New York. Missed my first partridge today. Crash.

Yours as ever
Stephen Crane

115. TO WILLIS BROOKS HAWKINS
ALS, NSyU.

Hartwood
Sullivan Co., N.Y.
[24 October 1895]

My dear Willis: The brown October woods are simply great. There is a kitten in the stables who walks like Ada Rehan and there is a dog who trims his whiskers like the late President Carnot's whiskers. Gypsey, cousin to Greylight and blood relative of the noble Lynne bel, who lost the Transylvania so capably at Lexington this season—well. Gypsey ran away with me. What can be finer than a fine frosty morning, a runaway horse, and only the still hills to watch. Lord, I do love a crazy horse with just a little pig-skin between him and me. You can push your lifeless old bicycles around the country but a slim-limbed thoroughbred's dauntless spirit is better. Some people take much trouble to break a horse of this or that. I dont. Let him fling himself to the other side of the road because a sumach tassle waves. If your knees are not self-acting enough for that sort of thing, get off and walk. Hartwood scenery is good when viewed swiftly.

I missed my first partridge yesterday. Keh-plunk. Bad ground, 'though. Too many white birches. I haven't written a line yet. Dont intend to for some time. Clip anything you see in the papers and send it. Remember me to everybody at Greene Ave. I have heard indirectly from Brentano's that the damned "Red Badge" is having a very nice sale

Yours as always
Stephen Crane

116. TO RIPLEY HITCHCOCK
ALS, NN.

Hartwood, N.Y.
Oct 29 [1895]

Dear Mr. Hitchcock: The story is working out fine.[1] I have made seven chapters in the rough and they have given me the proper enormous interest in the theme. I have adopted such a "quick" style for the story that I don't believe it can work out much beyond twenty-five thousand words—perhaps thirty—possibly thirty-five. Can you endure that length?—I mean, should you like the story otherwise, can you use a story that length?

Mr. Howells almost always speaks of my work in Harper's Weekly and, if you cared to, a book might be sent to him.[2]

I have lost a certain document relating to the making over of ownership of copyright. If you will send me another copy, I will sign it at once.

Yours sincerely
Stephen Crane

[1] *The Third Violet*.
[2] Howells reviewed *Maggie* in *Harper's Weekly* on 8 June and *The Red Badge* on 26 October 1895.

117. FROM GUSTAV A. ROEDELL
ALS, ViU.

Gallipolis, Ohio,
Oct. 30, 1895.

Mr. Stephen Crane,

My Dear Sir:

If it is not asking too much, dare I beg that you will do me the great honor to transcribe your poem, "He was a brave heart," to insert in my copy of *The Black Riders and Other Lines*?[1]

The favor would be valued more than I can say.

I have the honor to remain

Your obliged servant,
Gustav A. Roedell.

[1] The concluding stanza of "There was a man and a woman," No. LXI of *The Black Riders*.

118. FROM THE CORRESPONDING EDITOR OF *THE YOUTH'S COMPANION*
Letterhead: "The Youth's Companion." ALS, ViU.

Boston. October the 31st [1895]

Mr. Stephen Crane

My Dear Sir

In common with the rest of mankind we have been reading The Red Badge of Courage and other war stories by you. And our editors feel a strong desire to have some of your tales in The Youth's Companion.

I want to invite you to submit some of your work to The Companion for consideration.[1] While we have a number of standards inside of which all our stories have to fall I am confident that you would not find them a grave inconvenience. But to save you possible misdirection of effort, would you be so kind—(if our invitation is acceptable to you) to write me and let me send you a few hints as to the kind of stories we want and dont want.

Will you also let me say that for the higher grades of work the substantial recognition which The Companion gives to authors is not surpassed in any American periodical.

Very Truly Yours
The Corresponding Editor

P.S. For your address I am indebted to the politeness of Messrs Copeland and Day, the former of whom is one of our editors.

L. B.[2]

[1] None of Crane's work appeared in *The Youth's Companion* within his lifetime. "An Episode of War" was reprinted with textual variations from earlier publications in the 16 March 1916 issue of the magazine. An appended note reads that the story "was written for *The Companion* just twenty years ago this month."

[2] Probably either Louise Baker or L. J. Bridgman, both of whom were connected with the *Companion*.

119. TO WILLIS BROOKS HAWKINS
ALS, ViU.

Hartwood, Sul. Co., N.Y
Nov 1st. [1895]

My dear Willis: My correspondence—incoming—has reached mighty proportions and if I answered them all I would make Hartwood a better class office and my brother[1] a better class post-master for you know he is a postmaster, justice-of-the-peace, ice-man, farmer, mill-wright, blue stone man, lumberman, station agent on the P.J.M. and N.Y.R.R,[2] and many other things which I now forget. He and his tribe can swing the majority in the township of Lumberland. By that reference to my correspondents I meant the fellows before the war.

They're turning up. Heaven send them somebody to appreciate them more although it is true I write two or three perfunctory little notes each day.

There has been an enormous raft of R.B. of C. reviews and Appleton and Co have written me quite a contented letter about the sale of the book. Copeland and Day have written for my New York sketches and Appleton and Co wish to put my new story in their Zeit-Geist series, Which I leave you alone to pronounce. Devil take me if I give you any assistance.

That's enough about books.

On the bicycle question, I refuse to listen to you. In the old days at military school I once rode a wheel—a high one—about three miles high, I think. An unsmiling young cadet brought one into the armory one morning and as I was his senior officer I took it away from him. I mounted by means of a friend and rode around and around the armory. It was very simple.

When I wished to dismount however I found I couldn't. So I rode around and around the armory. Shafer, who was champion of Pennsylvania in those old high-wheel days, watched me and said I did some things on that wheel which were impossible to him. A group of cadets gathered in a corner and yelled whenever I passed them. I abjured them at intervals to let me off that wheel but they only hollered. At last, I ran into a bench and fell neatly on my head. It broke the machine, too, praise God. Some days later I whipped the boy who had loaned it me. Not for that, mind you, but for something else.

I am shooting a good deal. I beat my brother the last time out. That's a good deal.

I have another brother who is running for surrogate of Orange County and I haven't a doubt but that he will achieve a magnificent defeat. For he is a bold Democrat and they're rare birds in Orange.

Give my remembrances cordially to all your people and say that I regret the Apaches and the Pilgrims. Remember me too at the Lantern.

Yours as always
Stephen Crane

[1] Edmund Crane.
[2] The Port Jervis Midland and New York Railroad.

120. TO WILLIS BROOKS HAWKINS
ALS, ViU.

[about 2 November 1895]

Dear Willis: Here are two sample letters.[1]

S. C.

[1] Nos. 117 and 118.

121. TO LUCIUS L. BUTTON
Fragment of item 83, Catalogue 3827 (11-12 March 1930), American Art Association Anderson Galleries.

Hartwood, Sullivan County, N.Y., Nov. 3, 1896 [for 1895]

When I returned from Mexico I tried to look you up but you had incontinently vanished. . . . I am up here writing another book. . . .

122. FROM ELBERT HUBBARD
ALS on *Philistine* stationery, NNC.

East Aurora, N.Y.
Nov 4 '95.

Dear Mr. Crane:

The enclosed[1] sounds a bit formal, but it is all straight business and I trust you will see your way clear to accept.

The newspaper men of Buffalo and even that arrant varlet on the Rochester Chronicle will co-operate with us to make the dinner a big success, also the manager of the Associated Press. "The Red Badge" is a strong work—thoroughly well sustained. I congratulate you on it.

Sincerely Your friend
Elbert Hubbard

Send acceptance to me.

---

[1]No. 126. Crane copied Nos. 122 and 126 (ViU), writing at the top of No. 122 "Personal letter from Hubbard. Verbatim" and at the top of No. 126 "*Verbatim*" and sent both to Hawkins on 8 November. Both copies are inaccurate transcriptions containing minor errors. Crane occasionally copied out letters that praised him.

123. TO THE CORRESPONDING EDITOR OF *THE YOUTH'S COMPANION*
ALS, ViU.

Hartwood
Nov 5th [1895]

The Corresponding Editor,
The Youth's Companion,

My dear sir: I am very grateful for your letter of October 31st., and I am sure that I would be very glad to write for the Companion. My time is just now possessed by a small novel but in the future, I might perchance do a story that you would like. Such possible stories I would send to you, if I was informed of your literary platform and I would be happy to hear from you concerning it.

Very truly yours,
Stephen Crane.

124. TO POST WHEELER
TT, NSyU.

Hartwood Nov 5 [1895]

My dear Post: It is good of you to remember me so often. I saw the Town Topics review. Didn't I show it to you at the Club. I am working out-of-sight. Novel third done.

Yours as ever
Stephen Crane

125. TO AN UNKNOWN RECIPIENT
Inscribed on a copy of *Maggie*, CSmH.

With compliments.
Stephen Crane.

Nov 5. 1895

126. FROM THE COMMITTEE FOR THE PHILISTINE SOCIETY
ALS in Hubbard's hand, NNC.

East Aurora N.Y. Nov 5, '95

My Dear Mr Crane:

Recognizing your merit as a man and your genius as a poet, and wishing that the world should know you better, the Society of the Philistines tender you a dinner to take place at the Iroquois Hotel in Buffalo in about one month.

As soon as we receive your acceptance stating the date that suits you best we will send out invitations to 200 of the best known writers publishers and newspaper men of the United States and England.

We have already secured transportation for you and we further beg to assure you that you will be our guest as long as you remain here. We believe that aside from the charming friendly intercourse of the occasion that the dinner will be of very great value to your books and will lead to a wider recognition of your talent.

Pray favor us with an early answer giving date that suits you best. With high esteem, Dear Sir, we are,

> Elbert Hubbard
> H. P. Taber.
> W*m* McIntosh, Mgn Editor Buffalo News
> E R White, of the News
> A. G. Blythe Buffalo Express.

127. TO WILLIS BROOKS HAWKINS
ALS, ViU.

> Hartwood
> Nov 8 [1895]

Dear Willis: I sent down to Port Jervis to-day to get hung up for fifty cents worth of tobacco and on the same train with the tobacco came the enclosed interesting cummunications.[1] My dress suit took to the woods long ago and my 1895 overcoat is not due until 1896. I have not owned a pair of patent leather shoes in three years. Write me at once and tell me how to get out of the thing. Of course I am dead sore but I think if you will invent for me a very decent form of refusal, I will still be happy up here with my woods.

> Yours as always
> S. C.

[1] Nos. 122 and 126.

128. TO WILLIS BROOKS HAWKINS
ALS, ViU.

[Port Jervis, N.Y., 8 November 1895]

My dear Willis: I always considered Field[1] to be a fine simple spirit and I am glad his death makes you so sad.

I never thought him a western barbarian. I have always believed the western people to be much truer than the eastern people. We in the east are overcome a good deal by a detestable superficial culture which I think is the real barbarism. Culture in it's true sense, I take it, is a comprehension of the man at one's shoulder. It has nothing to do with an adoration for effete jugs and old kettles. This latter is merely an amusement and we live for amusement in the east. Damn the east! I fell in love with the straight out-and-out, sometimes-hideous, often-braggart westerners because I thought them to be the truer men and, by the living piper, we will see in the next fifty years what the west will do. They are serious, those fellows. When they are born they take one big gulp of wind and then they live.

Of course, the east thinks them ridiculous. When they come to congress they display a child-like honesty which makes the old east laugh. And yet—

Garland will wring every westerner by the hand and hail him as a frank honest man. I wont. No, sir. But what I contend for is the atmosphere of the west which really is frank and honest and is bound to make eleven honest men for one pessimistic thief. More glory be with them.

The novel is one-third completed.[2] I am not sure that it is any good. It is easy work. I can finish a chapter each day. I want you to see it before it goes to the Appletons.

Sometimes I go out sailing in a little boat here. The people are expecting my death shortly for the little boat leans like a shingle on a house—when she tacks—and the November winds are very strong.

My brother William went down in the Democratic wreck. Poor boy.

It is singular that the Republicans won in every place where it was to the glory of God that they should lose, and lost in every place where it was to the glory of God that they should win.

I am very contented here. For a while I felt incarcerated but not, now. Good-bye. My remembrances always to your Greene Ave castle.

Your friend—ever
Stephen Crane

[1] Eugene Field, who died on 4 November.
[2] *The Third Violet*. Crane sent the completed manuscript to Hitchcock on 27 December 1895, but Appleton did not publish the novel until May 1897.

129. FROM THE COMMITTEE FOR THE PHILISTINE SOCIETY

Elbert Hubbard, *The Members of the Society* (East Aurora: Roycroft Printing Shop, 1895) [one of three pamphlets commemorating the banquet].

East Aurora, N.Y., Nov. 10, 1895.

To Mr. Stephen Crane:

Recognizing in yourself and in your genius as a poet, a man whom we would like to know better, The Society of the Philistines desire to give a dinner in your honor early in the future. If this meets with your approval we should be glad if you will let us know upon what date you could conveniently come to us.

Elbert Hubbard.
H. P. Taber, Editor of the *Philistine*.
Samuel G. Blythe, of the Buffalo *Express*.
Wm. McIntosh of the Buffalo *News*.
Eugene R. White of the Buffalo *News*.
Philip Hale of the Boston *Journal*.
Nelson Ayres of the New Orleans *Picayune*.
L. H. Bickford of the Denver *Times*.
Marshall Cushing of the Washington *Capital*.
Walter Blackburn Harte of *Moods*.
John Northern Hilliard of the Rochester *Union and Advertiser*.

Committee for the Society.

130. TO ELBERT HUBBARD
ALS, Collection of Maurice F. Neville, Santa Barbara, California.

Hartwood, N.Y.
Nov 11th. [1895]

My dear Mr Hubbard: You must have known of course what an astonishment and delight the invitation of the Philistines would be to me and I need scarcely announce to you here that I have accepted it. Of course I am a very simple person and I am dejected when I think of the disappointment of my friends, the Philistines, if they have been good enough to form any opinion at all favorable of my ability or my personality. But I am delighted with the invitation of course and though I was amazed that I occurred to you at all, I was blissfully conscious of the honor. Name any date—as I have said elsewhere—and let me know quickly. Remember that I would come to Buffalo any time possible if I were to meet none of it's citizens but the courageous and stout warriors who conduct the Philistine Magazine. I am at Hartwood writing a novel which must end in forty-five more days but I have it over half finished. Until we meet—

Very sincerely yours
Stephen Crane

Hartwood is in Sullivan Co., N.Y.

131. FROM WILLIS B. HAWKINS
ALS, NNC.

875 Greene Ave., Nov. 11. [1895]

My dear Stephen: I intended to write to you last night, but the folks lured me into an amateur game of poker (penny ante) and I was so sleepy that I went to bed as soon as it was over. I am a bit rocky this morning—(up at the unreasonable, unreasonable hour of 7)—but I want this to get to you soon as possible so that you you may answer the Buffalo fellows without delay, for you must—you just *must*—accept their invitation. There is a business side of life that must not be wholly ignored. It hasn't a leg to stand on, and there's no honest reason for it's being, but here it is and—there you are. I could sit and give ten reasons why you must go to that dinner for one why you can't; and then, by gum, I can set even the one aside. You go ahead and accept. Tell me of the day you fix on, and I'll agree that you'll be togged properly for the occasion. Send me your chest measurement and your length of leg (from your crotch to your heel—you remember Lincoln's answer when he was asked how long an ideal soldier's leg should be)[1] and I'll find some way. Tell me, too, what size—anybody with an ear for rhyme would know that the next word is—shoe best fits you. I'm not one of those proper persons who get up early in the morning to write—even letters. I'll write the letter part later.

Yours, very sincerely, all the time,
Willis B. Hawkins

[1] Lincoln believed that a soldier's leg should be at least long enough to reach the ground.

132. TO WILLIS BROOKS HAWKINS
ALS, ViU.

[Hartwood, N.Y., 11 or 12 November 1895][1]

My dear Willis: Upon my soul when I first read your letter I was ashamed that I had written you about it at all. Then when I reflect I find I wrote you because the letter delighted and charmed me and I had to whoop it up to somebody. But heavens, to think you would allow me to make a victim of you! For, blast it all, on the strength of your letter I have accepted the invitation. At first, as I said, I was dismayed at your letter but, confound it, you might understand that I blush for myself more still when I think I was low enough to grab at your generosity.

I told the Philistines that any date in late November or early December would suit me. When they write, you shall hear from me at once. I shall go and I shall have a dandy time, I know, and am satisfied that it will do me an immense amount of good. My chest, bad luck to it, measures 35 inches—scant—and my leg is a 33—worse luck. And foot—rot it—is a seven. There! It is over. I feel as if I have told you that I am a damned thief.

Heaven send you rest, Willis, and in your old age may you remember how you befriended the greatest literary blockhead in America from himself.

The novel is exactly half finished. It seems clever sometimes and sometimes it seems nonsensical. I hope to show it you in less than two months. The Evening Post has come out very grandly in support of the Black Riders. And the Boston papers have said some fine things about the Red Badge.

What do you suppose made the Philistines do this dinner thing? Was it because I wrote for their magazine? You could have knocked me down with a gas-pipe when I got their bid. Until today I was very miserable about it for I of course was resolved to refuse the offer. But, bad luck to me again, I was delighted with your letter and accepted it "within-side" of thirty minutes.

The woods up here are all dun and dusk and purple save where there are pines or white birches. The little lake is like blue crystal.
I am as always Willis

Your good friend
Stephen Crane

[1]Dated "About November 15" in *Letters*, this letter was written a few days earlier. Crane wrote Hubbard on 15 November accepting 19 December as the date for the Philistine banquet; consequently, his statement here to Hawkins that "any date in late November or early December would suit me" would be inconsistent if it had been written on 15 November.

No. 132, which is Crane's hurried response to No. 131, was most likely written on 11 or 12 November. Crane could have gotten Hawkins' letter in the afternoon because same-day delivery was common between Hartwood and New York City. As soon as Crane received it, he wrote Nos. 130 and 132, saying to Hawkins that "on the strength of your letter I have accepted the invitation."

133. TO THE COMMITTEE FOR THE PHILISTINE SOCIETY BANQUET

Elbert Hubbard, *The Members of the Society* (East Aurora: Roycroft Printing Shop, 1895) [One of three pamphlets commemorating the banquet].

Hartwood, N.Y., Nov. 15, 1895.

To Mr. Elbert Hubbard, Mr. Harry P. Taber, Mr. Eugene R. White, Mr. Wm. McIntosh, Mr. Walter Blackburn Harte, Mr. S. G. Blythe, Mr. John Northern Hilliard, Mr. Philip Hale, Mr. Nelson Ayres, Mr. L. H. Bickford, Mr. Marshall Cushing, of the Society of the Philistines.

Gentlemen:

The only obstacle in the way of my accepting an invitation at once so cordial and so kind is the fact that an acceptance, it seems to me, is a tacit admission of my worthiness in the circumstances. Believe me, this sense of embarrassment that I should be at all considered as a fit person for such distinction is my solitary discomfort. But I have industriously blunted this sense and can say that it will deal me great pleasure to dine with the Society of the Philistines on Thursday evening, Dec. 19th.

I beg to thank you, gentlemen, and pray believe me that I am ever

Very Sincerely Yours,
Stephen Crane.

134. FROM ELBERT HUBBARD

ALS on *Philistine* stationery, ViU.

Nov 16, '95.

My Dear Mr Crane:

I am delighted with your letters of acceptance, and write now merely to acknowledge your letters and thank you. We want this dinner to be perfect and complete in all its appointments and therefore we will submit proof of invitations and list of invited guests to you for suggestion and revisal.

I feared you might think we were merely contemplating a pleasant meeting and dinner with you. But it is more than this—you represent a "cause" and we wish in a dignified, public (and at the same time) elegant manner to recognize that cause.

I fear it will be fully Dec 15th before arrangements can be fully perfected.

Will write you soon again and inform you of exactly what arrangements are being made.

Yours Truly
Elbert Hubbard

135. TO ELBERT HUBBARD
ALfrS, KU.

[after 16 November 1895][1]

two small bits which you may or may not care to use. If the Philistines might like it, I can send you a little sketch in prose—1000 words.[2]

I return you the letters. I am always afraid of losing them. By the way, if you cared to—I am sure William Heineman, 21 Bedford St., W.C., London, Eng., would be delighted at an invitation from you. He's my English publisher for the Red B. I am continually wondering how it is possible for me to repay you-all for your trouble

Yours sincerely
Stephen Crane

[1] As soon as Hubbard received Crane's acceptances to attend the banquet (Nos. 130 and 133), he began sending invitations to authors, journalists, and others who he felt might confer prestige upon a literary event. As responses arrived, Hubbard forwarded some of them to Crane, as indicated in Nos. 134 and 147.

[2] The sketch or one of the "small bits" may have been "A Great Mistake," which appeared in *The Philistine*, 2 (March 1896), 106-9.

136. TO WILLIS BROOKS HAWKINS
ALS, ViU.

Hartwood, N.Y.
Nov 15th. [for 17 November 1895][1]

Dear Willis: Herein enclosed letter of Hubbard. Write to me quick and tell me that you dont think I am a villian. Would you come out to Buffalo for the dinner?

I am getting frightened already. Imagine me representing a "cause."

Yours always
Stephen

[1]Crane enclosed Hubbard's letter of 16 November; and because he wanted Hawkins to respond as soon as possible, he most likely wrote to him on 17 November.

137. TO ELBERT HUBBARD
TT, CtU.

Hartwood, N.Y.
Nov. 18 [1895]

My dear Mr. Hubbard: Your photograph came today and I thank you heartily for it. I have none of mine own but I have been looking sideways at photograph galleries for some time and I am quite sure that I will be able to compass the thing before I come to Buffalo.

I am quite an old reader of your Little Journeys and I think them the best things that have been said.[1]

Yours very sincerely
Stephen Crane

[1]Commencing in January 1895 Hubbard wrote a series of 170 monthly *Little Journeys* sketches dealing with his visits to the homes of the great and near great. They were issued as chapbooks from Hubbard's press in East Aurora, New York, and were immensely popular.

138. TO WILLIS BROOKS HAWKINS
ALS, ViU.

Hartwood
Nov 19. [1895]

My dear Willis: I have no late news from Buffalo, although Hubbard sent me his picture some days ago. He is a clever-looking duck. I hope by all means you can come to the Buffalo dinner. For heaven's sake, begin to think about it now and then by the time the day comes around it will seem easy.

There is a clipping bureau in Boston which is said to only send in it's bills once in three months, so when they wrote me the other day I took them up. I got forty-one new reviews of the Red Badge. And, oh, say, most of 'em were not only favorable but passionately enthusiastic. They didnt skirmish around and say maybe—perhaps—if—after a time—it is possible—under certain circumstances—but.

No; they were cock-sure. The above is a fair sample of New York literary criticism. The fellows in Boston, ten of them,—had a real nice fit. In the west, the Chicago Post and the Minneapolis Tribune were the best but there were a lot of other good ones. About six in the patch are roasts. One is a copy of the Tribune's grind.[1] New York, throughout, has treated me worse than any other city. Damn New York. Except the Evening Post. The Evening Post has just reviewed The Black Riders beautifully.

There—I'm through talking about them but then you know there is nobody here whom one can talk to about them at all. It sounds sort of priggish, somehow. And it is I have no doubt. excepting that it is right to be elated when almost all the writers and reviewers seem to have really read the thing.

The new novel is two-thirds done.[2] I gave the first eighteen chapters to my brother Teddie[3] to read. He finished them up without a halt. He is an awful stuff in literature. I am a little dubious about his performance. Seems to me it throws rather a grimly humorous light on the situation. Understand, he thinks my style wouldn't be used by the devil to patch his trousers with. I think he—Teddie—discovered the fellow and the girl in the story and read on to find out if they married. He hung around for a time asking for more chapters but I sent him away.

Dont you forget to keep deciding every day that you are coming to the Buffalo thing.

I lost my temper to-day—fully—absolutely—for the first time in a good many years. I sailed the cat-boat up the lake today in the stiffest breeze we've had in moons. When I got near to the head of the lake, the boat was scudding before the wind in a manner to make your heart leap. Then we got striking snags—hidden stumps, floating logs, sunken brush, more stumps,—you might have thought ex-Senator Holman of Indiana[4] was there. Anything that could obstruct, promptly and gracefully obstructed. Up to the 5th stump I had not lost my philosophy but at the 22d I was swearing like cracked ice. And at the appearance of the 164th, I perched on the rail, a wild and gibbering maniac. It is all true. I cant remember when I was so furiously and ferociously angry. Never before, I think.

Teddie has a Belton setter named Judge. When the girls run Judge out of the kitchen, his soul becomes so filled with hate of the world, that, outside, he pounces on the first dog he meets. This is all right if it happens to be one of the hounds. They are only pups. He whales them and they roar. But sometimes the first dog he meets is the collie and the collie, after recovering from his surprise, simply wipes up the place with him. But this causes no change in Judge's way. Little dog, or big dog, hound or collie, put him out of the kitchen and he pounces on the first one. This is the way I felt up the pond. But there was nobody there.

Dont you miss the Buffalo dinner.

Yours always
S. C.

---

[1] The *New York Tribune* had not forgiven Crane for the embarrassment he caused them with his 21 August 1892 article on the parade of the Junior Order of United American Mechanics, and in its review of 13 October 1895, p. 24, called *The Red Badge* "a chromatic nightmare" that is as "tedious as a funeral march." The *Tribune* especially deplored the "anti-climaxes, produced by strivings for grotesque effect, the result of which is to make ridiculous some scenes which otherwise would not have been devoid of tragic power." In parting, Crane was warned that "the exaggerated common-places of Tolstoi, the brutal coarseness of Zola, and the reduplicated profanities of Maeterlink [sic], are not commendable ideals for the student of literary art. Nor is decadent morbidity destined to win a commanding place in literature."

[2] *The Third Violet.*

[3] Edmund Crane.
[4] William Steele Holman (1822-97) served in the House of Representatives, not the Senate.

139. TO THE EDITOR OF THE *CHAP-BOOK*
ALS, ViU.

Hartwood
Sul. Co., N.Y.
Nov 20 [1895]

Editor
Chap-book

Dear sir: I enclose a small thing.[1] Please let me hear of it at your earliest convenience. I also enclose stamp for it's return.

Very truly yours
Stephen Crane

[1] Crane's poem "In the night" appeared in the *Chap-Book*, 4 (March 1896), 372.

140. TO WILLIS BROOKS HAWKINS
ALS, ViU.

Dec 20. [for 20 November 1895]

Dear Willis: Date for dinner, Wednesday, Dec 18.[1] Don't say at Lantern Club that you are coming. Other invitations there supposed to be complimentary. Do you follow me?

Yours as ever
S. C.

[1]Crane misdated this letter and the date of the Philistine banquet, which took place on Thursday, 19 December 1895, at the Genesee House in Buffalo.

141. TO THE EDITOR OF THE *CHAP-BOOK*
ALS, ViU.

Hartwood,
Sullivan Co, N.Y.
[after 20 November 1895]

Editor, Chap-Book,

Dear sir: If the enclosed sketch is not available kindly return per stamps.

Very truly yours
Stephen Crane

142. TO THE EDITOR OF THE AMERICAN PRESS ASSOCIATION
ALS, MiU.

Hartwood,
Sul. Co., N.Y.
Nov 23d [1895][1]

Editor, American Press Association,

Dear sir: Stamps are enclosed for the return of this Ms if it is not found available.

Very truly yours
Stephen Crane

[1]The editorial department of the Association stamped the letter as being received on 21 November 1895. Though the last digit of the year might be a "3," "5" seems more likely because Crane was in Hartwood in November 1895.

143. TO LOUIS SENGER
ALS, NSyU.

Hartwood, N.Y.
Nov 23d [1895]

My dear Louis: I am about to finish my new novel—in eight days I think—and if you find yourself with a good deal of time, I would like to have you read it. Up here, I miss some little public to impale. Let me know if you possess any leisure and I will send or bring the thing to you.

I see you escaped with six dollars soon after election. Heaven guard us from such robbers.

Yours as always
Stephen Crane.

144. TO WILLIS BROOKS HAWKINS
ALS, ViU.

Hartwood
Nov 25. [1895]

My dear Willis: I have been frantically hustling of late to make some money but I haven't achieved a cent, mainly because I want it so badly. Frank Leslie's Weekly wrote me that my story was very stunning but that the tale "When Greek meets Greek" was going to run until February and they didnt feel justified in buying a serial at this moment. Irving Bacheller had tried hard to accept a story of mine, he said, but he said that he couldnt. Stone and Kimball wrote me that they wanted something for the Chap-book and I immediately fired something at them.[1] I hope for the Lord's sake, it goes, but it would be my luck if it didnt. I send you a clipping which may convey a general impression of Red Badge notices—outside of New York.²

I have send a little story to Irving but it is so tiny—the Lantern Club. will grab every cent. I tell you these things to convey a sense of how loyally and stoutly I have tried to pull you out of the hole you slid yourself into. When you dont write I begin to think you are disgusted with me. Adios.

Yours as ever
Stephen Crane.

¹See No. 139, n. 1.
²"An Extraordinary Work: Stephen Crane's Talent Recognized by the Reviews and Newspapers of the United States" (an undated clipping from the *Port Jervis Union* [November 1895]).

145. TO JAMES MACARTHUR¹

ALS, Collection of Stanley and Mary Wertheim, New York City.

Hartwood.
Sul Co., N.Y.
Nov 25 [1895]

Dear Mr. McArthur: I enclose a small thing as I remember you asked me for a contribution to the Bookman.² I enclose you stamps if you find the Ms unsuitable.

Yours sincerely
Stephen Crane

¹An assistant editor of the *Bookman* from 1895 to 1899.
²"The Judgment of the Sage" appeared in the *Bookman*, 2 (January 1896), 412.

146. TO LOUIS SENGER
ALS, NSyU.

Hartwood—Nov. 25th. [1895]

My dear Louis: You are a very amiable person. I will send the novel down by messenger to Will Parshal's office. I expect to finish it this week. As to your good invitation to come see you—I am expecting to break out of my asylum on Dec 17th, when I go to Buffalo for a few days. When I return, I shall be glad to take a moment's rest in Port Jervis. Adios.

Yours as ever
Stephen Crane.

147. TO ELBERT HUBBARD
ALS, Collection of Maurice F. Neville, Santa Barbara, California.

Hartwood, N.Y.
Nov 29. [1895]

Dear Mr Hubbard: I shall appear promptly in Buffalo on December 19th. The invitation reached me today and it made still greater reason for me to cudgel my brains, as to why you so distinguish me. I shall make a strong effort to appear as a man not altogether unworthy of this.

I see that you allowed me liberty in the matter of a speech. There is where you did another clever thing. I would be very bad at a regular speech but I will do my best in some way.

I am delighted with the entire affair although shaky still about my own part in it and, dear Mr Hubbard, believe me to be

Faithfully yours
Stephen Crane.

148. FROM SIDNEY S. PAWLING[1]

Letterhead: "Wm. Heinemann,/ Publisher/ 21 Bedford Street/ London/ W.C." ALS, NNC, copy in Crane's hand at NhD.

4th of December 1895

My dear Sir,

My partner Mr Heinemann has gone to Paris on business and so I have the pleasure of writing to you. We would like very cordially to express our appreciation of your book "The Red Badge of Courage" which we have purchased for England from Messrs. Appleton & Co of New York. We think so highly of your work—of its actuality—virility & literary distinction that we have been very pleased to take special pains to place it prominently before the British public. I have sent about one hundred gratis copies to the leading literary men of this country, & have personally seen some of the principal London reviewers. I have called Mr. Sheldon's attention to some of the excellent reviews obtained already—Mr. Sheldon represents Messrs. Appleton over here. I hope in the January number of our review "The New Review" to have a special article by the Hon George Wyndham MP on the book[2]—Mr. Wyndham is now secretary to Mr. A. J. Balfour the Leader of our House of Commons, & served as a soldier in Her Majesty's Guards: he has also done very excellent literary work. I think there is no doubt the book will obtain the success it so eminently deserves, & I have thus early made an opportunity to write to you to say how pleased we are to be identified with your work. I hope we shall in the future have the privilege of publishing your books in this country, and if there is any way in which we can be of service to you over here, I beg you will not hesitate to let us know.

Believe me
dear Sir
Yours obediently
Sidney S. Pawling

[1] Editor and partner in the firm of William Heinemann, Crane's English publisher.
[2] "A Remarkable Book," *New Review*, 14 (January 1896), 30-40. The *New Review* was the Heinemann house journal.

149. TO ELBERT HUBBARD
ALS, TxU.

Hartwood
Monday [9 December? 1895][1]

Dear Mr Hubbard: I am elated to find that none have yet confessed that they have never heard of me and wanted to know why in the devil you were going to dine me. I enclose you—or, send—you the letters in fear that I might lose them. I hope none of my friends—I mean the friends of my list—are to burden you? I was sure that they couldn't come but I have since reflected that it was a very ungraceful thing to send you such a hideously long list and I have been aroused at night by a dream of seeing them all writing acceptances.

Yours sincerely
Stephen Crane.

[1] Other possible dates are 25 November or 2 December rather than any other Monday in either of the two months. The tone of the letter suggests it was written after No. 135, in which Crane returned to Hubbard letters of acceptance to the banquet and asked that William Heinemann's name be added to the guest list. Crane was now clearly concerned about the "very ungraceful thing" he had done by giving Hubbard such a long list. Had No. 135 been written second, Crane would not have been so callous as to add nonchalantly Heinemann's name to the list.

If the letter is dated 9 December, there would have been time for the guests to respond to the invitations and for Hubbard to forward their acceptances to Crane. In addition, Hubbard's writing to Crane on 15 December that "All is well—it will be a select little affair—only twenty five—and all men who admire your work and recognize your genius" could be an attempt to allay Crane's concern.

150. TO LOUIS SENGER
TT, NSyU.

[10 December 1895]
Hartwood
Tuesday night

My dear Louisa:

I have arrived in Port Jervis. This is supposed to resemble one of Napoleon's previous bulletins. Come and see me.

Yours
S. C.

151. FROM JOHN NORTHERN HILLIARD
Letterhead: "The Union and Advertiser./ Daily and Weekly./ 'The People's Paper.'/ Rochester, N.Y." ALS, NNC.

Rochester, N.Y. December 14th 1895

Dear Sir

I am running in The Union a series of illustrated articles on American foreign Authors. Sketches of such writers as Eugene Field, Donald G. Mitchell, Hamlin Garland, Sara Orne Jewett, James Whitcomb Riley, W. D. Howells and others equally as noted have appeared. I should like to run a series of articles concerning yourself if you will send us a photograph as our portraits are printed in half tone and on excellent paper.

Please write your name across the photograph, that it may be reproduced with it. Also jot down some notes of your life and work, which will be written up in a sketch, which will include a review of your works. If you have a scrap of manuscript to send we will reproduce that, too.

This series is attracting considerable notice and comment in this part of the world. Trusting to hear from you as soon as convenient I remain

Very sincerely yours
John N. Hilliard
Editor

152. TO WILLIS BROOKS HAWKINS
ALS, ViU.

[Hartwood, N.Y., before 15 December 1895]

My dear Willis: You harrow me a little bit. My transportation is to be by the Erie. I was hoping all along that you were going to go by the Erie. You were to be the moral reinforcement which I sought. I cant come to N.Y., because it requires "dough." I have mapped out my two or three shekels so that I will return home smiling but broke and in the smoking-car. I bought to-day one full dress shirt and what goes with it. I have a damn fine hat. I have no overcoat save that little gauze one which you may remember. Nor no dress-suit. My brother has—(had)— a pair of patent leathers and I am sleeping with them under my pillow. I've got 'em.

There is a peach of a row on in Buffalo. The Saturn Club, the Browning Clubs, etc., have heard somehow of me and—Hubbard says—are planning to dine me. All the *Philistines* are hot. Wrote swearing letters to and fro to each other. Hubbard enclosed letters to me without comment. I of course wrote him that it would naturally be hard for me to offend people who only intended to be kind but that for my very short stay I would consider that I had engaged myself to the *Philistines*. I didnt see what else to do when I could percieve by their letters that the *Philistines* were likely to be very much injured. They called the others a "god damned lot of old tabies."

I enclose you copy of a London letter.

In the matter of the Saturn Club—I don't deride a dinner from the Saturn Club. No. But then I have to proceed by the atmosphere when I get there.

And now, Willis, old man, when I get in all this flumy-doodle business and see you behind there moving the scenes and knowing all the time what a damned fool I am and what a ridiculous hole I'm in, I get fair feeble-minded with dwelling upon it. I leave it all to you. For my part I wish the whole thing was in Ballywhoo because while I look forward to it as probably the greatest pleasure of my life, I feel as if I were astride of your shoulders. And if I could stop the thing now I would.

Yours alway
S. C.

I go to Port Jervis on Sunday My address—Port Jervis, N.Y c/—W. H. Crane

153. FROM ELBERT HUBBARD
ALS on *Philistine* stationery, NNC.

East Aurora, N.Y.
Dec 15, 1895.

Dear Mr Crane:

The dinner will take place at the *Genesee* Hotel in Buffalo. I will meet you at the Hotel Thursday Morning. The party whom we depended on for passes has promised to mail your pass to Hartwood, but I have pinned my faith to mortal man before and been disappointed so I enclose an X for RR fare if pass does not reach you.

All is well—it will be a very select little affair—only twenty-five—and all men who admire your work and recognize your genius.

The two Poems you sent us are most charming—thank you very much.

Sincerely Your friend
Elbert Hubbard

154. FROM ELBERT HUBBARD
ACS, NNC.

E Aurora Dec 16. [1895]

S. C.

Just this card to say that your letter of Saturday has reached me since I wrote this morning. Your Poems sent to me last week are all right Taber says and Taber he knows!

I will meet you at the *Genesee in Buffalo Thursday morning. My train reaches Buffalo at 8:40* so I'll be there about 9 oclock.

Hubbard

(I see the papers all over the country are "chewing" about the Dinner!)

155. FROM WILLIS BROOKS HAWKINS
MSL, NNC.

Tuesday Dec 17 [1895]

My dear Stephen:

I addressed a note to you at Hartwood last night. You may not get it in time, so I repeat its contents: I go by the central—*must*. I leave here Wed. night, reach Buffalo probably by noon Thursday. I shall go straight to the Genesee, where the dinner is to be, and shall ask for you. If you have not yet arrived I will wait for you at the Genesee. If I go out I will leave a note for you with the clerk. If you reach the Genesee before I do you either wait for me or leave a note for me. I shall express an overcoat to you this afternoon. In Buffalo we will fix up the dress suit question. You bring along your shirt, hat & shoes. I will attend to coat, vest and trousers.

I like this sorto' thing. Don't you let it bother you a bit. It isn't as if I were rich. It's one poor devil faking up a way for another poor devil to get his fingers into pie. I haven't had any fun at all lately, and this is a real enjoyment. We'll have a bully time. I wish I could go by the Erie, but I can't. Let me get you as soon as you reach Buffalo—before you fall into the hands of the Philistines if possible. It will be better so.

Your friend
Willis B Hawkins,
Humper[1]

[1] Presumably the secretary who transcribed and signed the letter.

156. TO WILLIS BROOKS HAWKINS
Letterhead: "Coming to Buffalo?/ Try the Genesee. . . ." ALS, ViU.

[19 December 1895]

Dear Willis: Back at four, old man

S. C.

157. TO DR. A. L. MITCHELL[1]
Inscribed in a copy of *The Red Badge of Courage*, InU.

To Dr. A. L. Mitchell
Stephen Crane

Buffalo, Dec 19th, 1895.

[1] Dr. Mitchell was a neighbor of Elbert Hubbard in East Aurora and a member of his Chautauqua reading circle.

158. TO ELBERT HUBBARD
Inscribed on a copy of *Maggie*, TxU.

[Buffalo, N.Y., about 20 December 1895]

My dear Hubbard: This tawdry thing will make you understand the full import of the words: "It is mor{e} blessed to give than to recieve." I am very sensible {o}f the truth of the sentence when I give book of mine

I am always
your friend.
Stephen Cran{e}

159. TO WILLIS BROOKS HAWKINS
ALS on a copy of the menu for the Philistine banquet, ViU.

East Aurora.,
Saturday [21 December]—1895.

Dear Willis: I am coming to New York on Tuesday morning.

Stephen Crane

160. FROM RIPLEY HITCHCOCK
Letterhead: "D. Appleton & Co.,/ 72 Fifth Avenue,/ New York." ALS, NNC.

Dec. 26 [1895]

My dear Crane,

Confusion to the printers! I have just received the printed responses to the invitations to your dinner and I find myself set down as referring to our "puppets." I used no such word, and I am disgusted. I may have said "writers" or "novelists" but how "puppets" came in I can't imagine. I owe you this explanation, and the printers owe one to me.[1]

The book is receiving admirable reviews in England. How is the new story coming on? My best wishes for the holiday season

Faithfully yours
Ripley Hitchcock

[1] In declining Hubbard's invitation to attend the Philistine Society banquet, Hitchcock had written H. P. Taber on 4 December that "At a time when so much is said regarding the predominating influence of foreign literature it is doubly grateful to meet with such a proof that American genius is appreciated and that our prophets when they prove themselves prophets are not without honor" (NNC). In Hubbard's souvenir menu of the banquet, *The Time Has Come*, Hitchcock's first use of "prophets" was misprinted as "puppets." At the top of Hitchcock's letter Crane wrote "Joke on Taber./ S. C."

161. TO RIPLEY HITCHCOCK
ALS, NN.

Hartwood, N.Y.
Dec 27, 95.

Dear Mr Hitchcock: I forward you today my new story: "The Third Violet," in the original manuscript for the typewriting was so bad I am obliged to consider the original better. Moreover as I am considering a start very shortly to some quarter of the world where mail is uncertain, I am in haste for your opinion. I was not in the least offended at the "puppet" thing. Thought it was all right.

Yours sincerely
Stephen Crane

162. TO RIPLEY HITCHCOCK
ALS, NN.

Please acknowledge reciept.

Hartwood
Friday [27 December 1895]

Dear Mr Hitchcock: Enclosed is "The Third Violet" in ms. There is only one. Typewriting is too new an art for the woods. If you think it well, have the thing type-writen—charged to my a/c.—and send me the type written one to save the story.

S. C.

163. TO DR. A. L. MITCHELL
Inscribed below a fair copy of "What says the sea, little shell?" InU.

To my friend, Dr. A. L. Mitchell.

Hartwood, N.Y. Dec 28, 1895.

164. TO JOHN PHILLIPS[1]
ALS, ViU.

Hartwood, N.Y.
Dec 30. [1895]

Dear Mr Phillips: Your project[2] it seems to me would require a great deal of study and a great deal of time. I would be required to give up many of my plans for this winter and this I am reluctant to do. I dont know how you would advise going about it but one of the first things I would want to do, would be to visit the battle-field—which I was to describe—at the time of year when it was fought. The preliminary reading and the subsequent reading, the investigations of all kinds, would take much time. Moreover, if I did not place the only original crown of pure gold on the heads of at least twelve generals they would arise and say: "This damned young fool was not there. I was however. And this is how it happened." I evaded them in the Red Badge because it was essential that I should make my battle a type and name no names but in your case, it would be very different. In the spring when a good deal of my work will be done and the anniversaries of the fights begin to occur, I think I would like to do the work and if you send me the name of the battle you first wish me to tackle I will try to do some reading on it. I am not very leisurely just now for I have a good many orders and requests, and I am busy at them.

Yours sincerely
Stephen Crane.

[1] Of the Phillips-and-McClure Syndicate.
[2] Phillips wanted Crane to write a series of sketches about Civil War battlefields. Although Crane visited Fredericksburg in January 1896, he did not involve himself further in the project.

165. TO CURTIS BROWN

Curtis Brown, *Contacts* (London: Cassell, 1935), pp. 223-24.

HARTWOOD, N.Y.
Dec. 31st, 1896. [for 1895]

MY DEAR CURTIS, Thank you for your kind words and for your *Sketch* clipping. I hear the damned book "The Red Badge of Courage" is doing very well in England. In the meantime I am plodding along. I have finished my new novel—"The Third Violet"—and sent it to Appleton and Co., as per request, but I've an idea it won't be accepted. It's pretty rotten work. I used myself up in the accursed "Red Badge."

Yours as ever,
STEPHEN CRANE.

166. TO NELLIE CROUSE[1]
ALS, NSyU.

Hartwood, N.Y.
Dec 31st., [1895]

Dear Miss Crouse: I embrace with pleasure the opportunities of the walrus. I knew little of the Philistines until they sent me this letter:[2] I was very properly enraged at the word "poet" which continually reminds me of long-hair and seems to me to be a most detestable form of insult but nevertheless I replied:[3] I am convinced that I would have written a worse letter if I had had the slightest idea that they were going to print it. I went to Buffalo and this is not at all what happened:[4]

However it is one man's idea of what happened and not altogether wrong in proper names. I had a good time and caused them considerable trouble in inventing nice things to say to me.

I do not suppose you will be overwhelmed with distinction when I tell you that your name is surrounded with much sentiment for me. I was in southern Mexico last winter for a sufficient time to have my face turn the color of a brick side-walk. There was nothing American about me save a large Smith and Wesson revolver and I saw only Indians whom I suspected of loading their tomales with dog. In this state of mind and this physical condition, I arrived one day in the city of Puebla and there, I saw an American girl. There was a party of tourists in town and she was of their contingent. I only saw her four times—one in the hotel corridor and three in the street. I had been so long in the mountains and was such an outcast, that the sight of this American girl in a new spring gown nearly caused me to drop dead. She of course never looked in my direction. I never met her. Nevertheless I gained one of those peculiar thrills which a man only acknowledges upon occasion. I ran to the railroad office. I cried: "What is the shortest route to New York." I left Mexico.

I suppose you fail to see how this concerns you in anyway! And no wonder! but this girl who startled me out of my mountaineer senses, resembled you. I have never achieved the enjoyment of seeing you in a new spring gown but this girl became to me not an individual but a sort of a symbol and I have always thought of you with gratitude for the peculiar thrill you gave me in the town of Puebla, Mexico.

The lives of some people are one long apology. Mine was, once, but not now. I go through the world unexplained, I suppose. Perhaps this letter may look like an incomparable insolence. Who knows. Script is an infernally bad vehicle for thoughts. I know that, at least. But if you are not angry at me, I should like you to tell me where Button is at. I lost him almost a year ago and I have never been able to discover him. I suppose it is his size. He could be so easily overlooked in a crowd.

Yours sincerely
Stephen Crane.

[1] Crane met Nellie Crouse, a prim, thoroughly conventional young woman from Akron, Ohio, at a tea given by Lucius Button in his New York City apartment for his Akron friends in January 1895. Crane was evidently smitten with Miss Crouse but waited to write to her until his fame as an author had been secured. Although he addressed seven fervent letters to her and she initially responded with long letters and a photograph, she ultimately remained impassive to his courtship.

[2] The letter of 10 November (No. 129) from the Committee for the Philistine Society, a copy of which Crane included.

[3] Crane attached a copy of his 15 November letter (No. 133).

[4] Crane attached a clipping of "The Philistines at Dinner" from the *Buffalo Evening News* of 20 December. The article listed the attendees, many of whom spoke about Crane. The guest of honor spoke "modestly and gracefully, saying he was a working newspaper man who was trying to do what he could 'since he had recovered from college' with the machinery which had come into his hands—doing it sincerely, if clumsily, and simply setting forth in his own way his own impressions."

167. TO WILLIS BROOKS HAWKINS
ALS, ViU.

Hartwood, N.Y.
Dec 31st. [1895]

Dear Willis: Back and retired once more to corduroys. I send overcoat tonight. Pray heaven I have not got you into trouble by keeping it too long. Write me your impressions of the dinner as soon as you get time. Hubbard and Taber think you are just the smoothest guy in the world. The reason I wrote you that I would be in NY was because they told me my passes would be over the Central but as it turned out, they were to Port Jervis over the Erie. I am very anxious to hear wether you are satisfied with the dinner. I did not drink much but the excitement soon turned everything into a grey haze for me and I am not sure that I came off decently.[1]

I sent my new novel down to Appleton's yesterday.[2] Will let you know it's reception. If you see Colonel Floyd give him my kindest regards. I think you and him made the big hit at Buffalo. The agony of the Indians over the fact that you left the boat in the middle of the Fox River may have led you to think differently but it is true. Write me soon.

Yours as ever
Stephen Crane

[1] Crane's diffidence contrasts sharply with the satiric tone of his letter to Nellie Crouse written the same day.
[2] Crane had sent Hitchcock the manuscript of *The Third Violet* on 27 December.

1896

168. TO WILLIAM DEAN HOWELLS
ALS, MH.

Hartwood, N.Y.
January 1st. [1896]

Dear Mr Howells: Every little time I hear from some friend a kind thing you have said of me, an interest which you have shown in my work. I have been so long conscious of this, that I am grown uncomfortable in not being able to express to you my gratitude and so I sieze the New Year's Day as an opportunity to thank you and tell you how often I think of your kind benevolent life.

Sincerely yours
Stephen Crane

169. TO JOHN NORTHERN HILLIARD[1]
Photocopy of ALS, CtU.

Hartwood, N.Y.
January 2d [1896]

Dear Mr. Hilliard: If you will pardon this kind of paper, I think I will be able to you more easily what you wish to know. However even then

I am not sure that I will succeed as I am not much versed in talking about myself. As to the picture I am sorry I cannot give you one but I haven't had a picture taken since early boyhood.[2]

Occasionally, interested acquintances have asked me if "Stephen Crane" was a nom de guerre but it is my own name. In childhood, I was bitterly ashamed of it and now when I sometimes see it in print, it strikes me as being the homliest name in created things. The first Stephen Crane to appear in America, arrived in Massachusetts from England in 1635. His son Stephen Crane settled in Connecticut and the Stephen Crane of the third American generation settled in New Jersey on lands that now hold the cities of Newark and Elizabeth. When the troubles with England came, he was president of both Colonial Assemblies that met in New York. Then he was sent by New Jersey to the Continental Congress and he served in that body until just about a week before the Declaration was signed, when the Tories made such trouble in New Jersey that he was obliged to return and serve as speaker in the colony's assembly. He died in the old homestead at Elizabeth when the British troops were marching past to what pappened to be the defeat at Trenton. His eldest son commanded the 6th New Jersey infantry during the Revolution and ultimately died the ranking Major-general in the regular army from an old wound recieved in the expedition to Quebec. The second son became the ranking commodore in the navy at a time when the title of admiral was unknown. The youngest son, while proceeding to his father's bedside, was captured by some Hessians and upon his refusing to tell the road by which they intended to surprise a certain American out-post, they beat him with their muskets and then having stabbed him with their bayonets, they left him dead in the road. In those old times the family did it's duty.

Upon my mother's side, everybody as soon as he could walk, became a Methodist clergyman—of the old ambling-nag, saddle-bag, exhorting kind. My uncle, Jesse T. Peck, D.D., L.L.D., was a bishop in the Methodist Church. My father was also a clergyman of that church, author of numerous works of theology, an editor of various periodicals of the church. He graduated at Princeton. He was a great, fine, simple mind.

As for myself, I went to Lafayette College but did not graduate. I found mining-engineering not at all to my taste. I preferred base-ball. Later I attended Syracuse University where I attempted to study literature but found base ball again much more to my taste. At Lafayette I joined the Delta Upsilon fraternity.

My first work in fiction was for the *New York Tribune* when I was about eighteen years old. During this time, one story of the series went into the *Cosmopolitan*. Previous to this I had written many articles of many kinds for many newspapers. I began when I was sixteen. At age of twenty I wrote my first novel—*Maggie*.[3] It never really got on the market but it made for me the friendships of W. D. Howells and Hamlin Garland and since that time I have never been conscious for an instant that those friendships have at all diminished. After completing *Maggie* I wrote mainly for the *New York Press* and for the *Arena* magazine. The latter part of my twenty-first year I began *The Red Badge of Courage* and completed it early in my twenty-second year. In my twenty-third year, I wrote *The Black Riders*. On the 1st day of November, 1895, I was precisely 24 years old. Last week I finished my new novel: "The Third Violet." It is a story of life among the younger and poorer artists in New York.

I have only one pride and that is that the English edition of *The Red Badge of Courage* has been recieved with great praise by the English reviewers. I am proud of this simply because the remoter people would seem more just and harder to win.

I live in Hartwood, Sullivan Co., N.Y., on an estate of 3500 acres belonging to my brother and am distinguished for corduroy trousers and briar-wood pipes. My idea of happiness is the saddle of a good-riding horse.

I am not so sure that the above is what you want but I am sure that it is the most complete I have ever written. I hope you will like and if you find that you need enlightenment on certain points, let me know. Please remember me to Mr Bragdon.[4] With assurances of my regard I am

Very sincerely
Stephen Crane

My father died when I was seven y'rs old.[5] My mother when I was nineteen.

[1]Crane is responding to Hilliard's 14 December 1895 request for autobiographical information (No. 151). Portions of this letter were published by Hilliard in an article, "The Hideousness of War: Stephen Crane and *The Red Badge*," *Union and Advertiser*, 8 February 1896, p. 2. A variant version of the letter was published in the 18 April 1900 edition of the *Rochester Post Express*, p. 4, with the spurious claim that it had been written a few weeks before. See Appendix B for a discussion of Crane's letters to Hilliard.

[2]Crane had a cabinet photograph made by the Lundeluco studio on Pike Street in Port Jervis in late 1892 or early 1893, and at the end of January 1896 he sent inscribed copies of this to Ripley Hitchcock and Dr. A. L. Mitchell. See Nos. 195-96. Corwin Knapp Linson took photographic studies for the oil portrait of Crane he painted in 1894. One of these was published in the February issue of the *Bookman*. While he was in Washington, D.C., in March, Crane had another cabinet photograph made, in high collar and cravat with his hair parted severely in the middle, by the Prince studio on Pennsylvania Avenue.

[3]"A Tent in Agony," one of the Sullivan County sketches, appeared in the December 1892 *Cosmopolitan* when Crane was twenty-one. *Maggie* was also completed around this time.

[4]Claude Bragdon (1866-1946), architect and theatrical producer, met Crane only once, at the Philistine Society banquet on 19 December 1895.

[5]Jonathan Townley Crane died on 16 February 1880, when Stephen was eight.

170. TO ELBERT HUBBARD[1]
ALS, ViU.

[Hartwood, N.Y., 2 January 1896]

My dear Haich: I read your "No Enemy" today.[2] I always find that I better appreciate what books are to us when I wait for the moment to come when I want a book and want it badly. This afternoon I read "No Enemy" at one sitting. I like it. Your manipulation of the life in Indiana and Illinois is out of sight. There are swift character sketches all through it that strike me as being immense. However, I sympathize with the clergyman in Chapter I. He stated his case rather badly but he was better than Hilliard. Hilliard proved in the rest of the book that he was not what he indirectly said he was in Chapter I. Hilliard is a bird. Yet in Chapter I he was a chump. Your flowers on the water—good god, that is magnificent. A thing that I felt in the roots of my hair. Hell and blazes, but I do envy you that paragraph.

The book strengthened me and uplifted me. It is a peach.³

Yours sincerely
Stephen Crane.

¹Hubbard wrote on the letter a now barely legible note to his sister Honor: "H H. Read and return. This fellow is spiritual and spirituable. Would you think it {*illegible words*} was here a{while?} with us. E. G. H." She responded, "This {letter?} not his poetry (?) proves it. H. H."

²Hubbard's novel, *No Enemy (but Himself)* (New York: Putnam's, 1894).

³The sincerity of Crane's praise of Hubbard's sensationalized adventure story is difficult to accept. The final paragraph of the novel, concerning flowers on the water, that Crane terms "magnificent" and ostensibly "felt in the roots of [his] hair" reads: "Flowers—flowers at this time of the year, and floating in the water! I have seen flowers in the gardens, flowers at banquets, flowers at weddings, flowers on graves—ah—there is the boat now; she must have been blocked by the ice" (p. 238).

171. TO CORWIN KNAPP LINSON
ALS, CCamarSJ.

Hartwood, N.Y.
January 4th. [1896]

Dear CK: The lot of truck which I left in your studio would be very acceptable to me just now if you will bundle them up and express them to me, C.O.D. I dont doubt but what you will be glad to see them out. There is some "lines" among them which I will be very glad to get; and also my contract with Copeland and Day, and with Appleton & Co. Please ship the whole business to me here at Hartwood. I am sorry to trouble you but I am too poor to come down to New York. Remember me to Jaccaci.¹

Yours as ever
S. C.

¹August F. Jaccaci, art editor of *McClure's Magazine* and later of *Scribner's Magazine*. Crane's muckraking essay, "In the Depths of a Coal Mine," appeared in the August 1894 issue of *McClure's* with illustrations by Linson. Linson wrote the following at the end

of the letter: "Note—The box of papers referred to was shipped to Steve by me from my studio in 'The Vandyke' on 8th ave. I was not in the building until the Fall of '95—therefore this dates this note as in Jan. 1896—I sent them to Hartwood—and shortly after—in Feb—I was off to Greece for the first Olympian games. with August F. Jaccaci, art Editor Scribners Magazine. Corwin Knapp Linson."

172. TO MR. RICHARDS
Fragment of an ALS, item 661, Catalogue 23, number 14, Paul C. Richards Autographs, Brookline, Massachusetts.[1]

Hartwood, N.Y.
January 4 [1896]

Dear Mr. Richards: I feel that it is perhaps unbecoming to feel immensely gratified at words concerning me in print but at the same time I cannot help from saying to you that of the notices of me which have appeared from time to time, the one in *The Tribune* of December 28, is the one I prefer above the others. I have friends who do not read many newspapers but who at the same time are interested in my prosperity and . . . I would like you to send . . . a few copies of the Dec. 28 issue of your paper.

Stephen Crane

[1] The catalogue description of this letter identifies Richards as "a reviewer."

173. TO NELLIE CROUSE
ALS, NSyU.

Hartwood, N.Y.
January 6th. [1896]

Dear Miss Crouse: Of course it was my original belief that you would not be offended at my letter. I had formed a much higher opinion. If you had rushed out and defended your dignity when it was not assailed,

170

I would have been grievously disappointed. I felt that I was doing something unusual but then I believed I saw in your eye once that the usual was rather tiresome to you. I am galloping all around the point of the argument but then—you know what I must mean—and it is awfully complimentary.

I am sorry you did not find the "two poems"—mind you, I never call them poems myself—in the *Philistine*.[1] No more did I. But as a matter of truth, the *Philistine* will have something of mine in every number in 1896 so if you ever see that little book again this year, you will on search discover the lost one.[2] I never encourage friends to read my work—they sometimes advise one—but somehow I will be glad to send you things of mine. Not because I think you will refrain from advising one either. But simply because I would enjoy it—sending them, I mean. I think your advice would have a charm to it that I do not find in some others.

I observe that you think it wretched to go through life unexplained. Not at all. You have no idea how it simplifies matters. But in your case I make humble concession and I am prepared to explain anything at all which I can find power to do. I have been told 84676 times that I am not of the cream of mankind but you make a sort of an inference that I might myself think I was of it, so I hasten to say that although I never line the walls or clutter the floors of ballrooms, my supreme detestation is dowdy women although they may be as intellectual as Mahomet. If you had seen me dashing through the back streets of Buffalo to escape the Browning Club, you would believe me. I am not sure that they were very anxious either, but then I was anxious, and I would not have been caught for a great deal.

When you said that Hitchcock mentioned me, I was alarmed for I thought you meant Ripley Hitchcock of New York and I knew just how he would mention anybody save himself and God.[3] I resolved to overthrow him on the first opportunity. But then I percieved you meant Hitchcock of Buffalo. His name, you understand, is Hitchy. If you had said that Hitchy mentioned me, I would have known at once.

I am sending you by this mail a newspaper clipping of "A Grey Sleeve." It is not in any sense a good story and the intolerable pictures make it worse. In England, it comes out in a magazine[4] and if I had a copy I would send you one, in order to make you think it was a better story but unfortunately I have not yet seen the English periodical.

I must here candidly say that I am not insanely desirous of knowing Button's location. Originally, it was a pretext. But still I am glad to know that you know where he is and I would be glad to have you find out for me, for he is as good an Indian as ever lived.[5]

I am not very much on newspaper work now but in the spring I am wanting very much to go to Arizona to study the Apaches more. There is a man in Boston who has been unwise enough to ask me to write a play for his theatre and I wish to have some Apaches in it. For instance the music of their scalp dance is enough to set fire to a stone church. And in this connection I intend going west on the Erie. This route leads through Akron, as I distinctly remember. Furthermore,—if I dont go to Arizona—I shall at any rate go to Buffalo and if you will please tell me that Akron is not far from Buffalo, I will make an afternoon—or possibly evening—call on you. Sure.

I am deeply interested concerning that lot of things which you say you wish to know. I pledge myself to " 'fess" if it ruins my egotism for a fortnight. Anyhow, it is a very comfortable and manful occupation to trample upon one's own egotism. When I reached twenty-one years and first really scanned my personal egotism I was fairly dazzled by the size of it. The Matterhorn could be no more than a ten-pin to it. Perhaps I have succeeded in lowering it a trifle. So you will please keep in mind that there is a young {*page torn*} corduroy-trousered, briar-wood-{smoking} young man—in Hartwood, N.Y. who is eagerly awaiting a letter from you.

Sincerely yours
Stephen Crane.

---

[1] Crane usually called his poems "lines." In part, this was a reaction against certain reviewers of *The Black Riders* who refused to accept his free-verse epigrams as poetry. More significant, in the context of his letter to Nellie Crouse, Crane wished to convey an image of himself as a conventional, ambitious young man who shunned the bohemian and effete appellation of "poet," which, as he wrote to her on 31 December 1895, he considered "a most detestable form of insult." The table of contents for the January 1896 *Philistine* lists "Two poems" by Crane, but only "I have heard the sunset song of the birches" appears in this issue. "What says the sea, little shell?" was published in the February issue, and this is probably "the lost one" to which Crane refers.

[2] Crane contributed to most, but not all, of the 1896 issues of the *Philistine*.

[3]Crane's resentment of Appleton editor Ripley Hitchcock at this time may have been fueled by Hitchcock's having forced him to excise key passages of *The Red Badge of Courage*. These passages slowed the pace of the action but contributed to the structural and thematic unity of the novel. In a copy of an 1896 issue of *The Red Badge* bearing Ripley Hitchcock's bookplate (NNC), his second wife, Helen Sargent Hitchcock, has written: "Two versions of this book written, Mr Hitchcock made Crane rewrite it and this was the first published version. A letter to Mr Hitchcock saying Crane is writing [in ink over penciled "is rewriting"] 'Maggie,' is in the Berg Collection in the New York Public Library." Nos. 199 and 203, the originals of which are in the Berg Collection, refer to revisions Crane was making in *Maggie*, which were also mandated by Hitchcock. Henry Binder advances the case for Hitchcock's intervention in the revision of *The Red Badge* in "The *Red Badge of Courage* Nobody Knows," *Studies in the Novel*, 10 (1978), 9-47. An edition of the novel edited by Binder (New York: Norton, 1982) restores the deleted passages. Donald Pizer challenges Binder's claim that Hitchcock forced Crane to revise the manuscript of *The Red Badge* in " '*The Red Badge of Courage* Nobody Knows': A Brief Rejoinder," *Studies in the Novel*, 11 (1979), 77-81; and Binder responds in "Donald Pizer, Ripley Hitchcock, and *The Red Badge of Courage*," *Studies in the Novel*, 11 (1979), 216-23. The question is controversial, and the exact nature of the editor's role in the revision of the book for publication remains a matter of scholarly debate. See also Stephen Mailloux, *Interpretive Conventions: The Reader in the Study of American Fiction* (Ithaca: Cornell University Press, 1982), pp. 160-65, 178-97; Hershel Parker, "*The Red Badge of Courage*: The Private History of a Campaign that—Succeeded?" *Flawed Texts and Verbal Icons: Literary Authority in American Fiction* (Evanston: Northwestern University Press, 1984), pp. 147-79; and Donald Pizer, "*The Red Badge of Courage*: Text, Theme, and Form," *South Atlantic Quarterly*, 84 (1985), 302-13.

[4]*The English Illustrated Magazine,* 14 (January 1896), 437-77.

[5]Crane occasionally referred to the artists, illustrators, and medical students with whom he lodged during his literary apprenticeship in New York as "Indians," probably a reference to their untrammeled, but hand-to-mouth, existence. Later, in England, he would use the term to describe the many uninvited guests who made deprivations upon his time and resources at Brede.

174. FROM RIPLEY HITCHCOCK
On Appleton's stationery, TLS, NhD.

January 6th, 1896.

Stephen Crane, Esq.,
Hartwood, N.Y.

Dear Mr. Crane:

We shall be happy to publish "The Third Violet" and I enclose agreements for your signature. I hardly know yet how we shall issue the book. It is rather short for the Town and Country Library and rather long for the 75 cent series. Perhaps we shall publish it at $1, but I can determine that better after obtaining an exact estimate of length from the printer.[1]

I wish you were here in the city for I should like to talk over the story with you. I should make any suggestions with the greatest diffidence, for your pictures of summer life and contrasting types and your glimpses of studio life are so singularly vivid and clear. I have found myself wishing that Hawker and Hollenden were a trifle less slangy in their conversation, and that the young lady who plays the part of the heroine was a little more distinct. You will pardon these comments I am sure, for I think you know my appreciation of your work and the value that I set upon the original flavor of your writing. Sometime, perhaps, we can talk the matter over. It will probably not be desirable to publish before March or April so that there will be plenty of time for the proof reading. I will let you know as soon as the style of the book is settled.

Very sincerely yours,
Ripley Hitchcock

[1] *The Third Violet* was serialized in various newspapers during October-November 1896 and published by Appleton in May 1897 for one dollar in the same tan buckram-binding format as *The Red Badge*, *Maggie* (1896), and *The Little Regiment*.

175. TO WILLIS BROOKS HAWKINS
ALS, ViU.

Hartwood
Tuesday [7 January 1896].

My dear Willis: No, you hadnt answered my last letter. Sometimes I dont need a reply because I know you are there and everything is all right. But this time I did need a reply because my sudden escape that day I was supposed to go to your house was upon my conscience very heavily and your majestic silence was a great trouble to me. However, I am perfectly contented with your reply and the way in which you appropriate 50% of the blame. I had been carefully abusing myself for the whole affair and was quite astonished and over-joyed when you volunteered.

I am writing a story—"The Little Regiment" for McClure.[1] It is awfully hard. I have invented the sum of my invention in regard to war and this story keeps me in internal despair. However I am coming on with it very comfortably after all.

The dinner scheme mingles my emotions.[2] In one sense, it portends an Ordeal but in the larger sense it overwhelms me in pride and arrogance to think that I have such friends.

By the way, you ought to see the effect of such things upon my family. Aint they swelled up, though! Gee! I simply cant go around and see 'em near enough. It's great. I am no longer a black sheep but a star.

Yours, always
S. C.

---

[1] "The Little Regiment" appeared in *McClure's Magazine*, 7 (June 1896), 12-22, and as the lead story in the volume of that name published by Appleton in December 1896. The English edition was delayed until February 1897.

[2] On Friday, 7 March 1896, Ripley Hitchcock gave a dinner for Crane at the Author's Club. Edmund C. Stedman, Edward Eggleston, and other writers were present.

176. TO LOUIS SENGER
ALS, NSyU.

[Hartwood, N.Y., 7 January 1896]

Dear L: Hope you will keep me posted on the Tribune's acrobatics.[1] Have sent for Munsey's.[2] The new novel accepted by Appleton's on Saturday. To be brought out in April or June.

Yours
S. C.

[1] The *Tribune*'s unflattering review of *The Red Badge of Courage* appeared on 13 October 1895, p. 24. In its "Literary Notes" column on 29 December 1895, p. 22, the *Tribune* vituperatively attacked the Society of the Philistines for tendering Crane a testimonial dinner: "But the Crane dinner redirects attention to the head and front of Philistine offending, the cause of it all, the irrepressible mediocrity which insists upon affronting public intelligence though the heavens cry out for shame. We had thought the 'Philistines' would help to quench the Minor Poet. Instead they give him a dinner and sing his praises to the moon!"

[2] See No. 177, n. 3.

177. FROM ELBERT HUBBARD
Letterhead: "The Philistine: A Periodical/ of Protest, East Aurora, N.Y."
ALS, NNC.

Jan 7, '96.

My Dear Poet:

Noxon is all right; I'm glad he knows I was sincere.[1] I would hate myself to my dying day had I said a trifling word at such a time. I can joke all day long, but there are times when I am in dead earnest. I have faith in you; and if you never write another page I have faith in you. That one last poem you sent us is a masterly thing and worth all the school-girl jingles ever pasted in yer grannys scrapbook.[2] That fourth stanza is sublime in its gentleness and strength!

Hubbard

(Munsy does you proud this month)[3]

[1] Frank Noxon, later a reporter for the the *Boston Herald,* was a member of the Syracuse University class of 1894 and a fraternity brother of Crane in Delta Upsilon. Noxon published a series of satiric sketches about a character named Clanginharp in early issues of the *Philistine* and attended the Philistine Society banquet at which Crane was roasted. He attributed Crane's eventual disillusionment with Hubbard to "the Fra's democratic prejudice against royalties." Noxon's reminiscences, "The Real Stephen Crane," appeared in the *Step-Ladder* (Chicago), 14 (January 1928), 4-9.
[2] "What says the sea, little shell?" *Philistine,* 2 (February 1896), 94-95.
[3] The "Literary Chat" column in *Munsey's Magazine,* 14 (January 1896), 503-4, deplores the excesses of Crane's style, especially in *The Black Riders.* "But in 'The Red Badge' there is a more substantial quality than mere eccentricity. His writings, to be sure, are an acquired taste. One must become hardened to having everything described as 'murder red,' and having one's composure startled by lurid similes. This achieved, there comes a realization that Mr. Crane possesses a power of his own, a forceful knowledge of truth, and an ability to portray it forcefully." The column concludes that Crane is "one of the most original writers of the day."

178. TO JOHN PHILLIPS
ALS, ViU.

Hartwood
January 9th. [1896]

Dear Mr Phillips: The only battle one could well do during this time of year is Fredericksburg. It was fought in December and no doubt the color of things there now would be the very same color of things of the days the battle was fought. I however could not arrange to go down there before the middle of February.[1]

Fredericksburg is to me the most dramatic battle of the war. The terrific assault of the Union army on the impregnable had something in it of the fury of despair. It had been goaded and hooted by the sit-stills until it was near insane and just as a maddened man may dash his fists against an iron wall, so did the Union army hurl itself against the hills back of Fredericksburg.[2]

If you intend to have me do the thing, let me know soon. I want to understand Fredericksburg completely as far as the books will teach it and then after that, the other things.

Yours sincerely
Stephen Crane.

[1] Crane toured Civil War battlefields in Virginia during the latter part of January 1896.
[2] The Battle of Fredericksburg, which occurred on 13 December 1862, resulted in one of the costliest defeats suffered by Union forces. Crane had modeled the action of *The Red Badge of Courage* upon another Confederate victory, the Battle of Chancellorsville, in which Lee defeated Hooker in early May 1863.

179. TO LOUIS SENGER
ALS, NSyU.

[Port Jervis, N.Y., 11 January 1896]

Dear Louis: Will you kindly loan your photograph of me to The Bookman?[1] Please send it to James MacArthur, c/o, Dodd Mead and Co., Fifth Ave., New York City.

Yours faithfully
Stephen Crane.

[1] The *Bookman*, 2 (February 1896), 470, used one of Corwin Knapp Linson's snapshots of Crane in an article on the Philistine dinner and Crane's newly acquired English reputation.

180. TO LOUIS SENGER
ACS, NSyU.

[Port Jervis, 11 January 1896]

Dear L: If you dont send the photograph, I will do you.

Very truly yours
Stephen Crane.

181. TO LOUIS SENGER
ACS, NSyU.

[Port Jervis, 11 January 1896]

Dear Louis: Have you sent it?

Sincerely yours
Stephen Crane

182. TO LOUIS SENGER
ACS, NSyU.

[Port Jervis, 11 January 1896]

Dear Louis: Why dont you send it?

Faithfully yours
Stephen Crane

183. TO LOUIS SENGER
ACS, NSyU.

[Port Jervis, 11 January 1896]

Dear Louis: Why the dickens have you not sent the picture to MacArthur, c/o Dodd, Mead and Co., New York City?

Yours
Stephen Crane

184. TO NELLIE CROUSE
ALS, NSyU.

Hartwood
January 12th. [1896]

Dear Miss Crouse: How dreadfully weary of everything you are. There were deeps of gloom in your letter which might have made me wonder but they did not, for by the same token, I knew of them long ago. As a matter of truth, I learn nothing new of you from your letters. They merely substantiate previous opinions.

For my own part, I am minded to die in my thirty-fifth year. I think that is all I care to stand. I dont like to make wise remarks on the aspect of life but I will say that it doesn't strike me as particularly worth the trouble. The final wall of the wise man's thought however is Human Kindness of course. If the road of disappointment, grief, pessimism, is followed far enough, it will arrive there. Pessimism itself is only a little, little way, and moreover it is ridiculously cheap. The cynical mind is an uneducated thing. Therefore do I strive to be as kind and as just as may be to those about me and in my meagre success at it, I find the solitary pleasure of life.

It is good of you to like "A Grey Sleeve." Of course, they are a pair of idiots. But yet there is something charming in their childish faith in each other. That is all I intended to say.

When I implored you to advise me, I knew very well you would not. But still I was crushed to an infinite degree when you suggested that I should take knowledge from the reviewers. Oh, heavens! Apparently you have not studied the wiles of the learned reviewer very much or you never would have allowed yourself to write that sentence. There is only one person in the world who knows less than the average reader. He is the average reviewer. I would already have been a literary corpse, had I ever paid the slightest attention to the reviewers. It may seem to you that I take this ground because there have been so many unfavorable reviews in America. Take this then from England:[1] Now I have never taken the trouble to look up a single one of these English reviews although I hear from all sides how enthusiastic they are. As for the English publishers I wrote them that I remembered thinking The Red Badge a pretty good thing when I did it, but that it had no attractions for me now and as for any other books I had not then the slightest knowledge of being able to write them. So, you see if I despise reviewers it is not because I have not recieved favorable notice in some quarters.[2]

I am dejected just now because I have to start for New York tonight and leave the blessed quiet hills of Hartwood. McClure is having one of his fits of desire to have me write for him and I am obliged to go see him. Moreover, I have a new novel coming out in the spring and I am also obliged to confer with the Appleton's about that.[3] But I am hanged if I stay in New York more than one day. Then I shall hie me back to Hartwood.

Why, in heaven's name, do you think that beer is any more to me than a mere incident? You dont, as a matter of fact. You were merely warning me. Teas bore me, of course, because all the girls gibber. But then you didn't mean that I might run into a regular tea.

Of course, I knew of the young man who wrote the back-hand. Not that he wrote a back-hand; but then I knew that he had come and gone. Writers—some of them—are dreadfully impertinent about knowing things. Once upon a time there was a young woman but her sister married a baronet and so she thought she must marry a baronet, too. I find it more and more easy to believe her stupid. This is rather lame consolation but I have known it to work.

Your admission that many people find you charming, leads me to be honest. So prepare. I called once in 34th St, when you were there didn't I? Well, I was rather bored. I thought you were very attractive but then I was bored, because I had always believed that when I made calls, I was bored. However to some sentence of mine you said: "Yes, I know," before I had quite finished. I dont remember what I had said but I have always remembered your saying: "Yes, I know." I knew then that you had lived a long time. And so in some semi-conscious manner, you stood forth very distinctly in my memory. In New Orleans I met a fellow—awful chump—who said he was from Akron, O.[4] After a decent interval, I mentioned my meeting you. I was delighted to find that he knew you. I said you were very charming and ultimately he said "rather queer girl, though." Of course he said you were charming, too, but then the slightly dazed manner in which he said "rather queer girl" impressed me. He apparently did not understand you and he being such a chump, I thought it a very good sign. You know the Mexican incident. It was very strange. When I arrived in New York I called at once at 34th St. Nobody was there. Long afterward, I sent the menu of that dinner in Buffalo.

There is the whole episode. You have been for me a curiously potential attraction. I tell it you frankly, assured that no harm could come from any course so honest. I dont know what it is or why it is. I have never analyzed it. Couldnt. I am bound to let my egotism have swing here and tell you that I am an intensely practical and experienced person, in fear you might confuse the word "poet" with various kinds of crazy sentiment.[5]

I have said sometimes to myself that you are a person of remarkably strong personality and that I detected it in New York in that vague unformulating way in which I sometimes come to know things; but then I dont even know this. In short, I want to be frank but I don't know precisely how. One thing however is certain. I would like to know you. And when Akron becomes possible to me, I shall invade Akron.

You will feel embarrassed. I'll bet on it. Here is a young man who proclaims an admiration of you from afar. He comes to Akron. You dont care either way but then you feel a sort of a moral responsibility. Great Scott! What a situation!

The Bookman next month is I believe going to use a photograph of me which is worse than one in the Chicago *Echo*. It is worse because it looks more like me. I shall expect an answer soon. You have not yet told me where is Button. I enjoyed your last letter immensely and understood your point-of-view exactly. I am going to take this letter to Port Jervis with me tonight so that your answer may come quicker.

Very sincerely yours
Stephen Crane.

[1] Here Crane attached to his letter a newspaper clipping: "The 'Red Badge of Courage' has fascinated England. The critics are wild over it, and the English edition has been purchased with avidity. Mr. Crane has letters from the most prominent of English publishers asking for the English rights to all of his future productions."

[2] *The Red Badge of Courage* received generally favorable reviews in newspapers throughout the United States following its publication by Appleton in October 1895. Estimates in American monthly magazines tended to be more qualified. British enthusiasm over the novel, heralded by Harold Frederic's article, "Stephen Crane's Triumph," in the 26 January 1896 *New York Times*, stimulated American reviewers to higher levels of praise. By March and April *The Red Badge* headed many best-seller lists, and there were fourteen printings in 1896.

[3] Either the expurgated *Maggie* brought out by Appleton in June or *The Third Violet*, which he had completed at the end of December but which was not published until May 1897.

[4] The "intolerable duffer" he had mentioned to Lucius Button in March of the previous year. See No. 81.

[5] Here, as in No. 166, Crane attempts to disassociate himself from the bohemian connotations of the word *poet*, which he, no doubt correctly, feared might alienate the unimaginative Middle Western beauty to whom he was futilely attempting to convey an image of stolid respectability. In the absence of external evidence for the existence of Beer's Helen Trent, it seems that Nellie Crouse was the only iron maiden of the 1890s to whom Crane ever paid court. His previous amorous experiences were with chorus girls, prostitutes, and Lily Brandon Munroe, an older married woman. Cora Taylor would require no stilted protestations of virtue.

185. TO VICTOR NEWMAN[1]

Inscribed in a copy of *The Black Riders*, VtMiM.

To Victor Newman.
Stephen Crane

January 25th, 1896
New York

[1]Newman was the roommate of Post Wheeler in 1894 "in an enormous loft in 23rd Street, a few doors west of Sixth Avenue, where Stevie camped out as often as not, sleeping on a divan in the front" (memorandum by Post Wheeler, 3 November 1947, NSyU).

186. TO NELLIE CROUSE
ALS, NSyU.

Hartwood, N.Y.
Sunday—[26 January 1896]

Dear Miss Crouse:

I am just this moment back to the hills. I was obliged to go down to Virginia from New York and so the time of my little journey was unduly prolonged.[1] I was impatient to get your letter and so had it forwarded to New York where I got it two days ago but was so badgered with silly engagements that I did not really own a minute in which I could reply. Sometimes people revenge themselves for delayed letters by calmly delaying the reply but I know you will not treat me to any such injustice.

I told you indeed that I was a practical and experienced person but your interpretation in this last letter was perhaps a little too wide. I did not say so to "warn" you. I mentioned it in a sort of a wonder that anyone so prodigiously practical and experienced should be so attracted by a vague, faint shadow—in fact a young woman who crossed his vision just once and that a considerable time ago. This is the thing that makes me wonder. Your letters, however, have reinforced me. I know much more of you now than I did before you amiably replied to my first letter and I know now that my instinctive liking for you was not a mistake.

I am afraid you laugh at me sometimes in your letters. For instance when you speak of a liklihood of being aghast at being left alone with such a clever person. Now that is really too bad of you. I am often marvelously a blockhead and incomparably an idiot. I reach depths of stupidity of which most people cannot dream. This is usually in the case of a social crisis. A social crisis simply leaves me witless and gibbering. A social crisis to me is despair. When I am really myself however, I am all right, being a good fellow, I think, and quite honest and simple. On most occasions I contrive to keep myself that way but sometimes the social crisis catches me unawares. The "Great Scott" in my letter was intended to show me stupid, witless, gibbering, despairing when I meet you in Akron. I only wish it could be in riding weather. I could bring some toys and I dare say I could rent some kind of a steed in Akron. My pilgrimage to the west via the Erie will please me immensely if it achieves a ride, a tea and *An Evening Call*, in Akron. Considering, February weather, I can forego the ride. The story "One Dash— Horses," which I sent you celebrates in a measure my affection for a little horse I owned in Mexico.[2] I just thought to tell you. I was about to say however that you must submit to my being quite serious over the stop-off at Akron. As sure as February appears you can expect to be bored by *An Evening Call*.

I have some friends departing for London on the 29th of February and as some people in London have requested me to come over and be looked at and as S. S. McClure, Limited, has requested me to go to London for him, I am mildly tempted, but expect to decline. Travelling is a great deal of trouble. If however you have in mind any new excursions to the land where all bad newspaper articles come from, you ought to let me know for then I would feel capable of overcoming my inertia.

You dont mean to soberly say that you thought I was anything but very ordinary when I called in 34th St? I was sure that on that occasion I was stupid. In truth I sometimes secretly wail over the fact that women never see the best traits of a man—not, at least, in our conventional intercourse. Many a duffer shines like a sun and many a brave man appears a duffer.[3] To offset this, women have a sort of an instinct of discovery. Still I am sure that no women—not even the women who have cared for me—ever truly knew the best and worst of me. There are three men in this world who know me about as I am but no woman does.

I see that I am in danger of wandering. I meant to say that in all social situations I am ordinarily conscious of being minute. At a dinner the other night in New York—the Lantern Club—they drank a very kind toast to me and to see all those old veterans arise and looked solemnly at me, quite knocked the wind from me and when it came my turn to get up I could only call them damned fools and sit down again. They were all old friends. At Buffalo however where everyone was strange, I was as cold as iced cucumbers when I arose and I said what I had to say very deliberately. The social crisis catches me sometimes and sometimes it doesnt. At Buffalo however I didnt talk as well as I could talk and to a woman I never talk as well as I can talk. Now that is exactly what I mean. And I never made a call, fought a tea, or sat on the sands by the mournful sea, that I didnt come away much discontented. So you see, when my mind recalled the evening on 34th St., I was always disgusted for I distinctly remembered that I was more than usually stupid on that occasion. And this is why I was bored then. It wasn't because I didn't know I was meeting a very charming girl, because I did know it. It was simply because it was my experience and, later, my habit to be bored when calling. Button, good a soul as he is, only dragged me forth on that call because he was exhibiting his literary friend. You know what I mean. It seems that to some men there is a mild glamor about their literary friends and they like to gently exhibit them. I was used to it and usually submitted as decently as possible. It is awfully nice to be exhibited like a stuffed parrot. They say that Davis enjoys it. I should think he would. He has, I believe, the intelligence of the average saw-log and he can no doubt enjoy anything.[4] And now with this illumination of the subject you will better understand why I say I was bored.

This is manuscript paper and I think it is perfectly plain. Otherwise several editors would by this time have tomahawked me. Your paragraph relating to the tangle of my letters was a remarkable case of supreme and undaunted assurance. I had been patiently and humbly working at your pages, fitting them this way and that way, trying them one way and then another, performing puzzle solutions on them and exhausting half the devices of the Chinese in efforts to form the proper sequence, when, glory to you, along you come with an ingenuous request to be more plain.

No, I know you are not cynical. But then you are very tired. I am, too, very tired. So you think I am successful? Well I dont know. Most people consider me successful. At least, they seem to so think. But upon my soul I have lost all appetite for victory, as victory is defined by the mob. I will be glad if I can feel on my death-bed that my life has been just and kind according to my ability and that every particle of my little ridiculous stock of eloquence and wisdom has been applied for the benefit of my kind. From this moment to that deathbed may be a short time or a long one but at any rate it means a life of labor and sorrow. I do not confront it blithely. I confront it with desperate resolution.

There is not even much hope in my attitude. I do not even expect to do good. But I expect to make a sincere, desperate, lonely battle to remain true to my conception of my life and the way it should be lived, and if this plan accomplish anything, it shall be accomplished. It is not a fine prospect. I only speak of it to people in whose opinions I have faith. No woman has heard it until now.

When I speak of a battle I do not mean want, and those similar spectres. I mean myself and the inherent indolence and cowardice which is the lot of all men. I mean, also, applause. Last summer I was getting very ably laughed at for a certain book called The Black Riders. When I was at my publishers yesterday I read long extracts from English newspapers. I got an armful of letters from people who declared that The Black Riders was—etc, etc,—and then for the first time in my life I began to be afraid, afraid that I would grow content with myself, afraid that willy-nilly I would be satisfied with the little, little things I have done. For the first time I saw the majestic forces which are arrayed against man's true success—not the world—the world is silly, changeable, any of it's decisions can be reversed—but man's own colossal impulses more strong than chains, and I percieved that the fight was not going to be with the world but with myself. I had fought the world and had not bended nor moved an inch but this other battle— it is to last on up through the years to my grave and only on that day am I to know if the word Victory will look well upon lips of mine.

It is a pretty solemn thing to talk thus and if you were not you, I would re-write that paragraph and write it much better but I know you will understand. To become frank still further, it seems to me that I like you wonderfully more, after confessing so unreservedly.

That trouble to locate Button. As I said, it was originally merely an expedient.

I am a very hurried writer but I hope my innumerable editings will not make you impatient.

I dont like to appear common-place but I remember that Button had your photograph and it seems to me that one who pays you such such reserved and unreserved, conditional and unconditional devotion as do I, might be one of the chosen. If you refuse, I shall go and slay Button for his impertinence.

I remain in the hope that you will do it. And remember that you are supposed to reply at once to this letter.

Yours sincerely
Stephen Crane.

[1]Crane studied the Virginia battlefields in preparation for the Civil War stories he was currently writing, some of which were incorporated into *The Little Regiment*. "A Mystery of Heroism" and "A Gray Sleeve," included in this collection, had already been published in newspapers in 1895.

[2]Syndicated by Bacheller, Johnson and Bacheller in two parts during the first week of January 1896 and included in *The Open Boat and Other Tales of Adventure* (1898). It appeared in the Heinemann house organ, *The New Review* (February 1896), and in the Heinemann book publication *The Open Boat and Other Stories* under the abbreviated title "Horses." Crane canceled the Americanism "One Dash" in the table of contents for the English edition.

[3]This and the other self-effacing and ingratiating comments that follow highlight Crane's insecurity in dealing with a "nice girl."

[4]Richard Harding Davis (1864-1916), journalist, novelist, and playwright, was a fellow correspondent with Crane in the Greco-Turkish and Spanish-American Wars. Clean-cut, priggish, and a self-styled soldier of fortune, Davis later became Charles D. Gibson's model for the upstanding, handsome young men who squired the famous Gibson Girl. Crane's deprecation of Davis to Nellie Crouse was most likely based upon his fear that she might find a writer cast in the Davis mold a more acceptable suitor than himself.

187. FROM WILLIAM DEAN HOWELLS
Letterhead: "40 West Fifty-Ninth Street." ALS, NNC.

Jan'y 26, 1896.

Dear Mr. Crane:

Your New Year's greeting was very pleasant to me, and I have been enjoying for your sake your English triumphs. I am glad you are getting your glory young. For once, the English who habitually know nothing of art, seem to know something.—For me, I remain true to my first love, "Maggie." That is better than all the Black Riders and Red Badges.

You have a lot of good work in you, and the whole of a long life to get it out.

I wish you could come sometime to see me.

Yours sincerely
W. D. Howells.

188. TO WILLIS BROOKS HAWKINS
ALS, ViU.

Hartwood, N.Y.
January 27th. [1896]

My dear Willis: There are none of my friends whom I could treat so shamefully and none who can make me feel so utterly dejected over it afterward. But oh you dont know how that damned city tore my heart out by the roots and flung it under the heels of it's noise. Indeed it did. I couldnt breathe in that accursed tumult. On Friday it had me keyed to a point where I was no more than a wild beast and I had to make a dash willy-nilly. It was a disgraceful retreat but I think you will understand me. I feel myself perfectly capable of any sacrifice for you now with the sting of that retreat still upon me. But as to that past thing I will have to throw myself upon your mercy. I am coming down again in about two weeks.

Yours invariably
S. C.

P.S.: I am expressing you the original ms of The Red Badge. Thought maybe you'd like it.[1] S. C. *Did* you see Sunday's Times.[2]

---

[1] Crane sent Hawkins the complete final manuscript of *The Red Badge of Courage*, consisting of 176 leaves written throughout in black ink on legal-cap paper with false starts inscribed on the verso of some of the leaves and portions of an earlier draft on 57 of the others. Hawkins had the loose sheets bound in a notebook. They are now preserved, disbound and laminated, at ViU.

[2] Referring to Harold Frederic's "Stephen Crane's Triumph," *New York Times*, 26 January 1896, p. 22. Frederic stressed the acclaim for *The Red Badge* by English critics.

189. TO WILLIAM HEINEMANN
ALS, Collection of the Newark Museum, Newark, New Jersey.

Hartwood
Sullivan Co., N.Y.
January 27th. [1896]

Dear Mr Heineman:

I have just read Mr George Wyndham's review and I feel glad to be able to write you that I think it a very wonderful thing.[1] Of course it is difficult for me to speak of The Red Badge of Courage as I wrote it when I was between twenty-one and twenty-two years of age and have lost sense of it's being of any value. Still I am conscious that Mr Wyndham has reproduced in a large measure my own hopeful thoughts of the book when it was still for the most part in my head. As near as a man can do it, he convinces me that the thing is in some ways an artistic success. As far as I know he is the one writer to arouse in me the joyful hope that perhaps the book is good. I wish you would extend to him a serious expression of my gratitude and appreciation. If it were not my own work that was under discussion I would give you many reasons for my thinking the article in The New Review a very remarkable essay.

Yours sincerely
Stephen Crane

P.S.: If you would care to send me two or three copies of The New Review, of January, I would be very glad. I trouble you only because being at Hartwood it would be immensely difficult to otherwise get them.

---

[1] George Wyndham (1863-1913) was a Member of Parliament who had seen action with the Coldstream Guards in the Suakim Campaign of 1885 and who had devoted himself mainly to literature since the Conservatives went into opposition in 1892. Sidney Pawling, partner in the firm of William Heinemann, engaged Wyndham to write an article about *The Red Badge of Courage* for the *New Review*. In his estimate, Wyndham called Crane "a great artist" and *The Red Badge* "a masterpiece." Crane's protrayal of war was "more complete than Tolstoi's, more true than Zola's." Above all, Wyndham realized that Crane went beyond surface realism "to recognize all life for a battle and

this earth for a vessel lost in space" ("A Remarkable Book," *New Review* [London], 14 [January 1896], 30-40; retitled "An Appreciation" and rpt. as the introduction to *Pictures of War* [London: Heinemann, 1898]).

190. TO RIPLEY HITCHCOCK
ALS, NN.

Hartwood, N.Y.
January 27. [1896]

Dear Mr Hitchcock: I fear that when I meet you again I shall feel abashed. As a matter of truth, New York has so completely muddled me on this last visit that I shant venture again very soon. I had grown used to being called a damned ass but this sudden new admiration of my friends has made a gibbering idiot of me. I shall stick to my hills.

I think it is as well to go ahead with The Third Violet. People may just as well discover now that the high dramatic key of The Red Badge cannot be sustained.[1] You know what I mean. I dont think The Red Badge to be any great shakes but then the very theme of it gives it an intensity that the writer cant reach every day. The Third Violet is a quiet little story but then it is serious work and I should say let it go. If my health and my balance remains to me, I think I will be capable of doing work that will dwarf both books.

Yours sincerely
Stephen Crane

[1] Following Crane's initial elation over the success of *The Red Badge*, his comments about the war novel assumed a more negative tinge as he came to realize that whatever he wrote subsequently would be compared to it and found wanting.

191. TO WILLIAM DEAN HOWELLS
ALS, MH.

Hartwood, N.Y.
Jan 27. [1896]

Dear Mr Howells: I had just become well habituated to abuse when this bit of a flurry about the red badge came upon me. I am slightly rattled and think it best to cling to Hartwood where if I choose to shout triumphant shouts none can hear me. However I have not yet elected to shout any shouts. I am, mostly, afraid. Afraid that some small degree of talk will turn me ever so slightly from what I believe to be the pursuit of truth, and that my block-head will lose something of the resolution which carried me very comfortably through the ridicule. If they would only continue the abuse. I feel ably to cope with that, but beyond I am in great doubt.

Yours sincerely
Stephen Crane.

192. TO S. S. McCLURE
ALS, ViU.

Hartwood, N.Y.
January 27th. [1896]

Dear Mr McClure: I think my retreat to Hartwood was quite a masterly move on my part for I feel so much more quiet and undisturbed and the noise of the trees cannot muddle me as does the city. I am getting the Fredericksburg row into shape.[1] I dont know how much you were going to pay me for the little "Three Miraculous Soldiers"[2] but if you can send me twenty-five more dollars to last until my February ship comes in, it would assist the Cranes of Sullivan County very greatly.

I think the agreement with you is a good thing. I am perfectly satisfied with my end of it but your end somewhat worries me for I am often inexpressibly dull and uncreative and these periods often last for days.

I see by Sunday's Times, that the Englishmen are mildly curious about me. Many of my friends—quite a number, I mean—are going to Europe on the 29th February. If you could think out some campaign for me I might go but I feel reluctant.

Whenever you have some article or other in mind, let me know at once. Beware only how you catch me up here without car-fare to N.Y. That is the spectre that perches on the back of the Crane "child of promise."

I think it will be of a great advantage to me to have you to invent subjects for me. By the way I would like to go to the scene of the next great Street-car strike. I feel I could do something then to dwarf the Red Badge, which I do not think is very great shakes.

Yours sincerely
Stephen Crane

---

[1] "The Little Regiment."

[2] Another of the stories collected in *The Little Regiment*. A shortened version of "Three Miraculous Soldiers" was first syndicated by McClure in a number of newspapers.

193. TO RIPLEY HITCHCOCK
ALS, ViU.

Hartwood, N.Y.
January 28. [1896]

Dear Mr Hitchcock: I forward you a copy of the ameteur photograph which the Bookman used.[1]

Sincerely
Stephen Crane.

---

[1] The *Bookman* reproduced a sketch of Crane by David Ericson to accompany a short essay on the young author's career by Harry Thurston Peck in its May 1895 issue, but by "ameteur photograph" Crane is referring to the study published in the February 1896 *Bookman* that he had described to Nellie Crouse as "worse than the one in the Chicago *Echo*. It is worse because it looks more like me." See No. 184.

194. TO S. S. McCLURE
ALS, ViU.

Hartwood, N.Y.
January 28. [1896]

Dear Mr McClure: I feel for you when I think of some of the things of mine which you will have to read or have read. If you dont like the enclosed please return it to me here.[1]

Sincerely
Stephen Crane

[1] Possibly "The Veteran," which was published in the August 1896 issue of *McClure's Magazine*.

195. TO RIPLEY HITCHCOCK
Inscribed on the verso of a cabinet photograph of Crane,[1] NNC.

Mr. Ripley Hitchcock
With the regards of
Stephen Crane

Hartwood, N.Y.
January 29, 1896.

[1] This is a copy of the identical photograph Crane sent to Dr. A. L. Mitchell on the same day. It was made at Lundeluco Studio in Port Jervis in 1892 or 1893 and shows the young Crane with full lips and without mustache.

196. TO Dr. A. L. MITCHELL
Inscribed on the verso of a copy of No. 195, InU.

To Dr A. L. Mitchell
Stephen Crane

Hartwood, N.Y., January 29, 1896.

My dear Docter: I was in Virginia when your letter came to Hartwood and so did not get it until yesterday. You delight me with your appreciation and yet too it makes me afraid. I did not bend under the three hills of ridicule which were once upon my shoulders but I dont know that I am strong enough to withstand the kind things that are now sometimes said to me. I have a desire to sit down and look at myself.

Always your friend
Stephen Crane

197. TO JOHN NORTHERN HILLIARD[1]
Quoted in the *New York Times,* Supplement, 14 July 1900, p. 466.

[January 1896?]

The one thing that deeply pleases me in my literary life—brief and inglorious as it is—is the fact that men of sense believe me to be sincere. "Maggie," published in paper covers, made me the friendship of Hamlin Garland and W. D. Howells, and the one thing that makes my life worth living in the midst of all this abuse and ridicule is the consciousness that never for an instant have those friendships at all diminished. Personally I am aware that my work does not amount to a string of dried beans— I always calmly admit it. But I also know that I do the best that is in me, without regard to cheers or damnation. When I was the mark for every humorist in the country I went ahead, and now, when I am the mark for only 50 per cent of the humorists of the country, I go ahead, for I understand that a man is born into the world with his own pair of eyes and he is not at all responsible for his quality of personal honesty.

To keep close to my honesty is my supreme ambition. There is a sublime egotism in talking of honesty. I, however, do not say that I am honest. I merely say that I am as nearly honest as a weak mental machinery will allow. This aim in life struck me as being the only thing worth while. A man is sure to fail at it, but there is something in the failure.

[1] The letter was probably written in response to further questions from Hilliard about Crane's literary career. Hilliard edited the *Rochester Post Express*.

198. TO RIPLEY HITCHCOCK
ALS, NN.

Hartwood, N.Y.
February 2d [1896]

Dear Mr. Hitchcock: I am very glad to hear you speak as you do concerning *Maggie*. I will set to work this month rewriting it. I have no more pictures until they come from New York where I sat the last time I was down. They should reach me soon. I was very much delighted with Frederick's letter in the Times.[1] I see also that they are beginning to charge me with having played base ball. I am rather more proud of my base ball ability than of some other things. I am coming down to New York this month and will come to see you first thing.

Yours sincerely
Stephen Crane

[1] "Stephen Crane's Triumph: London Curious about the Identity of America's New Writer," *New York Times*, 26 January 1896, p. 22.

199. TO RIPLEY HITCHCOCK
ALfr, NN.

[4-6? February 1896]

Dear Mr. Hitchcock: I am working at *Maggie*. She will be down to you in a few days. I have dispensed with a goodly number of damns. I have no more copies of the book or I would have sent you one.

I want to approach Appleton & Co on a delicate matter. I dont care much about money up here save when I have special need of it and just at this time there is a beautiful riding-mare for sale for a hundred dollars.[1] The price will go up each week, almost, until spring and I am crazy to get her now. I dont want to strain your traditions but if I am worth $100. in your office, I would rather have it now

[1] Crane paid Hubbard only sixty dollars for the horse, "Peanuts"—a gelding, not a mare—to which he had taken a fancy while visiting East Aurora in December 1895.

200. TO NELLIE CROUSE
ALS, NSyU.

Hartwood
February 5th. [1896]

Dear Miss Crouse: Your photograph came to-day. Of course you know how very grateful I am to you. I had expected to hear from you on Monday but that day as well as Tuesday were times of disaster. At noon today, however the coming of the portrait relieved me. I am sure now, still more, that you are precisely the kind of young woman I have judged you. However, you have awed me. Yes, indeed, I am awed. There is something in your face which tells that there are many things which you perfectly understand which perhaps I dont understand at all. This sounds very vague but it is nevertheless very vague in my mind. I think it means that I am a savage. Of course I am admittedly a savage. I have been known as docile from time to time but only under great social pressure. I am by inclination a wild shaggy barbarian. I know that I am hopelessly befogging my meaning but then at best my meaning is a dim thing. I intend to say at any rate that the light of social experience in your eyes somewhat terrifies this poor outer pagan.

Well, it is better that I should gibber in the above lines. Otherwise I would have bored you with long descriptions of how charming I think the portrait.

I am engaged in rowing with people who wish me to write more war-stories. Hang all war-stories. Nevertheless I submitted in one case and now I have a daily battle with a tangle of facts and emotions. I am however doing the thing in a way that is not without a mild satisfaction for me.

I believe I told you in my last chronicle—my letters arise almost to the dignity of chronicles; they are so long—that I might go over to England on the 29th. Well I've almost given up the plan. The publishers and things in London seem anxious for me to come, and people on this side furnish me with unlimited introductions. So the journey seems so easy and simple that I am quite out of the humor of it. I dont think I shall go until next fall. Do you come east in the summer? I hope so. I never work in the summer. It is one long lazy time to fool away. Just now we in Hartwood are being drearily snowed upon. Sometimes I am much agitated at the thought that perhaps the little train wont be able to struggle up the mountain and deliver my mail. As yet however nothing has happened to it. Did not you once ask me if Hartwood is out of the world? It is—very much. New York is only 104 miles but it is a terrible 104 miles, and the mail service is wretched.

I have about four new books coming out.[1] Sometimes I feel like sitting still and watching them appear. However, they are not good enough to delight me at all.

I wonder if you have a copy of *The Black Riders*. If you have not, let me know. I might as well let you know the worst of me at once. Although *Maggie* perhaps is the worst—or the most unconventional—of me.

I hope you will keep me no longer in anxiety by not writing. Of course I know that if you sent the picture you wouldn't write, and if you wrote, you wouldnt send the picture. So, possessing the picture I can forego the letter this week. Early next week, however, I shall not be so submissive. To add to the situation, no mail route, I imagine, can be so laboriously intricate as the way between Akron and Hartwood.

Yours sincerely
Stephen Crane.

[1] *George's Mother* was published by the Anglo-American firm of Edward Arnold in May in New York and in London the following month. *Maggie: A Girl of the Streets,* originally privately printed in 1893, was published by Appleton in June with revisions recommended by Ripley Hitchcock, which, as Crane acknowledged, gave the book "quite a new aspect" (see No. 203) and in the same month by Heinemann in London with the less suggestive subtitle, *A Child of the Streets.* Appleton published *The Little Regiment* in November. *The Third Violet* was serialized in various newspapers that month but did not appear in book form until 1897.

201. TO AN UNKNOWN RECIPIENT
Adrian H. Joline, *Meditations of an Autograph Collector* (New York: Harper, 1902), p. 14.

HARTFORD, N.Y., *February 6th.* [1896]

DEAR SIR,—I dont thing it possible to get my photograph. They have been mostly ameteur things.

Very truly yours,
STEPHEN CRANE.

202. TO RIPLEY HITCHCOCK
AL, NN.

Hartwood, N.Y.
February 7th. [1896]

Dear Mr. Hitchcock: I enclose you a letter from Syracuse written in the usual nervy vein of college editors. I am not trembling with anxiety to have them print my picture and I am sure it makes me apprehensive at a prospect of their reviewing the R.B. I have written them that I have requested you to send them a cut and a book but I don't request it.

203. TO RIPLEY HITCHCOCK
ALS, NN.

Hartwood,
Monday [10 February 1896]

Dear Mr. Hitchcock: I am delighted with your prompt sympathy in regard to the saddle horse. It is a luxury to feel that some of my pleasures are due to my little pen. I will send you *Maggie* by detail. I have carefully plugged at the words which hurt. Seems to me the book wears quite a new aspect from very slight omissions. Did you know that the book is very short? Only about 20000 words?

Yours sincerely
Stephen Crane.

204. TO NELLIE CROUSE[1]
ALS, NSyU.

Hartwood
Feb 11th. [1896]

Wherever that letter went is more than I can imagine. It certainly never reached Hartwood. I am grieved at the prospect of never seeing it but I console myself a little with the remembrance that you wrote it. There is some consolation in that, you know.

Your recent confession that in your heart you like the man of fashion more than you do some other kinds of men came nearer to my own view than perhaps you expected. I have indeed a considerable liking for the man of fashion if he does it well. The trouble to my own mind lies in the fact that the heavy social life demands one's entire devotion. Time after time, I have seen the social lion turn to a lamb and fail—fail at precisely the moment when men should not fail. The world sees this also and it has come to pass that the fashionable man is considerably jeered at. Men who are forever sitting with immovable legs on account of a tea-cup are popularly supposed to be worth little besides. This is true in the main but it is not without brave exceptions, thank heaven. For my part, I like the man who dresses correctly and does the right thing invariably but, oh, he must be more than that, a great deal more. But so seldom is he anymore than correctly-dressed, and correctly-speeched, that when I see a man of that kind I usually put him down as a kind of an idiot. Still, as I have said, there are exceptions. There are men of very social habits who nevertheless know how to stand steady when they see cocked revolvers and death comes down and sits on the back of a chair and waits.[2] There are men of very social habits who know good music from bad, good poetry from bad—(a few of 'em)—good drama from bad—(a very few of 'em)—good painting from bad. There are very many of them who know good claret and good poker-playing. There are a few who can treat a woman tenderly not only when they feel amiable but when she most needs tender-treatment. There are many who can ride, swim, shoot and sail a boat, a great many. There are an infinitismal number who can keep from yapping in a personal way about women. There are a large number who refuse to haggle over a question of money. There are one or two who invariably mind their own business. There are some who know how to be frank without butchering the feelings of their friends. There is an enormous majority who, upon being insured of safety from detection—become at once the most unconventional of peoples.

In short they are precisely like the remainder of the race, only they devote their minds to riding smoothly. A slight jolt gives them the impression that a mountain has fallen upon them.

I swear by the real aristocrat. The man whose forefathers were men of courage, sympathy and wisdom, is usually one who will stand the strain whatever it may be. He is like a thorough-bred horse. His nerves may be high and he will do a lot of jumping often but in the crises he settles down and becomes the most reliable and enduring of created things.

For the hordes who hang upon the out-skirts of good society and chant 143 masses per day to the social gods and think because they have money they are well-bred—for such people I have a scorn which is very deep and very intense. These people think that polite life is something which is to be studied, a very peculiar science, of which knowledge is only gained by long practice whereas what is called "form" is merely a collection of the most rational and just of laws which any properly-born person understands from his cradle. In Hartwood I have a great chance to study the new-rich. The Hartwood Club-house is only three miles away and there are some of the new rich in it. May the Lord deliver me from having social aspirations.

I can stand the society man, if he dont interfere with me; I always think the society girl charming but the type that I cant endure is the society matron. Of course there are many exceptions but some I have seen struck me afar off with the peculiar iron-like quality of their thick-headedness and the wild exuberance of their vanity.

On two or three occasions I had some things read at Sherry's and later by chance met people who had been there.[3] I distinctly remember some compliments paid me very graciously and confidently by a woman. Nothing so completely and serenely stupid have I ever witnessed. And the absolutely false tongue of her prattled away for ten minutes in more lies than are usually heard at one time. Of course it was nothing to me if she liked my stuff and it was nothing to her. She was merely being because she indifferently thought it to be correct at that moment, but how those old cats can stand up and lie until there is no breath left in them. Now, they think that is form, mind you, but, good heavens, it isnt. They think that a mere show of complacent idiocy is all that is necessary to a queen of society. Form really is truth, simplicity; when people surround it with falsity, interpret it as meaning: "lies," they become not society leaders but barbarians, savages, beating little silly tom-toms and flourishing little carved wooden goblins. They really defy every creed of this social god, the very diety which they worship.

I am rather apprehensive. I detest dogma and it strikes me that I have expressed too many opinions in this letter. When I express an opinion in writing I am in the habit of considering a long time and then formulating it with a great deal of care. This letter however has been so hasty that I have not always said precisely what I intended to say. But at any rate I hope it will be plain that I strongly admire the social god even if I do despise many of his worshippers.

As for the man with the high aims and things—which you say you like in your soul—but not in your heart—I dont know that he is to my mind any particular improvement on the society man.[4] I shouldn't care to live in the same house with him if he was at all in the habit of talking about them. I get about two letters a day from people who have high literary aims and everywhere I go I seem to meet five or six. They strike me as about the worst and most penetrating kind of bore I know. Of course I, with my meagre successes, would feel like an awful duffer if I was anything but very, very considerate of them but it is getting to be a task. Of course that is not the kind you meant. Still they are certainly people of high aims and there is a ridiculous quality to me in all high ambitions, of men who mean to try to make themselves great because they think it would so nice to be great, to be admired, to be stared at by the mob. "Well," you say, "I didnt mean that kind of high aim either." Tolstoy's aim is, I suppose—I believe—to make himself good. It is an incomparably quixotic task for any man to undertake. He will not succeed; but he will even succeed more than he can ever himself know, and so at his nearest point to success he will be proportionately blind. This is the pay of this kind of greatness.

This letter is certainly not a conscience-smiter but I hope you will reply to it at the same length that you claim for the lost letter.

I may go to Chicago in late February or early March—over the Erie's lines. I wish you would tell me more about your European trip. By the way, if you forbid me going over on the same boat, it must be because you think I am not clever.

Yours sincerely
Stephen Crane.

---

[1] The lack of salutation in this letter and in Crane's final letter to Nellie Crouse (No. 209) indicates he was no longer comfortable in addressing her formally as Miss Crouse. Yet, since he had met her only once and his passion was evidently unrequited, he was equally uncomfortable with her given name.

[2] Crane's embarrassing posturing in this letter is further evidence of his ineptitude in dealing with a conventional young girl.

[3] Some of the poems from *The Black Riders* were read before the Uncut Leaves Society at Sherry's by John D. Barry on Saturday evening, 14 April 1894.

[4]Nellie Crouse attempted to convey to Crane that although she admired him, she could not love him. Crane pointedly ignored the message.

205. TO ELBERT HUBBARD
ALS, ViU.

Hartwood, N.Y
Feb 13 [1896]

My dear H: I am going to pinch money this month from various places and will certainly be delighted to pay sixty bones for the mare. I will send you the check and you can board her out with some gentle people—if you will be so good—until I come after her in the spring.

My business is booming in great style.

Yours as ever
S. C.

206. TO THE EDITOR OF *THE CRITIC*[1]
ALS, ViU.

Hartwood, N.Y
Feb 15, 96.

Editor of the Critic

Dear sir: There is a very excellent photograph of me in the possession of Mr. King, the artist, c/ The Lantern Club, 126 William St., New York. It is a picture that has never been used for publication and is I think a very good portrait. I have forwarded him your letter with a request to send you a picture.[2]

I began writing for newspapers when I was 16. At 18 I did my first fiction—for the N.Y. Sunday Tribune—sketches. At 20 I began *Maggie* & finished it when I was somewhat beyond 21. Later in the same year I began *The R.B. of Courage* and finished it some months after my 22d birthday. *The Black Riders* were written in that year. When I was 23, I devoted most of my time to travelling for the Bachellor and Johnson syndicate and in writing short stories for English magazines. This winter I wrote a novel: "The Third Violet," which is to be published by the Appletons. Beforehand, however, they are to bring out in connection with William Heineman a new edition of *Maggie*. I am now finishing a novelette for S. S. McClure called The Little Regiment which represents my work at it's best I think and is positively my last thing dealing with battle.

When I look back on this array it appears that I have worked but as a matter of truth I am very very lazy, hating work, and only taking up a pen when circumstances drive me.

I live at Hartwood very quietly and alone, mostly, and think a good saddle-horse is the one blessing of life.

Sincerely yours
Stephen Crane

P.S. If in doubt concerning certain facts apply to S. S. McClure.

---

[1] Clarence Loomis Peaslee quotes from this letter or an identically worded one in his article, "Stephen Crane's College Days," *Monthly Illustrator,* 13 (August 1896), 30.

[2] *The Critic* (n. s. 25 [7 March 1896], 163) reproduced a portrait of Crane "from a photograph taken by Mr. F. H. King of this city. It is regarded by Mr. Crane as a good likeness, and has not hitherto been published." This highly mannered portrait, depicting a thin, aesthetic Crane in winged collar and cravat, seems to have been made in 1893 or early 1894, before Crane began to develop a mustache.

207. TO RIPLEY HITCHCOCK
ALS, NN.

Hartwood
Feb 15. [1896]

Dear Mr Hitchcock: I send you under two covers six edited chapters of Maggie to see if they suit. The remainder will shortly follow

Sincerely
S. C.

208. TO WILLIAM HEINEMANN
ALS, InU.

Hartwood
Sullivan Co., N.Y.
February 17. [1896]

Dear Mr Heineman: I was glad to get your opinion of the *Bookman*'s request. The furnishing of such matter is usually one of the odious necessities of the literary business and when it is not, I am only too happy to escape.

I am sending you today a copy of *The Black Riders*. I imagine that when you see the volume you wont care to publish it anywhere. If however I am wrong in this opinion, I will be only too happy to hear you say so.[1]

I have written very little of that sort of thing during the past year and they are all now out of my hands but if you wish to be protected by additional copy, I can perhaps contrive it in time.

I think some of my short stories are coming out in England but they are all stories which passed out of my hands before the publication of *The Red Badge*. My next thing is likely to be a re-print of *Maggie*. *Maggie* was born into a world of enemies three years ago but I have toned it somewhat at the request of the Appletons. It is perhaps only just to say that Mr Howells—our first critic, of course—has always solemnly sworn to the book's merit. He thinks it better than all The Black Riders and Red Badges. Kipling carried it in his pocket to England once—I have heard. Sort of a private view for some friends. For my own part, I hate the book.

I wish I could be sure that what I wrote about Mr Wyndham's article, really did gratify him.[2] If I could have talked to him—I think then I could have made him feel how generous and fine I thought it.

Yours very truly
Stephen Crane

[1] The English edition of *The Black Riders* was published by William Heinemann in November 1896.
[2] See No. 189.

209. TO NELLIE CROUSE
ALS, NSyU.

33 East 22d, NYC
March 1st [1896]

Do you know, I have succeeded in making a new kind of an idiot of myself. They had a winter party at Hartwood and after I had sat before twelve fire-places and drank 842 cups of tea, I said: "I shall escape." And so I have come to New York. But New York is worse. I am in despair. The storm-beaten little robin who has no place to lay his head, does not feel so badly as do I. It is not that people want to meet me. When that happens I can endure it. But it is that mine own friends feel bitterly insulted if I do not see them twelve times a day—in short they are all prepared to find me grown vain.

You know what I mean. That disgraceful Red Badge is doing so very well that my importance has widened and everybody sits down and calmly waits to see me be a chump

---

Dear me, how much am I getting to admire graveyards—the calm unfretting unhopeing end of things—serene absence of passion—

oblivious to sin—ignorant of the accursed golden hopes that flame at night and make a man run his legs off and then in the daylight of experience turn out to be ingenious traps for the imagination. If there is a joy of living I cant find it. The future? The future is blue with obligations—new trials—conflicts. It was a rare old wine the gods brewed for mortals. Flagons of despair—

Washington, D.C.[1]
March 18

Really, by this time I should have recovered enough to be able to write you a sane letter, but I cannot—my pen is dead. I am simply a man struggling with a life that is no more than a mouthful of dust to him.

Yours sincerely
Stephen Crane

The Cosmos Club
Washington

[1] This final letter to Nellie Crouse was completed in Washington, D.C., where Crane went in mid-March to study the political life of the city in preparation for a novel to be published by S. S. McClure. Finding Washington society impenetrable, he returned to New York at the end of the month, giving up all thoughts of the novel (see No. 222). While in Washington Crane resided at the Cosmos Club.

210. TO DAISY D. HILL
ALS, InU.

33 East 22d St.
[2 March 1896]

My dear Miss Hill: I have been wondering if you are not making game of me. And yet I suppose the egotism of the average man is large enough to make it all appear perfectly sincere. Assuming then that you mean what you say, your letter makes me mournful. In the first place, I am such a small pale-yellow person with a weak air and no ability of pose that your admiration, or whatever it may be—if admiration is too strong a term—causes me to feel that I am an impostor and am robbing you of something. Of course your letter appeals to me. It is the expression of a vibratory sensitive young mind reaching out for an ideal. But then I cannot for a moment allow you to assume that I am properly an ideal. Ye Gods! I am clay—very common uninteresting clay. I am a good deal of a rascal, sometimes a bore, often dishonest. When I look at myself I know that only by dint of knowing nothing of me are you enabled to formulate me in your mind as something of a heroic figure. If you could once scan me you would be forever dumb.

Your mind must be of a finer mold than the minds around you or the fingers of your soul would never so reach into the distance. This is why I am glad to write to you and tell you the truth as I know it. Of course, I wish for the sake of the episode that I could tell you that I *am* a remarkable person but, alas, poor romance, I am most hideously ordinary.

You offer me your photograph! Ah, my dear, you must be handsome or you would never make such an offer. And am I capable of refusing it?

As for mine, however, there are none in my possession. I have been supplying various good-natured periodicals until I am exhausted.

You wrote to me with such charming candor that I am perfectly incapable of becoming austere about it. You have trusted your frankness to my poor little honor and so the situation is something which I enjoy. Depend upon it, I shall protect you.

Yours sincerely
Stephen Crane.

211. FROM WALTER H. PAGE[1]
TL, MH.

2 March, 1896

Dear Sir:

I beg to ask, on behalf of the *Atlantic Monthly,* whether you have or are likely to have, a piece of fiction, preferably not longer than "The Red Badge of Courage", ready for publication during the last two or three months of the year? If you have, we shall be glad to communicate further with you.[2]

Very sincerely yours,
Walter H. Page.

Stephen Crane Esq./

[1] Associate editor of the *Atlantic Monthly.* Page assumed the editorship in 1898 upon the resignation of Horace E. Scudder but served for only a year, after which he became a partner in Doubleday Page & Company.

[2] In response to this request, Crane sent Page the manuscript of "An Indiana Campaign" and asked Ripley Hitchcock to forward the manuscript of *The Third Violet* to him.

212. FROM ELBERT HUBBARD
Letterhead: "The Roycroft Printing Shop/ At East Aurora,/ New York." ALS, NNC.

Mar 6, '96,

My dear C. S.

My friends have started the Opposition Co. But bless my soul they are none of them business men and none have capital. I hear you are going to give them Ms for a book, but look you Stephen! they never can or will pay you a dollar for it.[1] I do not think you would be o'er wise to let *me* publish a book for you much less these experimenters. You have fame enough to catch the big publishers and I believe if you stick close to Appletons they will do you mighty good service.

The trouble with these foolish boys here is that they think I'm making five hundred dollars a month out of this little business. The Philistine has boomed to the front to be sure, but it is not the Comstock Lode by a damn sight, as they would find if they paid the bills.

The horse is as fine as silk.[2] Don't bother about sending a check—just bring it when you come. I got a check from Putnams last week (royalty on Little Journeys that Hartwood people like) so am easy. I want a bit of a poem though for the May Philistine or a short prose sketch or something.[3]

With kindest greetings as ever

Sincerely Yours
Elbert Hubbard

[1] Because of disagreements with Hubbard, Henry P. Taber, who edited the first few issues of the *Philistine,* and a number of associates proposed to purchase the magazine from Hubbard and to establish a new firm that would publish books as well as the magazine. Taber and Eugene White met with Crane at the Hotel Imperial in New York, and Crane evidently promised them one of the books upon which he was then working, probably *The Little Regiment.* When the group returned to East Aurora, Hubbard reneged on his original decision to sell the *Philistine,* and the new publishing venture was dissolved.

[2] "Peanuts," the riding horse Crane purchased from Hubbard. Crane had a lifelong attachment to horses and dogs.

[3] Crane's Bowery sketch, "A Great Mistake," appeared in the March 1896 issue of the *Philistine* and his poem, "To the maiden," in the April issue. There was no contribution by Crane in the May 1896 *Philistine.*

213. TO VIOLA ALLEN
ALS, ViU.

> The Cosmos Club
> Washington, D.C.
> March 15th., 1896.

My dear Miss Allen: I am very glad to be able to forward you by this mail a copy of The Red Badge. My years at Claverack are very vivid to me. They were I believe the happiest period of my life although I was not then aware of it. Of course, you were joking when you inferred that I might not remember you. And Anna Roberts! And Eva Lacy! And Jennie Pierce! Alas, Jennie Pierce. You must remember that I was in love with her, madly, in the headlong way of seventeen. Jennie was clever. With only half an effort she made my life so very miserable.

Men usually refuse to recognize their school-boy dreams. They blush. I dont. The emotion itself was probably higher, finer, than anything of my after-life, and so, often I like to think of it. I was such an ass, such a pure complete ass—it does me good to recollect it.

> Yours sincerely
> Stephen Crane

214. TO WILLIS BROOKS HAWKINS
ALS, ViU.

> Cosmos Club
> Washington
> Mch 15. [1896]

Dear Willis: It was a woman! Dont you see? Nothing could so interfere but a woman.[1] How sorry I am that I treated you so badly and yet how full how absolute is the explanation—a woman. I shall want to know at once how angry you are. I am sure, of course that you have been very much offended but it is a woman, I tell you, and I want you to forgive me.

Yours as ever
Stephen Crane

[1] This may be Crane's first hint to Hawkins of his complex entanglement with Amy Leslie.

215. TO RIPLEY HITCHCOCK
ALS, NN.

The Cosmos Club
Washington, D.C.
[15? March 1896]

Dear Mr Hitchcock: Of course eccentric people are admirably picturesque at a distance but I suppose after your recent close-range experiences with me, you have the usual sense of annoyance. After all, I cannot help vanishing and disappearing and dissolving. It is my foremost trait. But I hope you will forgive me and treat me as if you still could think me a pretty decent sort of chap.

I am almost settled in Washington but for some time yet I hope to see the city in the manner of a stranger. My address will be the Cosmos Club. You must send me the edited Maggie.[1] I am going to settle down to New York work in lazy Washington. I have had enough tea.

Yours sincerely
Stephen Crane

[1] The revision of *Maggie* had already been completed. Crane is requesting proofs.

216. TO DANIEL G. THOMPSON
Letterhead: "Cosmos Club,/ Washington, D.C." ALS, NN.

March 21 [1896]

Dear sir: Allow me to express the great pleasure it gives me to be elected a member of the Author's Club and to say that I gratefully accept.

Sincerely yours
Stephen Crane

Mr Daniel G. Thompson.

217. TO RIPLEY HITCHCOCK
ALS, NN.

The Cosmos Club
Washington, D.C.
Mch 23d [1896]

Dear Mr Hitchcock: I will begin to drive Maggie forward. Is The Red Badge going yet? Greeley by the way told me yesterday that it had been filed in the "archives" of the war department.

Your man Marcus Benjamin has been awfully good to me here, putting himself out generously.

I am all very well and am gradually learning things. I have been already in a number of the senatorial interiors. But I want to know all the congressmen in the shop. I want to know Quay of Pennsylvania. I want to know those long-whiskered devils from the west. So whenever you see a chance to send me headlong at one of them, do so.

Do you think the Atlantic Monthly would like The Third Violet? I enclose a note from them.

Yours sincerely
Stephen Crane

218. TO IRVING BACHELLER
ALS, NCaS.

The Cosmos Club
Washington, D.C.
March 24th. [1896]

My dear Irving: I saw the professor's article in the Philadelphia Press[1] and I want to thank him through you for it. The tone of it was so generous and kindly throughout, that it was a genuine pleasure to me. Moreover he didnt try to appear as wise as all-hell. I suppose the American critic's first anxiety is to impress the reader with the fact that he knows everything. No doubt there are many of them that do know everything but then the positive tone grows exasperating at last. There was so little—not any of that falsely-solemn judgment in the professor's article and so I think it was a great thing.

Sincerely yours
Stephen Crane

[1] In "Rise to Fame of Stephen Crane," *Philadelphia Press*, 15 March 1896, p. 34, Professor Charles K. Gaines, who had interviewed Crane at the Lantern Club, emphasized the two strains in Crane's heritage, the soldier and the clergyman, which contributed to the thematic background of *The Red Badge of Courage*.

219. TO DEWITT MILLER[1]
TT, NSyU.

The Cosmos Club
Washington, D.C.
March 24, 1896

Mr. Dewitt Miller,

Dear Sir:

Maggie was privately printed some years ago and I have no copy at hand. The new edition will be brought out by Appleton & Co.

Sincerely yours,
Stephen Crane

---

[1] Jahu Dewitt Miller (1857-1911) was a noted lyceum lecturer and book collector. Crane may have met him at Pennington Seminary. Miller was graduated from there in 1881 and lectured at the school at least once annually from 1887 to 1890. Miller eventually managed to obtain a copy of the 1893 *Maggie*, had it rebound, and sent it to Crane for his inscription. See No. 251.

220. TO LOUIS SENGER
ALS, NSyU.

The Cosmos Club
Washington, D.C.
March 24th [1896]

Dear Louisa: I forgot to tell you that I have come to Washington for a long stay. Otherwise I would be happy to hear the S.U. glee club. So glad the young woman has all her mothers and fathers. Give my regards to the Van Ettens. I have heard nothing from Williams but have written him again. Excuse this haste.

Yours
S. C.

221. TO RIPLEY HITCHCOCK
ALS, NN.

>The Cosmos Club
>Washington, D.C.
>March 26. [1896]

Dear Mr Hitchcock: I have not told you that I am beset—quite—with publishers of various degrees who wish—or seem to wish—to get my books and who make me various offers. Some of them are little firms but I think nearly every representative American house has made overtures of some kind to me as well as five or six London firms. I have not thought it worth while to talk much about it and in fact this letter contains the first mention of it, I believe. I have not considered at all the plan of playing one house against another but have held that the house of Appleton would allow me all the benefits I deserved. Without vanity I may say that I dont care a snap for money until I put my hand in my pocket and find none there. If I make ill terms now there may come a period of reflection and so I expect you to deal with me precisely as if I was going to write a *great* book ten years from now and might wreak a terrible vengeance on you by giving it to the other fellow. And so we understand each other.

As for Edward Arnold, his American manager is an old school-mate and ten-year's friend of mine and he conducted such a campaign against me as is seldom seen.[1] He appealed to my avarice and failing appealed to my humanity. Once I thought he was about to get "The Little Regiment," when you stepped in and saved it. Finally I thought of a satirical sketch of mine—an old thing, strong in satire but rather easy writing—called Dan Emmonds—and I gave it to him.[2]

You know of course that my mind is just and most open but perhaps in this case I violated certain business courtesies. But, before God, when these people get their fingers in my hair, it is a wonder that I escape with all my clothes. My only chance is to keep away from them.

I sent you three pictures yesterday

It would oblige me very much if you would have a check for my initiation fee sent to the secretary of the Author's Club.

>Yours sincerely
>Stephen Crane

[1]Harry Thompson, who had attended Claverack College and Hudson River Institute with Crane.

[2]Crane's allusion to "Dan Emmonds" as "a satirical sketch" has caused much creasing of scholarly brows. A professionally made ten-page typescript of a voyage fantasy with this title is preserved at Columbia University. It was first published by R. W. Stallman in "New Fiction by Stephen Crane," *Studies in Short Fiction*, 1 (1963), 1-7. George Monteiro has called attention to repeated references in various periodicals during the spring of 1896 to a forthcoming Crane novel entitled *Dan Emmonds* and an announcement in the Arnold catalogue of August 1896 that *Dan Emmonds* would be published in the fall ("Stephen Crane's 'Dan Emmonds': A Case Reargued," *Serif*, 6 [1969], 32-36). *George's Mother* had appeared under the Arnold imprint in June. Most likely, the typescript at Columbia is a transcript that Cora had made while Crane was in Cuba of the opening pages of a novel Crane began in the spring of 1896 but did not continue. Cora unsuccessfully attempted to market this confused fragment as a sketch. See *Works*, X, pp. 292-95, and No. 328, n. 4.

222. TO RIPLEY HITCHCOCK
ALS, NN.

> The Cosmos Club
> Washington, D.C.
> March 30. [1896]

Dear Mr Hitchcock: You may see me back in New York for good by the end of this week. These men pose so hard that it would take a double-barreled shotgun to disclose their inward feelings and I despair of knowing them.

> Yours sincerely
> Stephen Crane.

223. TO COPELAND AND DAY
ALS, VtMiM.

The Cosmos Club
Washington, D.C.,
March 31st. [1896]

Copeland and Day,

Dear sirs: I will be very glad if Mr Heineman gets the book.

As for the additional matter, that will be very hard. I dare say five or six of the best of the rejected matter would be the best plan.[1] Have you the ms? I'm sure I dont know where it is.

Sincerely yours
Stephen Crane

[1] Heinemann's English edition of *The Black Riders,* in a flexible black morocco binding, has essentially the same text as the American edition published more than a year earlier. No additional poems were used.

224. TO WILLIS BROOKS HAWKINS
ALS, ViU.

Cosmos Club
Washington, D.C.
March 31 [1896]

My dear Willis: You are the only friend I ever had who possessed the decency to forgive me for being an ass and your value has doubled in my eyes. I intend to come back to New York this week. Washington pains me. By the way, the three who I would like to see at the dinner[1] are my brother, for one, William H Crane, Port Jervis, N.Y., Col. Floyd, and Underwood Johnson of the Century.²

Will probably see you at Lunch on Saturday.

Very much yours
S. C

¹The Lantern Club gave a dinner in Crane's honor on 7 April 1896. William Dean Howells, the principal speaker, lauded Crane for taking "the right course in looking at and describing men and things as they are" (*New York Sun,* 8 April 1896, p. 3).

²Robert Underwood Johnson (1853-37) was associate editor of the *Century Magazine.* He had been coeditor (with Clarence Clough Buel) of the magazine's *Battles and Leaders of the Civil War,* 4 vols. *(1887-88).* In 1909 he succeeded Richard Watson Gilder as editor of the *Century* and held that position until 1913.

225. TO THE EDITOR OF *THE YOUTH'S COMPANION*

ALS illustrated as item 185 in Catalogue 220, Paul C. Richards Autographs, Templeton, Massachusetts.

The Cosmos Club
Washington, D.C.
[March 1896]

Dear sir: I enclose you a small sketch.¹ I would like your judgment upon it that I may find out how my kind of work gets along in the Companion office.

If you like it, you may keep it. It was written for you.

I have some thought of writing a Part II to it but that is a matter the next two weeks will decide. As it stands it is of course complete.

Pray let me hear from you at your earliest convenience.

Sincerely yours
Stephen Crane
(over)

As for the title—make it, perhaps, which labels them as *real accounts*?

This lieutenant is an actual person.

[1] Between November and March 1896, Crane wrote "An Episode of War" and sold it to *The Youth's Companion*. Although an advertisement in the *New York Press* (28 November 1896, p. 5) listed Crane as one of the ten "Leading Writers" for the magazine, the editors apparently after acceptance found the story unsuitable. Its sardonic treatment of war was probably too harsh for a family magazine, and to recover payment the publisher, Perry Mason & Co., sold the English rights and sent a copy of the story to *The Gentlewoman*, which published it in the December 1899 issue. "An Episode of War" finally appeared in the 16 March 1916 issue of *The Youth's Companion*.

226. TO MR. SHIPMAN[1]
ALS, ViU.

33 East 22d
[March 1896]

Dear Mr Shipman: Hope you can find it your heart to pardon. I indeed feel too ill this morning to leave the house. Many many regrets.

Yours sincerely
Stephen Crane.

[1] Though Shipman has not been identified, the envelope was addressed to him at the Player's Club in New York City.

The Tenderloin

In the spring of 1896 Crane again began to explore the New York scene, and now he shifted his attention from the Bowery to the Tenderloin, the vast amusement area of the City lying roughly between Fifth and Ninth Avenues from Madison Square to 49th Street. Like the Bowery, the Tenderloin was cluttered with theaters, saloons, gambling dens, and houses of prostitution. Sixth Avenue, the Main Street of the district, was lined with bars in which the orgy of drinking was at its worst on Sundays, when bartenders worked in four consecutive shifts, openly defying the blue laws that prohibited the sale of alcoholic beverages on the Sabbath. The Tenderloin differed from the Bowery chiefly in that it catered to New Yorkers of all social strata, including solid middle-class citizens. Despite the efforts of the reform government that had defeated Tammany Hall in the 1894 elections to eliminate corruption of city officials in the Tenderloin, an established system of bribery still assured police protection to the bordellos, opium dens, and card parlors, although they were required to operate in a more covert and restricted fashion than in palmier days. The name "Tenderloin" was bestowed upon the area by Police Inspector Alexander "Clubber" Williams, who, when transferred from a quiet precinct to this graft-ridden center of vice, is reported to have said, in effect, "For some time now I've had to be content with the cheaper cuts of meat, like round steak. From now on, I'm sure I'll have a more generous diet of thick, juicy tenderloin."

Crane's interest in the Tenderloin centered on its inhabitants, not only the déclassé forced through reduced circumstances to live in the district like the tiny old lady of his sketch "A Detail," who in her faded innocence approaches two streetwalkers on Sixth Avenue to inquire where she might secure employment, but also the "sporting" people, the chorus girls, confidence men, gamblers, and prostitutes who were at home in the Tenderloin. As in the Bowery, Crane empathized with the essential isolation of these pariahs. The people of the Tenderloin, he wrote in "Opium's Varied Dreams" (*New York Sun*, 17 May 1896), "are at once supersensitive and helpless, the people who think more upon death and the mysteries of life, the chances of the hereafter, than any other class, educated or uneducated."

In September 1896 Crane agreed to write a series of feature articles about demimonde life in the Tenderloin for William Randolph Hearst's *New York Journal*. Out of this came "The 'Tenderloin' as it Really is," "In the 'Tenderloin,' " and "Yen-Nock Bill and His Sweetheart." At 2 A.M. on 16 September Crane emerged from the Broadway Gardens with two chorus girls he had been interviewing for the *Journal* series and Dora Clark, a known streetwalker. While Crane escorted one of the girls to a cable car, Dora Clark and the other woman were arrested for soliciting two passing men by Patrolman Charles Becker, later notorious for complicity in the murder of his gambling partner, Herman Rosenthal, and the first New York City policeman to be executed in the electric chair. The chorus girl was freed when Crane gallantly supported her claim that she was his wife, but Dora Clark spent the night in a jail cell. The next morning, Crane appeared in her defense at the Jefferson Market Police Court, a "reluctant witness," as he reported in his account of the hearing, "Adventures of a Novelist," in the *Journal* for 20 September. Considering the prudery of the age and the vindictiveness of the New York police force, Crane's action required considerable courage. When Dora Clark brought charges of false arrest against two policemen in the Tenderloin precinct, Crane again testified in her behalf at a Police Department trial. The widespread publicity attendant upon this case, especially the charges of immorality heaped upon Crane by defense witnesses, was devastating to his reputation, already tarnished by rumors that he was a drug addict and an alcoholic. Theodore Roosevelt, the Chairman of the Board of Police Commissioners, had expressed admiration for *The Red Badge*, but he henceforth shunned Crane, who found himself persona non grata with the police, subject to arrest at every turn. Realizing he could no longer function successfully as a journalist in New York, Crane was glad to accept

Irving Bacheller's offer to go to Cuba to report on the rebellion. Except for a few brief visits in 1897 and 1898, he never returned to the City. Even on these occasions the enmity of the police pursued him, and attempts were made to lock him up on flimsy, fraudulent charges.

227. TO RIPLEY HITCHCOCK
ALS, NN.

165 W 23d
Thursday [2 April 1896]

Dear Mr Hitchcock: I am engaged on the preface.[1] Dont let anyone put chapter headings on the book. The proofs make me ill. Let somebody go over them—if you think best—and watch for bad grammatical form & bad spelling. I am too jaded with Maggie to be able to see it.

Yours
Crane

[1] Crane's preface to *Maggie* has not survived.

228. TO WILLIAM HOWE CRANE
ALS, ViU.

[early April 1896]

Dear Will: Dont forget the dinner on the 7th. I've sent in your name. Dr Goode of the Smithsonian wanted me to give him a list of our family. Will you get this filled out, and send it to me? I thought I knew more about the tribe.

Yours as ever
Stephen

229. TO WILLIS BROOKS HAWKINS
ALS, ViU.

[early April 1896]

Dear Willis: I am returned. Can—will—you bring the boys over for a little fiesta de poke tonight. Charley, Fairman & you will do if you cannot raise more

Yours
S. C

230. TO WILLIS BROOKS HAWKINS
ALS, ViU.

Shanley's
[early April 1896]

My dear Willis: Howard was not at home. Ans- by this boy if you corraled him later.

Yours
S. C.

His address is #10 West 19.

231. FROM WALTER H. PAGE
TL, MH.

7 April, 1896.

Dear Mr. Crane:

I have been somewhat long in replying to your very courteous response to my inquiry, because when your letter came, with "An

225

Indiana Campaign", Mr. Scudder was away from home, and I wished him to read it before I wrote you my own impressions about it, with reference to use in *The Atlantic Monthly*. In the meantime there has come, by your very kind request, the manuscript of "The Third Violet", from Mr. Hitchcock, which also I have read with pleasure.[1]

Not only have both these manuscripts been read, but I have had time to think over the practicability of publishing them in *The Atlantic*—at a sufficient distance from my reading of them to have a clear judgment.

And I think that neither of them quite fits *The Atlantic*—the shorter story because, vividly and excellently as it seems to me you have written it, in substance it is somewhat too slight for our more or less serious pages, and "The Third Violet" because it is not quite the kind of story with which you ought to make your appearance in *The Atlantic Monthly*. There are certain incidental disadvantages, too, about our use of the longer story: we infer from Mr. Hitchcock's letter to us that Messrs. Appleton & Co. expect to publish it in the fall, and we might not be able to use it in *The Atlantic* in time. This, however, I need not, perhaps, have mentioned; for the main matter is that you will have a story—I hope at an early time—which you yourself would prefer should be your first contribution to *The Atlantic*.[2]

Please accept our thanks for your very prompt and generous response to my inquiry, and let me look forward to the pleasure not only of hearing from you regarding future work, but to meeting you, to talk over *The Atlantic* and its possible needs, some time when I am in New York.

I send both manuscripts back today—the longer one to Mr. Hitchcock, the shorter one enclosed herewith.

Very truly yours,
Walter H. Page

Stephen Crane, Esq.

---

[1] See No. 211.

[2] None of Crane's works appeared in the *Atlantic*. "An Indiana Campaign" received newspaper syndication through the Bacheller, Johnson and Bacheller syndicate and was reprinted in a slightly different text in the *Pocket Magazine* (September 1896) before it was included in *The Little Regiment*. *The Third Violet* was also published in a number of newspapers previous to book publication by Appleton in May 1896. Page wrote to Reynolds on 6 April 1898 declining "The Blue Hotel" for the *Atlantic*.

232. TO POST WHEELER
Inscribed on the back of a photograph, NSyU.

To Post Wheeler
From his friend
Stephen Crane

April 14th, 1896

233. TO THE EDITOR OF THE *NEWARK SUNDAY CALL*
"A Genuine Jerseyman," *Newark Sunday Call*, 3 May 1896, p. 20.

[165 West 23d Street, New York City, 29 April 1896]

I was born in Newark on the 1st of November, 1871. The house was No. 14 Mulberry place. My father was the Rev. J. T. Crane, D.D., presiding elder of the Newark district. The family moved from there to Bound Brook. My great great great grandfather was one of the seven men who came and solemnly founded Newark. He was Jasper Crane. His farm came into the southwest corner of Market and Broad streets. His son Stephen Crane,[1] moved to Elizabeth, where my grandfather and my father were born. During the Revolution the Cranes were pretty hot people. The old man Stephen served in the Continental Congress (for New Jersey), while all four sons were in the army. William Crane was Colonel of the Sixth Regiment of New Jersey Infantry. The Essex Militia also contained one of the sons.

I am not much on this sort of thing or I could write more, but at any rate the family is founded deep in Jersey soil (since the birth of Newark), and I am about as much of a Jerseyman as you can find.

Sincerely yours,
"STEPHEN CRANE."

[1] Stephen Crane (1709-80), a delegate from New Jersey to the Continental Congress, was not the son of Jasper Crane, a member of a collateral branch of the Crane family who died in 1681.

234. TO SADIE SIESFELD[1]
Inscribed on recto of a photograph of Crane, NhD.

To Kid
From Stephen Crane

April 29—1896.

[1] Sister of Amy Leslie.

235. TO VIOLA ALLEN
ALS, NSyU.

165 West 23d
Thursday—[late April 1896]

My dear Miss Allen: As you permit, I will very gladly come on the evening of the first Sunday in May. Is that right?

Yours sincerely
Stephen Crane

236. TO THE *BOOK BUYER*
ALfrS reproduced in holograph in *Book Buyer*, 13 (April 1896), 140.

[April 1896]

I have never been in a battle, of course, and I believe that I got my sense of the rage of conflict on the football field.

Stephen Crane

237. TO ELBERT HUBBARD
ALS, NhD.

> 165 West 23d St.,
> New York City
> [April 1896]

My dear Hub: I've been a rampant wild ass of the desert with my feet never twice in the same place but at last I am settled down finally & feel that my first occupation should be the writing of a profound apology to you for my curious silence. I expect to be in East Aurora in about 2 weeks—at least if I am still at liberty to purchase that noble horse? At that time we will chew the rag at great length and finally decide all these contested points.

> Yours always
> S. C.

238. TO ALFRED
MSL, ViU.

> [April 1896?]

My Dear Alfred:

Call and see me at the Union Leaugue Club. I have been unusually busy for quite a few days & have been unable to get around to your home

> Sincerly
> Stephen Crane

239. FROM P. VERDI
ALS, NSyU.

[April 1896?]

My dear Mr Crane

I am very sorry that I have an engagement for the early part of the evening. If you need to see me before going away you might come here at about half-past nine.

Yours in haste
P. Verdi

240. TO THE EDITOR OF *DEMOREST'S FAMILY MAGAZINE*
"A Remarkable First Success," *Demorest's Family Magazine*, 32 (May 1896), 399-400.

[late April-early May 1896]

I have heard a great deal about genius lately, but genius is a very vague word; and as far as I am concerned I do not think it has been rightly used. Whatever success I have had has been the result simply of imagination coupled with great application and concentration. It has been a theory of mine ever since I began to write, which was eight years ago, when I was sixteen, that the most artistic and the most enduring literature was that which reflected life accurately. Therefore I have tried to observe closely, and to set down what I have seen in the simplest and most concise way. I have been very careful not to let any theories or pet ideas of my own be seen in my writing. Preaching is fatal to art in literature. I try to give to readers a slice out of life; and if there is any moral or lesson in it I do not point it out. I let the reader find it for himself. As Emerson said, "There should be a long logic beneath the story, but it should be kept carefully out of sight."[1]

Before "The Red Badge of Courage" was published I often found it difficult to make both ends meet. The book was written during this period. It was an effort born of pain, and I believe that this was beneficial to it as a piece of literature. It seems a pity that this should be so,—that art should be a child of suffering; and yet such seems to be the case. Of course there are fine writers who have good incomes and live comfortably and contentedly; but if the conditions of their lives were harder, I believe that their work would be better.

Personally, I like my little book of poems, "The Black Riders," better than I do "The Red Badge of Courage." The reason is, I suppose, that the former is the more ambitious effort. In it I aim to give my ideas of life as a whole, so far as I know it, and the latter is a mere episode,—an amplification. Now that I have reached the goal for which I have been working ever since I began to write, I suppose I ought to be contented; but I am not. I was happier in the old days when I was always dreaming of the thing I have now attained. I am disappointed with success. Like many things we strive for, it proves when obtained to be an empty and a fleeting joy.

---

[1] Although Crane misquotes from Emerson's "Intellect," he preserves the essential meaning of the passage: "We want in every man a long logic; we can not pardon the absence of it, but it must not be spoken. Logic is the procession or proportionate unfolding of the intuition; but its virtue is as silent method; the moment it would appear as propositions and have a separate value, it is worthless." A sketch in Crane's Notebook, "The Art Students' League Building," quoted an aphorism presumably from Emerson chalked on an old beam in a remote studio: "Congratulate yourselves if you have done something strange and extravagant and broken the monotony of a decorous age." Kenneth W. Cameron could not find a source for this quotation in Emerson's works, and it is apparently apocryphal. See Clarence O. Johnson, "Mr. Binks Read Emerson," *American Literary Realism: 1870-1910*, 15 (1982), 104-9.

241. TO J. HERBERT WELCH
Quoted in J. Herbert Welch, "The Personality and Work of Stephen Crane," *Leslie's Weekly*, 23 May 1896, pp. 372-73.

[late April-May 1896]

I can't do any sort of work that I don't like or don't feel like doing, and I've given up trying to do it. When I was at school few of my studies interested me, and as a result I was a bad scholar. They used to say at

Syracuse University, where, by the way, I didn't finish the course, that I was cut out to be a professional base-ball player. And the truth of the matter is that I went there more to play base-ball than to study. I was always very fond of literature, though. I remember when I was eight years old I became very much interested in a child character called, I think, Little Goodie Brighteyes, and I wrote a story then which I called after this fascinating little person. When I was about sixteen I began to write for the New York newspapers, doing correspondence from Asbury Park and other places. Then I began to write special articles and short stories for the Sunday papers and one of the literary syndicates, reading a great deal in the meantime and gradually acquiring a style. I decided that the nearer a writer gets to life the greater he becomes as an artist, and most of my prose writings have been toward the goal partially described by that misunderstood and abused word, realism. Tolstoï is the writer I admire most of all. I've been a free lance during most of the time I have been doing literary work, writing stories and articles about anything under heaven that seemed to possess interest, and selling them wherever I could. It was hopeless work. Of all human lots for a person of sensibility that of an obscure free lance in literature or journalism is, I think, the most discouraging. It was during this period that I wrote "The Red Badge of Courage." It was an effort born of pain—despair, almost; and I believe that this made it a better piece of literature than it otherwise would have been. It seems a pity that art should be a child of pain, and yet I think it is.[1] Of course we have fine writers who are prosperous and contented, but in my opinion their work would be greater if this were not so. It lacks the sting it would have if written under the spur of a great need.

But, personally, I was unhappy only at times during the period of my struggles. I was always looking forward to success. My first great disappointment was in the reception of "Maggie, a Girl of the Streets." I remember how I looked forward to its publication, and pictured the sensation I thought it would make. It fell flat. Nobody seemed to notice it or care for it. I am going to introduce Maggie again to the world some time, but not for a good while. Poor Maggie! she was one of my first loves.

I suppose I ought to be thankful to "The Red Badge," but I am much fonder of my little book of poems, "The Black Riders." The reason, perhaps, is that it was a more ambitious effort. My aim was to comprehend in it the thoughts I have had about life in general, while "The Red Badge" is a mere episode in life, an amplification. A rather interesting fact about the story is that it lay for eight months in a New York magazine office waiting to receive attention. I called on the editor[2] time and again and couldn't find out whether he thought it a good story or whether he intended to publish it or not, so at last I took it away. Now that it is published and the people seem to like it I suppose I ought to be satisfied, but somehow I am not as happy as I was in the uncertain, happy-go-lucky newspaper-writing days. I used to dream continually of success then. Now that I have achieved it in some measure it seems like mere flimsy paper.

[1]Crane reiterated this statement in letters to other editors. Cf. Nos. 240 and 352.
[2]S. S. McClure. Crane has amplified the time that McClure held *The Red Badge* from six months to eight.

242. TO LUCIUS L. BUTTON
Inscribed in a copy of *A Souvenir and a Medley*, NSyU.

[after 1 May 1896]

Go to hell!
C.

243. TO CHARLES J. PIKE[1]
Inscribed on a copy of *Maggie* (1893), NSyU.

To my friend
Charles J. Pike.
Stephen Crane

May 10th, 1896.

[1] Pike explained years later how he got a copy of *Maggie:* "I knew Crane intimately. He lived for eighteen months or more with me, in my studio on the third floor front of the old building that stood just where the Sacho building now stands—on the corner of 33rd and 6th ave New York. My copy of 'Maggie' was Stephen Crane's own personal signed copy, which he occasionally opened. He had promised to give me a copy of 'Maggie', but being unable to find a new one, he ultimately gave me his own. . . . Although I cannot prove it, I have always believed that this copy of 'Maggie' was the *last* (1st edition) Stephen Crane ever owned and used personally" (NSyU).

244. FROM ELBERT HUBBARD
ALS, NNC.

May 19, 96

My dear Steve:

I have Col Higginsons Ms on "The Red Badge."[1] It is very choice and exceedingly sympathetic. He makes the point that the book is not written from the patriotic broadness of the great General Mc Clurg[2] but from that of Henry Fleming, and as such is true to life.

I'm going to sail for Europe on the 27*th:* will be in New York in a few days and will hunt you up for a quiet little chat.

Yours ever
Hubbard

[1] Thomas Wentworth Higginson, "Book and Heart: A Bit of War Photography," *Philistine,* 3 (July 1896), 33-38.
[2] A. C. McClug, in "The Red Badge of Hysteria," *Dial,* 20 (16 April 1896), 227-28, characterized Crane's Civil War novel as "a vicious satire upon American soldiers and American armies."

245. TO JOSEPH B. COOKE
Inscribed in a copy of *The Red Badge of Courage* (1895), Collection of Daniel G. Siegel, Weston, Massachusetts.

To Joseph B. Cooke.
Stephen Crane,

New York City,
May 20, 1896.

246. TO COPELAND AND DAY
Letterhead: "Wm. H. Crane,/ Attorney & Counselor at Law,/ Port Jervis, N.Y. . . . ."
ALS, ViU.

Port Jervis, N.Y.
May 29 [1896]

Dear sirs: If it is convenient for you at this time I would greatly like a settlement in the matter of *The Black Riders*.

Sincerely yours
Stephen Crane

247. TO RIPLEY HITCHCOCK
ALfr, NN.

Port Jervis, N.Y.
May 29 [1896]

Dear Mr Hitchcock: I have again taken to the woods and I shall try to remain here, for I am certainly unable to withstand the fury of New York. Are you bringing out *Maggie* soon? I am planting some financial seed up here and I would

248. TO EDDIE[1]

Inscribed in a copy of *George's Mother*, NhD.

To my friend Eddie
in memory of our days
of suffering and trouble
in 27th St.
Stephen Crane

New York City
June 14. [1896]

[1] Perhaps Elisha J. Edwards ("Holland") of the *New York Press,* who had occasionally provided Crane with a place to sleep in his room on West 27th Street during the peripatetic years of 1892-93 and who had praised *The Red Badge* in the *Philadelphia Press* on the day the final installment of the novel appeared in that paper, 8 December 1894.

249. TO JOHN THOMAS LEE[1]
ALS, ViU.

Hartwood N.Y.
July 2d, [1896]

To John Thomas Lee: I am grateful for your kind words concerning my work.

Sincerely yours
Stephen Crane

[1] A book collector.

250. FROM E. S. GOODHUE
ALS, NNC.

Koloa
Kauai
July 3 1896.

Mr. Stephen Crane

Dear Sir:—

I have the honor to inform you that you have been elected to honorary membership in the Kauai Kodak Klub. As a member you are cordially invited to visit Hawaii when we will be pleased to entertain you.

Ours is an Outing club that meets under the Monkey Rod tues to compare snap shots, read books written by an honorary member and talk about pleasant subjects generally. Among our members are Mark Twain, C. D. Warner, Sir H. Irving, Sir E. Arnold, W. D. Howells, J. Jefferson, T. B. Aldrich & many more.[1]

If you have a Kodak please tell us some of your experiences.

Yours respy
E. S. Goodhue MD,
Koloa
Kauai

[1]Sir Henry Irving (1838-1905) was a well-known British actor; Sir Edwin Arnold (1832-1904), a poet and journalist known for his travel books and his epic poem, "The Light of Asia"; and Joseph Jefferson (1829-1905), an American actor most famous for his stage portrayal of Rip Van Winkle.

251. TO DEWITT MILLER
Inscribed in a rebound copy of *Maggie* (1893), PEL.

It is indeed a brave
new binding[1] and I
wish the inside were

braver.
Stephen Crane

Mr. Dewitt Miller
July 3d, 96.

[1] This copy of the 1893 *Maggie* in wrappers was rebound by Clarke & Co. of Cincinnati with additional blank leaves. The inscription appears upon one of these leaves bound between the front wrapper and the title page.

252. TO RIPLEY HITCHCOCK
AL, NN.

Hartwood
Saturday [4 or 11 July 1896]

Dear Mr. Hitchcock: Through the fault of the U.S.P.O. Dept.—no less—proofs did not reach me until today.[1] I return them herewith. I have asked Arnold's to come up here and I will reiterate to you.—
The copy was not complete. Used June McClure's.[2]

[1] *The Little Regiment*.
[2] The title story, "The Little Regiment," appeared in the June 1896 issue of *McClure's Magazine*.

253. TO HERBERT P. WILLIAMS[1]

Photostatic copy of the holograph, CtU.

165 West 23d
[before 6 July 1896]

My dear sir: If you will come tomorrow about 3 o'clock I will talk as well as I am able.

Sincerely yours
Stephen Crane

Mr Herbert P. Williams

[1] Williams interviewed Crane for an article, "Mr. Crane as a Literary Artist," *Illustrated American,* 20 (18 July 1896), 126. Because one of the three letters Crane wrote to him is undated and another misdated, the sequence of events leading up to the article needs clarification. Williams interviewed Crane in late June or early July before Crane left for Hartwood. After writing the article, he had some doubts about certain observations or statements and conveyed them to Crane, asking him also for pictures. Crane replied on 6 July, saying he would not have pictures for "some weeks." Because Williams could not wait, he sent Crane the proofs for the article. Though they arrived too late for any corrections, Crane indicated in the 8 June (for 8 July) letter what he would have changed.

254. TO HERBERT P. WILLIAMS

ALS, Collection of Stanley and Mary Wertheim, New York City.

Hartwood, N.Y.
July 6th. [1896]

My dear Mr Williams: You are at liberty to write what you think best. As to the pictures however it will take some weeks to provide them. If you care to wait, let me know at once.

Pray excuse haste.

Yours cordially
Stephen Crane

255. TO HERBERT P. WILLIAMS
ALS, UPB.

Hartwood, N.Y.
June 8 [for 8 July 1896]

Dear Mr Williams:

The interview in my opinion is a very good one. I received the proof too late to make any corrections but for your satisfaction I enclose it to show you the only corrections I would have made. I am much indebted to you. I dont know when I will reach Boston but when I do I would like to see you.

Yours sincerely
Stephen Crane.

256. TO DANIEL APPLETON
ALS on Appleton's stationery, InU.

July [16, 1896]

Dear Mr Appleton: I have written to Arnold that your arrangement with Heineman concerning The Little Regiment and The Third Violet must stand—that it was a prior and just contract and that I intend to see that Heineman's rights in the books shall be guarded.[1]

Very truly
Stephen Crane

---

[1] Crane found it necessary to assure Ripley Hitchcock and Daniel Appleton that he would not again breach ethics by violating his agreement with Appleton & Co. and the agreement they had made with Heinemann regarding English rights to Crane's books, as he had done by allowing Edward Arnold to publish *George's Mother* on both sides of the Atlantic.

257. FROM THEODORE ROOSEVELT
Letterhead: "Police Department/ of the City of New York. . . ." TLS, NNC.

July 20th 1896.

Stephen Crane, Esq.,
c/o S. S. McClure,
141 E. 25th St.,
New York

Dear Mr. Crane:—

Court opens at ten, but eleven o'clock would be the time for you to come around. I have much to discuss with you about "Madge."

Sincerely yours,
Theodore Roosevelt

258. FROM WILLIAM DEAN HOWELLS
ALS, NNC.

Far Rockaway, [Long Island]
July 30, 1896.

My dear Mr. Crane:

I send you my notice of your last books, which has been vexatiously delayed.[1] It ought to have been out a month ago.

We are hoping for a little glimpse of you here before the season is over.

Yours cordially
W. D. Howells.

[1] "New York Low Life in Fiction," *New York World,* 26 July 1896, p. 18.

241

259. TO HAMLIN GARLAND
ALS, CLSU.[1]

[165 West 23d Street, New York City, July 1896]

Dear Mr Garland:

Just heard you were in town. I want you to dine tonight with me at the Lantern Club. Sure!! Roosevelt expects to be there. He wants to meet you. Dont fail. I will call here at six—again.

Yours
Crane

[1] Crane left this note at Garland's hotel together with an inscribed copy of *George's Mother*. See No. 260.

260. TO HAMLIN GARLAND
Inscribed in a copy of *George's Mother*, CLSU.

To Hamlin Garland
of the great honest West
From Stephen Crane
of the false East.

New York City
July, 1896.

261. TO HARRY P. TABER
Inscribed on a copy of *Maggie* (1893), MH.

[July? 1896]

My dear Tabor: I wrote this book when I was very young so if you dont like it, shut up. But my best wishes go with it. Stephen Crane.

262. TO E. S. GOODHUE
ALS, NSyU.

Hartwood.,
Sullivan Co.,
New York State
Aug 3*d*, 96.

E. S. Goodhue, M. D

Dear sir: I acknowledge with gratitude your kind favor of July 3d in which you inform me that I have been made an honorary member of the Kanai[1] Kodak Club and I accept the distinction with many thanks. Cordial greetings to all Kodak Klubers.

Very truly yours
Stephen Crane

[1] Crane misread Goodhue's handwriting (No. 250) and wrote "Kanai" instead of "Kauai."

263. TO PAUL LEMPERLY[1]

Library of the Late Paul Lemperly, Lakewood, Ohio (New York: Parke-Bernet, 1940), p. 39.

New York City
[3? August 1896]

Dear Mr. Lemperly:

I shall be glad to inscribe the copy of Maggie as you suggest.

Stephen Crane

[1] Paul Lemperly (1858-1939), a book collector in Lakewood, Ohio. For Crane's inscription in Lemperly's copy of the 1893 *Maggie,* see No. 273.

264. FROM WILLIAM RANDOLPH HEARST

Telegram, NNC.

Aug 11 1896

New York 11
To Stephen Crane
Crane Postal Office

How much money do you require[1]

W R Hearst

[1] On 20 September 1896, Hearst's *New York Journal* announced a forthcoming series of articles by Crane upon the life of the metropolitan policeman. The September 1896 issue of *Book News* reported that Crane was writing a story or group of stories about the police; however, No. 277 shows that he was really hired to write about the Tenderloin district, not the police, in New York City. Crane published Tenderloin sketches in *Town Topics* and in the *Journal,* but none about the police.

265. TO WILLIAM DEAN HOWELLS
ALS, MH.

McClure's Magazine
August 15—[1896]

Dear Mr Howell's: I was away in the country when your essay appeared in the World—so deep in the woods in fact that word of it was much belated.[1] It is of course the best word that has been said of me and I am grateful in a way that is hard for me to say. In truth you have always been so generous with me that grace departs at once from my pen when I attempt to tell you of my appreciation. When I speak of it to others however I am mightily fluent and use the best terms every time. I always thank God that I can have the strongest admiration for the work of a man who has been so much to me personally for I can imagine the terrors of being indelibly indebted to the Chump in Art or even to the Semi-Chump in Art.

I would like to know Mr Cahan.[2] I am reading his book and I am wondering how in the name of Heaven he learned how to do it. I am going tomorrow on a business journey and shall be gone until Wednesday. Upon my return I shall call at Far Rockaway and I hope then you will tell me where to find him. I have a delicious feeling of being some months ahead of him in the recognition, critically, and I would like to take some trouble in looking him up at his home.

Sincerely yours
Stephen Crane

[1] Crane was at the summer camp he frequented with Louis Senger and other Port Jervis friends (1894-96) at Twin Lakes in Pike County, Pennsylvania when Howells' essay, "New York Low Life in Fiction," appeared.

[2] In his *World* essay Howells compared Crane with Abraham Cahan (1860-1951), a Russified Jewish immigrant, and said that Crane and Cahan had drawn the most accurate pictures of East Side life in fiction. Cahan's *Yekl: A Tale of the New York Ghetto* was published in 1896. In this year he also became editor of the *Jewish Daily Forward*. Cahan's masterpiece, *The Rise of David Levinsky* (1917), is a fictional chronicle of the Americanization of Eastern European Jews in the decades following the great pogroms.

266. FROM WILLIAM DEAN HOWELLS
ALS, NNC.

Far Rockaway,
August 15, 1896.

Dear Mr. Crane:

Come a week from the time you mention—that is, come Wednesday the 25th, and spend the night and the next day with us, so as to get in two sea baths. Take the 3:20 p.m. train from the L.I.R.R. station at the East 34th st. ferry, and you will arrive here at 4:10; we will meet you and go at once to the beach with you.

Cahan lives at 213 East 6th st. He will be glad to see you, and is a fine fellow—school teacher, and editor of the Yiddish socialist paper.

We all join in regards to you.

Yours cordially
W. D. Howells.

267. FROM WILLIAM SCHUYLER[1]
ALS, NNC.

5858 Clemens Ave
St Louis Mo
Aug 16 1896.

Dear Mr. Crane:

Ever since last February when Mr Hamlin Garland, then visiting at my house, quoted some of your verses, & especially since I have read your "Black Riders" over & over—I have wished to write to you.

However a dislike of forcing myself upon another's attention has prevented me from writing until now I have at last a good excuse.— I have set to music three of your poems, & expect at a near date to publish them. To do this, I need your permission to use the words. Will you kindly grant it? I have so far set "Then came whisperings in the winds," "On the horizon the peaks assembled," & "I was in the darkness."

In conclusion permit me to express the great admiration I feel for your work. You are a true poet of the soul. You have dared to express the thoughts & feelings that so many of us entertain but have not the power or the courage to utter. Besides, you have chosen a form singularly suited to the ideas & you have an infallible scent for the right words—the words needed for the full & clear expression of your great thoughts

Yours sincerely
Wm Schuyler

If you so desire I should send you a copy of the songs—

[1] Between 20 February and 1 May 1897, Schuyler published five of Crane's poems set to music in *The Criterion,* a St. Louis weekly. They were subsequently issued as *Songs from Stephen Crane's* Black Riders: *Music by William Schuyler* (St. Louis: Thiebes-Stierlin Music Co., 1897). The poems were "Should the wide world roll away," "There came whisperings in the winds," "There was, before me," "I was in the darkness," and "On the horizon the peaks assembled." See No. 274.

268. TO WILLIAM DEAN HOWELLS

Inscribed in a copy of an 1896 issue of *The Red Badge of Courage* with the name "Mrs Mary Fleming" on the flyleaf, NN.[1]

To W. D. Howells this small and
belated book as a token of the ven-
eration and gratitude of Stephen Crane
for many things he has learned
of the common man and, above
all, for a certain re-adjustment of his point of view victoriously
concluded some time in 1892.

August 17, 1895. [for 1896][2]

[1] Howells never received his presentation copy of *The Red Badge of Courage*. A letter from Victor S. Sicilia of Evansville, Indiana, to Max Herzberg, President of the Stephen Crane Association of Newark, New Jersey (19 August 1931), describes this book and

an uninscribed copy of the first edition of *Maggie,* both of which are in his possession, and requests an estimate of their monetary value. Sicilia explains that "These books were given to my grandmother by Stephen Crane, whose brother Ed Crane was married to my mother's sister. As we understand it, my grandmother went east some years ago for a visit, and Stephen was there at the time and gave the books to her, which she brought home with her and they have been in the family since that time" (NjN, copy in NSyU).

[2] On the second front flyleaf Crane transcribed his poem "Do not weep, maiden, for war is kind," dating it also "1895," which refers to the year of the poem's composition.

269. FROM JAMES T. WHITE & CO.[1]
Letterhead: "James T. White & Co. . . . New York." TLS, NNC.

August 17, 1896.

Mr. Stephen Crane, Newark, N.J.

Dear Sir,—

We wish to have a biographical sketch of yourself for publication in the National Cyclopedia of American Biography, a prospectus of which we herewith enclose. This is a national publication and will be the biographical authority for the next century, and we do not want to have your biography omitted. We will therefore be greatly obliged if you will send us a sketch at your earliest convenience, or the material from which one can be prepared. A proof will be submitted to you before going to press.[2]

Trusting to hear from you at an early date, we are

Very truly yours,
James T. White and Co.

[1] James T. White (1846-1920) was a poet and publisher.

[2] A two-page preprinted form, "Biographical Notes for *The National Cyclopaedia of American Biography,*" stamped 7 July 1900 was filled out on Crane's life and his family's genealogy. The first page is in an unknown hand; the second, in Cora's. She did not answer the questions concerning when and where she was married and listed her residences before marriage as Boston and Athens.

Crane's biography did not appear in the *Cyclopedia* until volume 10 (1900), p. 113. Earlier volumes had entries on his father and Stephen's Revolutionary namesake.

270. FROM THEODORE ROOSEVELT
TLS on stationery of the New York City Police Department, NNC.

Aug. 18, 1896.

My dear Mr. Crane:—

I am much obliged to you for "George's Mother" with your own autograph on the front. I shall keep it with your other books. Some day I shall try to get you to write your autograph in my "Red Badge of Courage", for much though I like your other books, I think I like that book the best. Some day I want you to write another story of the frontiersman and the Mexican Greaser in which the frontiersman shall come out on top; it is more normal that way![1] I wish I could have seen Hamlin Garland, but I am leaving in a few days for a three weeks trip to the West.

This evening I shall be around at the Madison Square Garden to see exactly what the Police do. They have a very difficult task with a crowd like that, because they have to be exceedingly good humored with the crowd, and they also have to please the Managers of the meeting who know nothing about crowds, and yet they have to control twenty thousand people. I will say one thing for them at the Bryan[2] meeting; we have not had a single complaint of clubbing or brutality from any man claiming to have suffered; the Managers of the meeting and the Manager of the Garden have both written us in the warmest terms.[3]

I hope soon to see you again.

Sincerely yours,
Theodore Roosevelt

Stephen Crance, Esq.,

[1] Roosevelt had read a manuscript of "A Man and Some Others" in which an American sheepherder is killed by a group of Mexican rivals. This story was not

published by the *Century* until February 1897 because Richard Watson Gilder objected to language in the story that he considered inappropriate, especially the use of the exclamation "B'Gawd!" Reynolds negotiated with Crane, for whom this was a sticking point, and what was finally printed, whether Crane consented or not, was "B'—!" Subsequent Crane biographers have followed Thomas Beer's assertion (Beer, p. 137) that the *Century* delayed publication of "A Man and Some Others" because Gilder was appalled by the effect Crane's row with the New York police over the Dora Clark incident, which ended Roosevelt's friendship for him, would have upon readers of a family magazine (Berryman, p.135; Stallman BIO, p. 219). But, as J. C. Levenson has demonstrated, "Gilder did not see the manuscript until two weeks after the Dora Clark affair had broken in the papers, he accepted it while the furor was at its height, and he conducted his single-minded campaign for verbal decency at a time when Crane's misadventure was still alive in the press though he took no notice of the event" (*Works*, V, p. lii).

[2] William Jennings Bryan, Democratic Presidential candidate in 1896.

[3] Aware of reports that Crane was investigating the New York City Police force, Roosevelt attempted to deflect negative criticism by extolling the performance of the police in difficult situations.

271. TO WILLIAM DEAN HOWELLS
ALS, MH.

Hartwood, N.Y
Saturday [21 August 1896]

Dear Mr Howells: Just received your note and I shall be very glad to come out on Wednesday afternoon. I think however that I shall be obliged to return to New York Wednesday night.

Sincerely yours
Stephen Crane

250

272. FROM W. B. HARTE
Letterhead: "The Lotus,"[1] ALS, NNC.

24. August 1896.

144 East 54th Street
New York Cit.

Stephen Crane Esq
New York.

My dear Sir:

I called at the office of McClure's Magazine hoping to have the good fortune of finding you in, but I could learn nothing very definite about your hours of dropping in, or anything of your address. So I again write under cover of McClure's, supposing your mail matter held there for you.

I should like to hear whether you can bring yourself to sacrifice time and labor to do a story for *The Lotus* at a figure I can pay. I should be greatly pleased to get you into one of the forthcoming numbers. It is the intention of the Proprietors to make the little periodical a creditable and decent thing, & an attempt will be made to give it a very distinct character among contemporary periodicals. For this reason we wish to interest you in it.

Yours faithfully
W B Harte.

---

[1] *The Lotus* (1895-97) began as a bimonthly edited by undergraduates of Kansas colleges and issued in a Roycroft-type format. In May 1896 it left the colleges, became a monthly, and greatly improved the quality of its contents. Walter Blackburn Harte edited it for a year, but it could never compete successfully with Hubbard's *Philistine*.

273. TO PAUL LEMPERLY

Inscribed in a copy of *Maggie* (1893), ViU.

"And the wealth of the few
shall be built upon the
patience of the poor."
Prophecy not made B C 1090
Stephen Crane

New York
Aug 29, 1896

274. FROM WILLIAM SCHUYLER
ALS, NNC.

5858 Clemens Av.
St Louis Sept 6. 1896

Mr. Stephen Crane

Dear Sir.

Your kind letter was received day before yesterday. I have written to Copeland & Day, & hope I shall receive a favorable answer. Since writing to you, I have set another one no. XXI, & now have my inner ear listening for themes for one or two more nos X & XXIII, and now my idea is to publish a little book of six songs—Those of your poems whose subjects are suited to musical treatment give such a superb opportunity to the composer that I only wish you would write more—

And now I wish to make another request—believe me I shall not feel hurt at your refusal—for I know your time is precious—I have consented to deliver a lecture before the Eliot Society of this city on "Stephen Crane & his Verse"—I have the "Black Riders" & have read two other poems—one in the Chap Book—If you could tell me where others (if they are published) are to be found—or if you could tell me how you came to choose the form you have used—It would be a great favor. Mr.

Garland told me about your bringing the verses to him before they were published—which was a most interesting item.

I intend to have the songs published here in St Louis by Thiebes & Stierlin, & will send you them as soon as they come out. If I hold to my present idea of a set of six, I must wait for the other two to come to me—which may be a little while. If however you would like to see what sort of stuff my work in them is—I would gladly send you MS. copies of those already finished. Hoping that you will not abandon writing such poems—& thanking you for your kindness

I remain yours sincerely
Wm Schuyler

275. TO BELLE WALKER
ALS, NhD.

141 East 25th St
New York City
Sept 8th. [1896]

Dear Miss Walker: I think the motif of the story is properly strong. "You will never hold the cross toward me." That, I think is very effective. One thing I must say at once: Take the diamond out of that man's shirt immediately. Dont let him live another day with a diamond in his front. You declare him to be very swell and yet you allow him to wear a diamond as if he were a saloon proprietor or owned a prosperous livery stable. It is of the utmost importance that you remove the diamond at once for our fin de siecle editors have keen eyes for that sort of a mistake.

Frankly I do not consider your sketch to be very good but even if you do me the honor to value my opinion, this need not discourage you for I can remember when I wrote just as badly as you do now. Furthermore there are many men, far our superiors who once wrote just as badly as I do today and no doubt as badly as you.

Yours sincerely
Stephen Crane

276. TO PAUL REVERE REYNOLDS[1]
TT, ViU.

Sept. 9th/96.

Dear Mr. Reynolds,—

I leave you a story of something over 5000 words, which I like you to sell if you can.[2] It is one of the best stories that I have done and the lowest price that I could take for it would be $350. I think it is worth more however, if it once strikes the right place, but don't sell it please to some publication that will print it in 1897 and pay in 1898. There are so many of that kind of offices and I would rather take the bottom price if it was represented by cash. Please let me know within a couple of days whether you also arrange for the English rights. My English Market has always been pretty good and I would not care to have both English & American rights sold for 350. but I would expect for the English rights about 25 pounds. I wish you therefore every luck with the story and please let me hear from you when convenient. Don't go to Bacheller or McClure.

Yours truly,
(signed) Stephen Crane.

Dictated by S. C.

---

[1] Paul Revere Reynolds (1864-1944), Crane's literary agent in America. At one time or another Reynolds served as agent for many of the important writers of his day. Among his clientele were H. G. Wells, Edith Wharton, Jack London, Émile Zola, George Bernard Shaw, Arnold Bennett, and Willa Cather. Crane met him at a party given by Irving Bacheller in early 1896, and Reynolds remained Crane's American agent until July 1899, after which James B. Pinker assumed control of his affairs on both sides of the Atlantic.

[2] "A Man and Some Others."

77. FROM H. R. HUXTON
TLS, NNC.

19 West 31st Street
N.Y., September 10th, 1896.

(Confidential)

Dear Mr. Crane:—

I managed to catch Mr. Hurst on a stairway for a moment this afternoon and spoke to him about your doing novelettes based upon real incidents of New York life. He said to go ahead and that he would decide afterwards whether to use them in the Sunday or in one of the daily editions. I am sure that if you read the police news in next Sunday and Monday mornings' papers and go to Jefferson Market Police Court on Monday morning, you will get the material for a good Tenderloin story to start with. I suppose that if you are going there on Monday you would be glad to have a reporter, who knows the ropes, meet you there.

Please let me know how I can best oblige you in this connection, and believe me, dear Mr. Crane,

Yours very sincerely,
H R Huxton

278. FROM PAUL REVERE REYNOLDS

Letterhead: "Paul R. Reynolds,/ Representative of/ Cassell & Co., Limited,/ Wm. Heinemann,/ Sampson Low, Marston & Co., Limited,/ Of London./ . . ./ No. 70 Fifth Avenue,/ New York," TLS, NNC.

New York, Sept. 11th [1896]

Stephen Crane Esq.
Sullivan County N.Y.

Dear Mr. Crane,—

I received your story, also your letter for which many thanks. I have spoken to one of the large papers down town and they have asked me to let them consider it for a day or two. I should be glad to try and handle the English rights for you. And will try to get you 25 pounds. I will write you again soon and let you know how the thing progresses. I will also write to London and place the story there.

Very truly yours,
Paul R. Reynolds

I am writing to a literary agent in London tonight about your story.

279. FROM WILLIAM HOWE CRANE

Letterhead: "The Hartwood Club." TL, NNC.

September 12th, 1896

Dear Stephen: An invitation to Cousin George's wedding arrived for you and I presume you received it in time. I could not attend on account of my arm. So I presume we were not represented. The splints come off my arm tomorrow; but it will be some time before the arm will be strong enough to do any work—hold a gun, for instance. I will try hard, however, to have it in shape for the deer-shooting in October.

There is a flock of wild ducks in the pond at Hartwood, which it will take the three of us to circumvent. When will you come up to do it? Your letter about money arrived all right. Hurrah for Bryan!

Yours ever, Will.

Did you hear that Lew Senger has a badly sprained ankle? He is going about on crutches.

280. FROM H. R. HUXTON
TLS, NNC.[1]

19 West 31st Street.
New York, September 13th, 1896.

Dear Mr. Crane:—

Your pen slipped and your note to me was addressed to 19 West *21st* street and the postoffice people did not deliver it very promptly.

I wrote to the city editor of the Journal this morning and he sends me word that a reporter will ask for you at Shanley's tomorrow, Monday, morning at a quarter before nine. I am sorry that I did not have time to go down to the editorial rooms this morning and attend to the matter myself, but I have no doubt they will send you some one who has all the facilities.

Believe me, dear Mr. Crane,

Yours very sincerely,
H R Huxton

[1] Crane wrote on the verso of the letter, "The Third Violet is really the history of the love of one of the younger and brilliant American artists for an heiress of the ancient New York family kind. The girl spends her summer near the home."

281. TO LUCIUS L. BUTTON
TT, NSyU.

> Hartwood
> Sullivan Co. N.Y.
> Nov. 3d '96

My dear Button: When I returned from Mexico, I tried to look you up in New York but you had incontinently vanished. I heard latter [sic] that you were in Rochester so I fire this small note in that direction or perhaps I had better try Norwich. I think, upon consideration, I will. I am up here writing another book. Let me know where you are and when you intend going to New York so we may clash.

> Yours as ever
> Stephen Crane

282. TO THE *NEW YORK JOURNAL*[1]
ALS reproduced in facsimile in the *New York Journal,* 8 November 1896, p. 14.

> [before 8 November 1896]

It is a condition of most of us who are in journalism that we do not know how to define it because your newspaper seems to change and advance each day.

> Stephen Crane

[1] The *New York Journal* celebrated its first birthday on 8 November with contributions from Crane, William Dean Howells, Edgar Saltus, and Julian Ralph. Crane's note appeared under the heading "A Birthday Word from Novelist Stephen Crane."

283. TO HARRY THOMPSON[1]

ALS, Collection of Stanley and Mary Wertheim, New York City.

[26 or 27 November 1896]

My dear Harry: If you have any copies of George's Ma send one by boy, please. I am going today or in the morn'g at the latest

Yours
Crane

[1] American manager of Edward Arnold, publisher of *George's Mother*.

284. FROM YONE NOGUCHI[1]

ALS, NNC.

Nov. 28th '96 Sausalito Calif.

Oh My dear Stephen Crane:

I love you: I admire you: Would you like to be my friend—will you not? Is it too much rude to speak out boldly about that? Why, I don't think so! I am Yone Noguchi, a little Japanese who live at present at pacific Coast, of course you know—. I regret verily much, some uneducated (in poetry) people compares me with you—I don't like such comparison, as perhaps you don't. I am entirely stranger to you, but I hope that you would like to be my real friend in heart: So I boldly write to you, asking the friendship between you and me. My poetical book is going out perhaps with the next week from the lark—you know, Gelett Burgess.[2] then I would like to send one copy of them to you—will you, my dear Crane, kindly give to me your "black rider," if you have one of them in your shelf? Don't you wonder of me—so rough, so bold! If you will read my lines, you may know what kind of people I am. I write this humble little letter to you, asking simply the real friendship. Would you like to write me soon, accepting my offer? Why, you will not like to be my friend! I love you: I admire you: but I do not know what I love with you or what I admire with you: Still I like very much, you would like to be my friend. I am ever yours truly

Yone Noguchi

I left for little while Mr. Joaquin Miller's cottage, and I am living alone delighted w. a grand view of Sausalito here. I await your answer. How bold youth I am!

Yone

[1] Yone Noguchi (1875-1947), a Japanese poet and professor of English literature at Keio Gijuku University in Tokyo, lived in California for three years with Joaquin Miller. Noguchi enclosed samples of his poetry, which show a striking resemblance to that of Whitman. *The Bookman,* 4 (1896), 287-88, printed a biographical sketch of Noguchi.

[2] Gelett Burgess published in San Francisco a little magazine, *The Lark,* which printed Noguchi's poetry.

Jacksonville and the Commodore

Following a mysterious explosion in its engine room, the filibustering steamer *Commodore,* carrying men and munitions from Jacksonville to the Cuban rebels, foundered fifteen miles off the coast of Florida on the morning of 2 January 1897. Stephen Crane, en route to report the insurrection for the Bacheller-Johnson syndicate, and three other survivors—Captain Edward Murphy, Steward C. B. Montgomery, and William Higgins, an oiler—battled heavy seas for almost thirty hours in a ten-foot dinghy until it capsized in the surf on the beach at Daytona. Ironically, Higgins, the most able seaman and best swimmer aboard the tiny craft, drowned. For Crane, this struggle for survival with the elements and its irrational denouement confirmed his view of the essential conditions of life itself and was fictionalized, with very little alteration of the actual circumstances, in his finest short story, "The Open Boat."

Crane had arrived in Jacksonville during the last week of November and, along with other correspondents eager to get to Cuba, registered at the St. James Hotel as "Samuel Carleton." On 29 November, mistakenly believing, as he was to do on a number of subsequent occasions, that departure for the war zone was imminent, he hired a stenographer-typist and dictated some urgent letters. One of these, to his brother and attorney William Howe Crane, recapitulated to the best of his memory the terms of a lost copy of the will that William had drawn up for him to sign. Another, which is probably no longer extant, went to Amy Leslie, the flamboyant drama critic of the *Chicago Daily News,* who had been Crane's mistress in the months preceding his departure from New York and who may have told him shortly before he left that she was pregnant with his child. A third letter, to Willis Brooks Hawkins, advised him that Crane had appointed him one of his literary executors and especially enjoined him "to help Amy in what is now really a great trouble." Hawkins was skeptical. A note by Marlene Zara in the Ohio State University Library reads, "Mrs. Anthony told me that Hawkins told her that Amy Leslie had 'framed' Crane, saying she was pregnant, in an effort to get Crane to marry her." The recent death of Amy's four-year-old son was undoubtedly another cause for her emotional distress.

Financial involvement further complicated the Crane-Leslie relationship. On 1 November 1896 Amy entrusted Crane with a sum she later claimed was $800. Between 5-25 November Crane deposited $776.50 with William Clarke & Sons, Bankers, whose offices were in the *Tribune* building, although much, if not all, of that sum may have come from royalties on the five books he then had in print. *The Red Badge of Courage* alone went through fourteen printings in 1896. During the same period Crane wrote checks totaling $775, including one on 25 November to "Willis Brooks Hawkins, Agent" for $500, which he gave to Hawkins that same day to disburse in smaller amounts to himself or Miss Leslie as needed. The bank assessed Crane a service charge of $1.50, and his account balanced. Until March 1897 Hawkins reluctantly performed the role of middleman. Plagued with continual demands for small sums, he paid out $325.95 to Amy and $151.05 to Crane, leaving himself $4.00 out of pocket. In April 1897 Crane sent two more checks of $100 each for Amy, but they did not reach her. Hawkins, in disgust, had repudiated the function of intermediary and returned one of the checks; he probably never received the other. Hawkins' refusal to act further precipitated a lawsuit against Crane by Amy Leslie for the recovery of $550, and her attorney, George Mabon, obtained a warrent of attachment for that sum on 3 January 1898 from the Supreme Court of the State of New York, but the controversy was eventually settled without trial by agreement between Mabon and William Howe Crane.

While sending fervent assurances of devotion and loyalty to Amy Leslie, Crane was in early December 1896 cultivating a new love affair with the madam of one of Jacksonville's most fashionable houses of assignation. Cora Howarth Murphy Stewart, thirty-one years old to Crane's twenty-five and the veteran of two unsuccessful marriages, was operating her thinly disguised brothel, the Hotel de Dream, under the cognomen of Taylor. Cultured beyond the demands of her profession, Cora had literary interests. Crane inscribed copies of his books to her and presented her with a copy of the first American edition of Rudyard Kipling's *The Seven Seas* (1896). Despite the intensity of his passion for Cora, Crane languished in Jacksonville, playing poker at the St. James and frequenting waterfront taverns with other journalists and adventurers awaiting the opportunity to sail for Cuba. He relieved the tedium in part by reading Louise de la Ramee's two-volume illustrated edition of *Under Two Flags* (1896) and uncharacteristically praised this high-flown romantic novel as voicing "the old spirit of dauntless deed and sacrifice which is the soul of literature in every age." This appreciation of "Ouida's Masterpiece" (*Book Buyer*, January 1897) was the only book review he ever wrote other than his general evaluation of Harold Frederic's work (*Chapbook*, 15 March 1898).

The wreck of the *Commodore* considerably damaged Crane's chances of reaching the scene of the insurrection. Revenue cutters enforced American neutrality laws by a relatively effective blockade of the Florida coast; but when Crane boarded the ill-fated *Commodore* on New Year's Eve, her cargo of arms and ammunition for the Cuban insurgents had been cleared by United States customs officials for transportation to Cienfuegos, Cuba (*Florida Times-Union*, 1 January 1897, p. 6). Very likely on this occasion, she reached the open sea only with the collusion of certain Coast Guard officials, for she twice ran aground on sand bars on the morning of 1 January, and in the first instance was actually towed into safe waters by the revenue cutter *George S. Boutwell*, whose captain was well aware of her reputation as a filibustering vessel. But such an opportunity was not to be afforded to Crane again. A week after the *Commodore* sinking he was in Port Jervis. According to Louis Senger, "he looked like a man from a grave. He jerked and thrashed in his sleep, and sometimes he cried out in anguish." In Hartwood he frenziedly wrote "The Open Boat," and after a visit to New York City he returned to Jacksonville to begin a futile search for another ship to take him to Cuba. He also occupied himself with the revision of "The Open Boat," consulting with Captain Murphy to assure that his recollection of their experience in the dinghy was accurate, since this was "A Tale Intended

To Be After the Fact." On 11 March 1897 he wrote to his brother William, with considerable hyperbole, that "I have been for over a month among the swamps further south wading miserably to and fro in an attempt to avoid our derned U.S. navy. And it cant be done. I am through trying. I have changed all my plans and am going to Crete." Crane signed with Samuel S. Chamberlain, managing editor of Hearst's *New York Journal,* as a correspondent to report the impending Greco-Turkish War. He also negotiated an independent contract with the McClure syndicate, which sold his dispatches to other American newspapers and to the *Westminster Gazette.* He did not marry Cora because she could not obtain a divorce from her aristocratic British husband, Captain Donald William Stewart, who was on Colonial service in Africa and who, in any event, held strict Anglican convictions about the sanctity of marriage. Stephen managed to persuade Chamberlain to send Cora to Greece with him as the *Journal's* first woman war correspondent.

285. TO WILLIAM HOWE CRANE
TSLS, ViU.

Jacksonville, Fla., Nov. 29, 1896.

Mr. William H. Crane,
Port Jervis, Orange Co., N.Y.

My dear Will:

The very thing that I apprehended came to pass in a violent manner and I was off to Cuba before I had a chance to even inform you of it from New York. I fooled around town for over a month expecting to go at any time, but also expecting to get sufficient notice. But at a time when I was not looking I suddenly received orders to skip and I left New York that very night.[1]

As a matter of fact the will is lost. I have not time now to wait for a copy of the document from you and I shall have to let it go. I do not know that this letter would stand for anything in Court and I am quite sure that I do not remember the exact terms of the will, although it was perfectly satisfactory to me. If I remember it the important terms were as follows:

First. I hereby appoint my brother William H. Crane as sole executor of my estate.

Second. I hereby bequeath to my brother William H. Crane one-third of all my estate.

Third. I hereby bequeath to my brother Edmund B. Crane one-third of all my estate.

Fourth. I hereby bequeath to my brother George P. Crane one-sixth of all my estate.

Fifth. I hereby bequeath to my brother J. Tounley[2] Crane one-sixth of all my estate.

This is the way we arranged matters I remember when going down on the train and it suited me exactly. Of course there are several little details which I would like to have seen carried out and I intended to speak to you of them when I saw you next. For instance my saddle horse[3] I would not like to have sold. I would prefer that he would be kept in easy service at Hartwood and have him cared for as much as possible by Ed himself, or by somebody whom it is absolutely certain would not maltreat him. As for the furniture of mine at Hartwood I would like that all to go to Ed except small things which the other members of the family might care to keep as mementoes of me.

I have arranged with Appleton & Co. that the money due me in February should be paid to you and that you should simply give receipt for it.

As far as my literary affairs go, I wish to appoint as my literary executors W. D. Howells, Hamlin Garland, Willis B. Hawkins and Ripley Hitchcock. They will no doubt be good enough to trouble themselves with my affairs. Of course Mr. Howells would be the chief one to decide upon the book publication of various collections of my stories which have appeared only in serial or magazine form. In my desk at Hartwood you will find a list of stories which I think is correct. The gathering of them will make considerable work, but there are some of them which I would hate to see lost. Some of my best work is contained in short things which I have written for various publications, principally the New York Press in 1893 or thereabout. There are some fifteen or twenty short sketches of New York street life and so on which I intended to have published in book form under the title of "Midnight Sketches."[4] That should be your first care and after that sketches of outdoor life such as "One Dash Horses", "The Wise men", "The Snake" and other stories of that kind could also be published in book form if the literary executors thought that they were up to my standard. There will be a story in the January or February Century which also could go very well with this collection.[5]

I have said everything now which strikes me as being of importance and all I can add now is my love to you and Cornelia[6] and all the babies.

I forgot to mention the Dora Clark case. If I should happen to be detained upon my journey, you must always remember that your brother in that case acted like a man of honor and a gentleman and you need not fear to hold your head up to anybody and defend his name. All that I said in my own article in the Journal is absolutely true, and for my part I see no reason why, if I should live a thousand years, I should be ever ashamed or humiliated by my course in the matter.[7]

I close now with warmest expression of affection for you and yours.

Your brother,
Stephen Crane

---

[1]Crane had received the first of a number of false reports that a filibustering ship was available to take him to Cuba. He left New York on 26 or 27 November accompanied by Amy Leslie, who traveled with him as far as Washington, D.C. As the second letter he wrote to Amy from Jacksonville (No. 287) on 29 November reveals, Crane believed he would be off to Cuba the next day, but he was subjected to many delays before he sailed aboard the *Commodore* on 1 January 1897.

[2]Stephen and William familiarly referred to their brother Jonathan Townley as either "Tounley" or "Twonley." In this instance, though, the stenographer might have misspelled the name. See Nos. 27, 332, and 585.

[3]The horse, Peanuts, which Crane had bought from Elbert Hubbard earlier in the year.

[4]Nine of Crane's New York City sketches were grouped under this title in *The Open Boat and Other Stories* (London: Heinemann, 1898). They are not present in the American edition of *The Open Boat and Other Tales of Adventure* (New York: Doubleday & McClure, 1898).

[5]"A Man and Some Others," *Century,* 53 (February 1897), 601-7.

[6]William's wife.

[7]For a full treatment of the episode, see Olov W. Fryckstedt, "Stephen Crane in the Tenderloin," *Studia Neophilologica,* 34 (1962), 135-63.

286. TO WILLIS BROOKS HAWKINS
TSLS, ViU.

Jacksonville, Fla., Nov. 29, 1896.

Mr. Willis B. Hawkins,
#141 East 25th St.,
New York City.

My dear Willis:

I am here in Jacksonville and feeling very good. I am very much obliged to you for allowing me to plant certain responsibilities upon your noble shoulders and I know that you will carry it out with every consideration for your old friend.[1] By the way, I have planted another responsibility upon your noble shoulders. I have just written to my brother Will that in case my journey was protracted by causes which you can readily imagine, I wish you to serve with Mr. Howells, Mr. Garland and Mr. Hitchcock as my literary executors.

In case you see Amy from time to time encourage her in every possible way. Of course feminine nature is mighty peculiar and she might have that singular ability to get rid of mournful emotions which is possessed by a great many of her sex, but I was positively frightened for the girl at the moment of parting and I am afraid and worried now. I feel that no one hardly could need a friendly word more than this poor child, and I know you are just the man to do it in a right way if the chance presents itself. Hooke fastens his intellect so securely to some damned molecule that he loses sight of a broad question and I do not think he is very efficient as a bracer.[2] It broke my heart to leave the girl but I could feel comparatively easy now if I could feel that she had good friends. There is not one man in three thousand who can be a real counsellor and guide for a girl so pretty as Amy, and this will present itself to your mind no doubt as a reason for supposing that Charley would not be very capable in the position. Her sister is a good hearted sort of a creature, but she is liable to devote most of her attention to herself and besides that Amy is mentally superior to her in every way. The sister is weak, very weak, and so I am sure that she would be of no help to Amy in what is now really a great trouble.[3] I do not want to bore you with any of my affairs but I am obliged to feel that you are about the only man who could possibly help me and do it in the way that would count for some good, so just remember this and when you think some times of your friend remember that he has left behind him one to whom he would count favors done as favors done to himself. By my remarkable use of bad English in parts of this letter you can see that I am dictating and you know very well that I am not used to dictation because my brain is too slow, but I have no doubt you will be able to make out what I mean.

Yours always
Stephen Crane

My best to old Bill Fairman.[4]

[1] The disbursement of funds deposited with him by Crane to Amy Leslie and to Crane himself.
[2] Charles W. Hooke, an author of mysteries who, along with Crane and Hawkins, was a member of the Lantern Club on William Street.
[3] Amy lived with her sister, either a Mrs. O'Brien or Mrs. Siesfeld, at 266 West 25th Street in New York City. Crane may here be alluding to Amy's purported pregnancy.
[4] Leonard "Bill" Fairman, one of Crane's poker-playing friends.

287. TO AMY LESLIE
Letterhead: "The St. James,/ Jacksonville,—Fla. . . . ." AL, NhD.

Sunday—[29 November 1896]

My Blessed Girl: I have dictated a long letter to you today but as it was dictated to a stenographer I could not very well tell you in it how much I loved you and how sorrowful I am now over our temporary separation. The few moments on your train at Washington were the most painful of my life and if I live a hundred years I know I can never forget them. I want you to be always sure that I love you. We start tomorrow night probably but if you have written today I will get it before the boat sails. Be good, my darling, my sweet. Dont forget your old hubber. I think of you at all times and love you alone.

Your lover.

P.S.: We are at the St James and my name is Samuel Carleton. I must hurry this to get it off on the northern mail. Be brave, my sweet.

288. TO AMY LESLIE
Letterhead: "Pullman's Palace Car Company," ALS, Collection of Robert Stallman, Jr., New York City.

Sunday night [29 November 1896]

My dearest: Two letters will reach you soon after this one. Just happened to get time to send this to you on the northern mail which leaves in ten minutes. God bless you and keep you safe for me. Yours with all the love in the world.

S.

289. TO CORA TAYLOR
Inscribed on a flyleaf from a book, NNC.

To C. E. S.[1]

Brevity is an element
that enters importantly
into all pleasures of
life and this is what
makes pleasure sad
and so there is no
pleasure but only sad-
ness.

Stephen Crane

Jacksonville, Fla
Nov [for December] 4th, 1896.

[1]Cora Ethel Stewart. Cora's married name as the wife of Captain Donald William Stewart, her second husband. Cora adopted the surname Taylor for business purposes.

290. TO CORA TAYLOR
Inscribed in a copy of *George's Mother*,[1] NhD.

To an unnamed sweetheart
Stephen Crane

Nov [for December] 4,/96

[1]This is probably the copy of *George's Mother* that Crane requested from Edward Arnold's manager, Harry Thompson, shortly before Crane left for Florida. See No. 283.

291. TO AMY LESLIE
AL on stationery of the St. James Hotel, NhD.

[11 December 1896]

My own Sweetheart: I have not written until now because every moment we have expected to get off and I have wished to save my last word here for you. We have had a great deal of trouble to get a boat ready and I think within 24 hours we will be on our way to Cuba. It breaks my heart to think of the delays and to think that I might have had you with me here if I had only known. There is a great deal of work attached to the affair and I have hardly had time to breathe but always I think of you, night and day, my own love. Remember me sweetheart even in your dreams. From now on I will have time to write oftener and you may expect to hear now every day until starting from your poor forlorn boy. I know you wont forget me. I know you love me and I want you always to remember that I love you.

Your lover

292. TO AMY LESLIE
ALS on stationery of the St. James Hotel, NhD.

Saturday—[12 December 1896]

My Beloved: It has been altogether a remarkable series of circumstances which has delayed us here so long and it breaks my heart to think that I might have had you with me a few days longer—as I wrote you yesterday. The boat we are going over on is a yacht chartered by the world.[1] We have had an awful lot of work in getting her ready for the voyage. We are troubled occasionally by Spanish spies. They follow us a good deal but they seem very harmless. At any rate the people down here are so thoroughly Cuban in their sympathies that they hammer thunder out of a Spanish spy about every other day. So we have loads of friends and you need not fear any harm to me. You have doubtless read in the newspapers the reports of Maceo's death.[2] If they are true, it will change our plans considerably and we will land somewhere in the eastern part of the island. I have had my picture taken here on horseback. I will send you one today. Do not forget that I love you dearly.

Sunday—Today we are spending in misery at the hotel with a strict rule about drinking and no one to play with. I can do nothing but think of you. I love you, my sweetheart, my sweetheart.

Monday: Seems sure that we leave tomorrow. I love you, mine own girl. Be good and wait for me. I love you.

S

[1] I.e., the *New York World*.
[2] General Antonio Maceo, the Cuban revolutionary leader, was killed on 7 December 1896.

293. TO WILLIS BROOKS HAWKINS
Telegram, NhD.

[Jacksonville, Florida to New York City] Dec. 24, 1896

Leave soon telegraph Frankly amys mental condition. Also send fifty[1] if possible. Will arrange payments from appleton troubled over Amy.

Crane

[1] Hawkins wired the money on 28 December. For an explanation of the significance of the receipt for the money, see Joseph Katz, "Some Light on the Stephen Crane-Amy Leslie Affair," *Mad River Review*, 1 (1964-65), 53, n. 20.

1897

294. MORTON[1] TO CORA
ALS, NNC.

9 pm [2 January 1897]

My dear Miss Cora

I am very sorry that I have no encouraging word to send you. The eleven men who were saved have arrived in town. One of them saw Mr Crane get out of his berth and dress himself with that same non-plussed manner, characteristic of him. He entered the boat containing the 16, which is reported to have swamped.[2] There is conflicting rumors as to the empty boat being washed ashore. Some say it has been washed ashore at Port Orange—others say not. The Operator at New Smyrna tells me that he has it pretty straight that it came in, bottom up. God save Crane if he is still alive

You are welcome

Morton

[1] Room clerk at the St. James Hotel in Jacksonville.
[2] Crane did not board the boat that was swamped but waited until the *Commodore*'s ten-foot dinghy was lowered and with the ship's captain, the steward, and an oiler spent almost thirty hours drifting along the Florida coast until the dinghy was beached at Daytona. See "Stephen Crane's Own Story," *New York Press*, 7 January 1897, pp. 1-2; rpt. *Works*, IX, pp. 85-94.

295. MORTON TO CORA CRANE
ALS, NNC.

[2-3 January 1897]

Have just conversed with Phonse Fretol.[1] He fears the worst. Carter[2] is here telling us the story from what he gathered from the rescued

M.

[1] Alphonse W. Fritot, manager of the Jacksonville Terminal for the Florida East Coast Railway and an owner of the tugboat *Three Friends*, which searched for survivors of the disaster. He also sent Cora notes (NNC) concerning Crane.
[2] W. R. Carter, editor and publisher of the *Jacksonville Evening Metropolis*.

296. FROM CORA TAYLOR
Telegram, NNC.

[Jacksonville to Daytona, Florida] Jan 3 1896 [for 1897]

Telegram received. Thank God your safe have been almost crazy

C. T.

297. FROM MORTON
Telegram, NNC.

[Jacksonville to Daytona, 3 January 1897]

The wake held at the St James last night turned into a Jubilee today. Just carried the news down home[1] all well there, congratulations from the gang

Morton

[1] To the Hotel de Dream.

298. FROM MORTON
Telegram, NNC.

[Jacksonville to Daytona, 3 January 1897]

I am right here within call anything I can do command me

Morton

299. FROM MORTON
Telegram, NNC.

[Jacksonville to Daytona, 3 January 1897]

Marshall[1] Wires "Congratulations on plucky and successful fight for life. Dont wire. But write fully from Jax. will wire money today" 4 telegrams here for you nothing important except above.

Morton

[1] Edward Marshall, at this time foreign correspondent for Hearst's *New York Journal*. Later in 1897 he became Sunday Editor of the *New York World*, but in June 1897 he rejoined the *Journal* staff and went to Cuba to report the Spanish-American War.

300. FROM CORA TAYLOR
Telegram, NNC.

[Jacksonville to Daytona] Jan 3 1896 [for 1897]

Come by special today never mind overcharges answer and come surely

C. T.

301. FROM THE ASSISTANT MANAGER OF THE ST. JAMES HOTEL
Telegram, NNC.

[Jacksonville to Daytona, 4 January 1897]

Cora will be there on noon train

M. St James

302. TO LILLIAN BARRETT[1]
Recorded in Richmond Barrett to David A. Fraser, 29 March 1964, NSyU.

Stephen Crane, Able Seaman, SS Commodore. January 4, 1897.

[1] A nine-year-old autograph collector who was staying at the St. James with her family. Crane's inscription might also be classified as an autograph sentiment. Another such example is tipped into a copy of *The Little Regiment* (NSyU): "May you never lack autographs/ Stephen Crane."

303. TO THE *NEW YORK WORLD*

Telegram cited in "Stephen Crane Safe," *New York World*, 5 January 1897, p. 1.

[Jacksonville to New York City, 4 January 1897]

I am unable to write a thing yet but will later.

304. FROM JAMES HAMILTON

Telegram, NNC.

[Detroit to Jacksonville], 1/5 1897

Was Alan P. Gilmour or George E Starr[1] on board Commodore answer my expense.

James Hamilton

[1] Possibly the George E. Starr (1873-1945) who was assistant to the Treasurer of the Curtis Publishing Company in Philadelphia.

305. TO THE *ATLANTA JOURNAL*

Atlanta Journal, 6 January 1897, p. 1.

ST. JAMES HOTEL, JACKSONVILLE, FLA., January 6 [1897]

To the Atlanta Journal:

Seven of the Commodore's men are now unaccounted for. The ship was probably not scuttled.[1] I will stay in Jacksonville until another expedition starts for Cuba.

STEPHEN CRANE

[1] There had been newspaper speculation that sabotage caused the sinking of the *Commodore*.

306. TO WILLIS BROOKS HAWKINS
Telegram, ViU.

[Jacksonville to New York City], 1/7 1897

Thanks awfully old man[1] greeting to club[2] send mail here

Crane

[1] Upon hearing that Crane had been saved, Hawkins forwarded him some money.
[2] The Lantern Club.

307. TO CHARLES F. POPE[1]
Inscribed in an 1896 copy of *The Red Badge of Courage*, NSyU.

Charles F. Pope
With the regards of
Stephen Crane

Jacksonville, Fla., Jan. 8. 1897.

[1] Pope (1843-1922) was a wealthy businessman known as "the glucose king" because of his financial success in the sugar industry.

308. FROM WILLIS B. HAWKINS
AL, NhD.[1]

Sign o' the Lanthorn.
New York, Jan'y 8, 1897.

Mr. Stephen Crane,
Jacksonville, Fla.

Dear friend and brother: A very large meeting at the Sign o' the Lanthorn, Tuesday evening, January 5, 1897, appointed a special committee to express to you its unanimous sentiment of praise and congratulation—praise for your manly bearing in the presence of great danger, and congratulation for your deliverance from that danger. I am instructed by the special committee to inform you that resolutions to this effect are being engrossed for presentation to you.

[1] This letter, probably unsent, is affixed to the front endpaper of *The Lanthorn Book*, Copy 23 (New York: The Sign of the Lanthorn, 1898).

309. TO CORA TAYLOR
Inscribed on a flyleaf from a book, NNC.

[January 1897]

To C. E. S.[1]

Love comes like the tall
swift shadow of a ship at
night. There is for a moment, the music of the water's
turmoil, a bell, perhaps, a
man's shout, a row of gleam-
ing yellow lights. Then the

slow sinking of this mystic
shape. Then silence and a
bitter silence—the silence
of the sea at night.

Stephen Crane[2]

[1] Cora Ethel Stewart.
[2] This inscription is a paraphrase of Crane's poem "I explain the silvered passing of a ship at night."

310. TO LYDA[1]
Inscribed in a copy of *Maggie* (1896), NNC.

To Lyda
From her friend
Stephen Crane

Jacksonville, Fla.
February 18,
1897

[1] Lyda de Camp, madam of a brothel on Ward Street (popularly known as "the line") in Jacksonville.

311. TO RIPLEY HITCHCOCK
Telegram, NN.

[St James Hotel, Jacksonville to New York City], Feby 24 1897

Wire here Heinemans payment little regiment or maggies very important

Stephen Crane

312. TO WILLIAM HOWE CRANE
ALS on stationery of the St. James Hotel, ViU.

March 11 [1897]

My dear Will: I suppose that you have again felt assured that I was the worst correspondent in the world but really I have been for over a month among the swamps further south wading miserably to and fro in an attempt to avoid our derned U.S. navy. And it cant be done. I am through trying. I have changed all my plans and am going to Crete.[1] I expect to sail from NY one week from next Saturday.[2] Expect me P.J. on Thursday. Give my love to all and assure them of my remembrances

Yours as ever
Stephen

[1] Crane reached Crete only accidentally when the *Guadiana,* in which he was sailing from Marseilles to Piraeus, changed course to deliver mail to the Allied Fleet, which was blocking the Cretan ports and anchored in Suda Bay at noon on 7 April 1897. The *Guadiana* departed three hours later, without Crane's having set foot on the Island. Crane reported his impressions of the formidable array of Allied warships, the Concert of Powers, in his first dispatch from Athens, "An Impression of the 'Concert,'" *Westminster Gazette,* 9 (3 May 1897), 1-2.

[2] Crane sailed from New York City to Liverpool aboard the *Etruria* on 20 March 1897 on the first leg of his journey to the Greek-Turkish War front.

313. TO WILLIAM HOWE CRANE
Letterhead: "The S. S. McClure Co./ 141-155 E. 25th St., New York," TLS, ViU.

Mch. 16, 1897.

My dear Will:—

After all, I do not think I can do anything except come to Port Jervis for about two hours. I am going to sail for Havre on the French line Saturday, and as I am in the middle of a story which I am bound to finish before I leave,[1] my time is most tragically short.

When I start for Port Jervis I will telegraph you, and if then you can get Teddy down for an hour or two, I would like to see him and you and chin until my train goes East again.

I think probably I will come tomorrow, Wednesday.

Yours affectionately
S.

[1]"Flanagan and His Short Filibustering Adventure," a second attempt to capitalize on the *Commodore* experience that falls far short of the artistic achievement of "The Open Boat."

314. TO EDMUND B. CRANE
TT of an inscription in Captain Charles King's *An Army Wife* (1895), NSyU.

E. B. Crane from Stephen March 19, 1897 on his departure for bretn

The Greco-Turkish War

As he later told Joseph Conrad, the experience of war in Greece proved to Crane that *The Red Badge* was "all right." Indeed, Crane's dispatches to the *New York Journal* from the combat zone reflect the pattern of enthusiasm, disillusionment, and final reconciliation experienced by Henry Fleming, the young protagonist of the war novel. In "The Spirit of the Greek People," a report datelined 18 April 1897, the day Turkey declared war, but not published in Crane's lifetime, he exulted in "the blare of bugles, the great roaring cheers of recruits mingled with the loud approbation of the populace" in the crowd assembled in Athens' Constitution Square before the Royal Palace. He was present at the commencement of hostilities in Epirus and the three-day bombardment of Arta by the Turks, which resulted in the panic-stricken retreat of the Greek army across the Arta River on 29 April; but in his cable from Athens on the day of that debacle ("Stephen Crane Says Greeks Cannot Be Curbed," *New York Journal,* 30 April 1897, p. 1), Crane again considered himself "fortunate enough to arrive at the capital in time to witness another popular outburst of the Athenians." In jingoistic terms he asserted that "this is not a king's war, not a parliament's war, but a people's war."

The jubilation of the Athenians notwithstanding, the thirty-days struggle evolved into a series of retreats and rear-guard actions on the part of the Greeks at Pharsala, Velestino, and Domoko and ended in their complete humiliation. Interviewing soldiers in the field, Crane discovered that many of them felt that they had been betrayed by their foreign-born king, who was under the control of the Powers, and that

283

their commander-in-chief, Prince Constantine, had been given orders to retreat each time victory seemed to be within his grasp. Hampered by illness, Crane witnessed only the second battle of Velestino among the major engagements, and here he found combat curiously exhilarating. The roll of musketry fire was "a beautiful sound—beautiful as I had never dreamed. It was more impressive than the roar of Niagara and finer than thunder or avalanche—because it had the wonder of human tragedy in it. It was the most beautiful sound of my experience, barring no symphony. The crash of it was ideal." Crane acknowledged that the men who died there would have been less sanguine ("Crane at Velestino," *New York Journal*, 11 May 1897, p. 1); but the actualities of war became more shocking to Crane when on 18 May he was aboard the hospital ship *St. Marina*, which left Chalkis for Athens crammed with soldiers wounded at Domoko. There were 800 bleeding men in the hold, and "Those who died, and there were not a few, could not be removed, and the corpses lay among the living men, shot through arm, chest, leg or jaw." Near the hatch, in a cameo horror reminiscent of *The Red Badge*, Crane could see "a man shot through the mouth. The bullet passed through both cheeks. He is asleep with his head pillowed on the bosom of a dead comrade." Crane concludes this dispatch with the balanced perspective that "There is more of this sort of thing in war than glory and heroic death, flags, banners, shouting and victory" ("Stephen Crane Tells of War's Horrors," *New York Journal*, 23 May 1897, p. 35). Only in "Death and the Child," his finest Greco-Turkish War story, did Crane approach the coalescence of irony, satire, and realism that distinguishes *The Red Badge of Courage*.

For at least three days after the 19 May armistice, Stephen and Cora remained in Athens. Obviously, Crane had little appreciation for classical antiquities. "Athens is not much ruins, you know," he reflected laconically in a letter to his brother William. Along with John Bass, the *Journal*'s chief correspondent in Greece, the Cranes had cabinet photographs taken at the studio of C. Boehringer, splendidly attired in the costumes of what well-dressed war correspondents should wear. They then departed, separately, as they had come to Greece, for refuge in England.

315. TO WILLIAM HOWE CRANE
Letterhead: "Grand Hotel D'Angleterre/ Athens (Greece) . . .," ALS, NNC.

April 10 [1897]

My dear Will: I arrived in Athens three days ago[1] and am going to the frontier shortly. I expect to get a position on the staff of the Crown Prince. Wont that be great? I am so happy over it I can hardly breathe. I shall try—I shall try like blazes to get a decoration out of the thing but that depends on good fortune and is between you and I and God.[2] Athens is not much ruins, you know. It is mostly adobe creations like Mexico although the Acropolis sticks up in the air precisely like it does in the pictures. I was in Crete but saw no fighting. However the exhibition of foriegn war-ships was great. The reputation of my poor old books had reached a few of the blooming Greeks and that is what has done the Crown Prince business for me. If I get on the staff I shall let you know at once. They say I've got a sure thing. They like Americans very much over here anyhow, or rather they hate all the others and so we have an advantage. It really isnt so much for a foriegner of standing to get on the staff but then it sounds fine and it really is fine too in a way and I am so happy tonight I can hardly remain silent and write I hope and pray that you are all well and that I see you all again. Love to everyone

Yours affectionately
S.

Write to me here.

---

[1] Most probably, the *Guadiana* arrived at Piraeus, the port of Athens 150 miles to the northwest of Crete, on the morning of 8 April.

[2] Considering Crane's lack of military qualifications, it is unlikely he would have been considered for a position on the Greek general staff, and there is no evidence to support his expectation that such an ambition would be fulfilled. It seems paradoxical that a writer who had exposed the futility of war and expressed an extremely cynical attitude toward heroism should lust for a decoration, but Crane's vainglorious boasts must be evaluated in the perspective of his guilt feelings over his youthful bohemianism and his desire to ingratiate himself with William, the stern paterfamilias, seventeen years his senior and a community leader and magistrate in Port Jervis who was always known as Judge Crane.

316. TO WILLIS BROOKS HAWKINS
ALS on stationery of the Grand Hotel, ViU.

[18 April 1897]

Willie: Have mailed at 25th St—one hundred for Amy—

Yours
S

A draft on Cooks[1]

[1] Amy Leslie moved from her sister's house on West 25th Street in New York City to 42 West 29th Street in late February or early March. Crane was unaware of her change of address, and his draft, which she never received, may have miscarried.

317. TO WILLIS BROOKS HAWKINS
ALS on stationery of the Grand Hotel, ViU.

[18 April 1897]

Dear Willie Have mailed you Cooks draft for one hundred for Amy[1]

C

[1] This note was sent to Hawkins c/o the Bacheller Syndicate, New York City, while No. 316 was sent to him at the Lantern Club.

318. TO WILLIS BROOKS HAWKINS
ALS on stationery of the Grand Hotel, NhD.

April 27 [1897]

Dear old man: I enclose a pony[1] for Amy. Give her my love Tell her there is lots more coming. Just off again to see fight I love Amy.

Yours
S.

Tell Fairman go to hell[2]

---

[1] A slang expression for £25. An unknown hand has scrawled "$100 ck" on this letter, but with the rate of exchange standing somewhat above $4.85 to the pound in spring 1897, the amount Crane actually sent was approximately $122. Amy Leslie did not receive this check either. On 28 December 1897 Hawkins wrote to her attorney, George Mabon, that he had returned the second sum entrusted to him by Crane for Amy "and declined to make any further disbursements for him."

[2] Leonard Fairman, a mutual friend of Crane and Hawkins, at times acted as an intermediary between Hawkins and Amy Leslie.

319. FROM EBAN ALEXANDER[1]
Letterhead: "American Legation/ Athens," ALS, NNC.

May, 5, 1897.

Dear Mr Crane,

Just as I am going out, I find the books you have been so good as to send me.

I should like to have them anyway, but they are all the more to me because of the friendly feeling that told you to give them to me.
I thank you heartily.

Your friend sincerely,
E. Alexander.

[1] United States Minister to Greece, Rumania, and Serbia, 1893-97. The first American edition of *Active Service* (New York: Stokes, 1899) was dedicated to Alexander. In his correspondence, Alexander referred to Cora as "Mrs. Stewart" or "Lady Donald Stewart," reflecting his knowledge that the Cranes were not married.

320. TO S. S. CHAMBERLAIN[1]

Inscribed on a cabinet photograph of Crane in war correspondent's uniform,[2] Collection of Stanley and Mary Wertheim, New York City.

> To S. S. Chamberlain
> With many regards
> Stephen Crane
>
> Athens
> May 20/97

[1] Managing Editor of the *New York Journal* who was responsible for Crane's assignment to Greece as a war correspondent for the newspaper.

[2] This inscription is on a copy of one of a group of cabinet photographs of Crane, Cora, and John Bass taken in the C. Boehringer studio in Athens during the second week of May 1897. The field uniforms worn by the correspondents and the false rocks upon which they are sitting are obviously studio props.

321. FROM IMOGENE CARTER[1]

Inscribed on a photograph of Cora in war correspondent's field dress, NSyU.

> Athens
> May 22 97
>
> To me old pal Stevie with best wishes—Imogene Carter

[1] The pen name used by Cora to byline dispatches from Greece published in the *New York Journal* and later a series of London columns that appeared, in part, in the *New York Press* (unsigned) between 15 August and 10 October 1897. One of the Greek reports, which was unfinished and not submitted to the *Journal*, has two of its manuscript leaves

rewritten with revisions in Crane's hand. Both Cora's Greek dispatches and London articles reveal internal stylistic evidence of Crane's participation, either through dictation or revision. See No. 334, n. 5.

Ravensbrook

Crane's settlement with Cora in England at Ravensbrook, Oxted, Surrey, in June 1897 was not an act of expatriation but of exile. Stephen's brothers and their prudish wives would have never welcomed the "hostess" of a Jacksonville pleasure resort to Hartwood or Port Jervis, but the literary group among whom Crane settled in England had less stringent conceptions of marriage. Harold Frederic, Ford Madox Ford, and H. G. Wells lived with women who were not their wives, and Henry James was tolerant, if not approving, of deviations from Victorian morality. To conceal his liaison with Cora from his family, Crane gave his publishers, William Heinemann, rather than Ravensbrook as his return address in letters to his brothers.

Crane's period of residence at Ravensbrook was among the happiest and most productive of his life, although he was increasingly beset by money worries. The most important of the literary friendships he made at this time was with Joseph Conrad, whom he met in October 1897 at a luncheon in London given by Heinemann's editor, Sidney Pawling. The Heinemann house organ, the *New Review,* was serializing Conrad's *The Nigger of the "Narcissus,"* and reviewers were suggesting that Conrad was a pendant of Crane. Although Conrad resented these innuendoes and would later assume a patronizing attitude toward Crane, at this time he greatly admired the young American and actually looked up to him as the superior writer. Another significant relationship was with the Scottish-born Robert Barr, who had spent his youth in Canada and had also lived in Detroit, where he edited the *Free Press.* Barr had gone to England to become a novelist, and, with Jerome K. Jerome, he founded the *Idler* magazine. After Crane's death, Barr would complete *The O'Ruddy* (1903). The Cranes welcomed visits to Ravensbrook from Edward and Constance Garnett, the Fords, Harold Frederic and his mistress Kate Lyon, the Barrs, and the Conrads. Less desirable were the hordes of tourists, fledgling writers, and journalists who crowded into the villa, so that Crane occasionally had to sequester himself in a London hotel room in order to work. He wrote prolifically, both what was intended to be remunerative hackwork such as "London Impressions," "Irish Notes," and "The Scotch Express" and some of his finest stories, "The Bride Comes to Yellow Sky," "Death and the Child," "The Blue Hotel," and "The Monster," which Frederic urged him to burn.

Despite literary friendships, public adulation, and artistic success, Crane gradually became restless. He was increasingly plagued by financial problems fueled by his own and Cora's extravagance. During the summer of 1897 he entertained the idea of foreign correspondence from South Africa or the Sudan, and in late October the Bacheller Syndicate proposed he go to the Klondike. Crane had been critical of British imperialism in a satirical undergraduate sketch, "A Foreign Policy in Three Glimpses." Early in 1898 he wrote a comic playlet, "The Blood of the Martyr," about German imperialism in China, which was published in the Sunday Magazine section of the *New York Press* on 3 April 1898. Yet, on 14 April, three days after Congress passed resolutions recognizing Cuba's independence from Spain, Crane sailed from Queenstown to New York on the *Germanic* and, shortly after reaching home, attempted to enlist in the Navy. When he failed to meet the physical requirements, he accepted a commission as a war correspondent for Pulitzer's *World*. On 24 April, the day Spain declared war against the United States, Crane left for Florida to join the scores of correspondents gathered at Key West and the port of Tampa with the army massing to invade Cuba.

322. TO EDMUND B. CRANE
TT by Edith F. Crane, OU.

[June 1897]

My dear Ted; Can you find among my possessions a story called "The Wise Men" and another story called "The Five White Mice"?[1] If so send them to me as soon as possible.

My love to everybody.

Yours hurriedly
but with all love.
S.

c/o William Heinaman
21 Bedford St. W.C., Londaon.

[1] "The Wise Men" (*Ludgate Monthly,* April 1898, pp. 594-603) and "The Five White Mice" (*New York World*, 10 April 1898, p. 32, of the Sunday Supplement) were written at Hartwood in late spring and summer 1896. Both stories grew out of Crane's Mexican experiences and featured as main characters two "Kids" from New York and San Francisco.

323. TO MR. HARRIS[1]
Inscribed in a copy of *The Third Violet*,[2] NhD.

Dear Mr Harris: This book
is even worse than any
of the others.
Stephen Crane

London, June, 1897.

[1] Probably Frank Harris (1856-1931), Irish-American author of the notorious *My Life and Loves*, 4 vols. (Paris: privately printed, 1922-27). Harris was a friend of Harold Frederic and a powerful literary force in the London of the 1890s as editor of the

Fortnightly and subsequently the *Saturday Review*. He inscribed to Crane a copy of *Elder Conklin and Other Stories*, 2nd. ed. (London: Heinemann, 1895): "To Stephen Crane/ from the author./ June '97."

[2]This inscription appears on the half title of a copy of the first English edition of *The Third Violet* (London: Heinemann, 1897). On the front pastedown is inscribed "For Stephen Crane's friend George Huling with regards of Mrs Stephen Crane," and the front flyleaf bears the signature "Mrs Stephen Crane."

324. FROM EBAN ALEXANDER
ALS on stationery of the American Legation in Athens, NNC.

July 14, 1897.

My dear Crane,

It would be altogether lovely to drop in and see you and Mrs. Stewart, as you kindly ask me in your letter of the second instant to do. Perhaps I can, but the chances are that luck won't run that way. I am hoping to be allowed to leave here by August 1st, and, in fact, have engaged passage by the Spree from Cherbourg for August 8th. If everything goes right, I may be in London on the 6th or 7th,[1] and, if so, I shall certainly shake hands with you.

I have missed both of you sorely. Several times I have wished (almost) that you hadn't come at all. Not quite.

I hear that Rockhill[2] has been named for this post. He is a capital fellow, no end better minister than I could ever be.

However—

I fancy that you have settled down in England. It is a decent country to live in, but the clear sky of Greece is lacking. Also the infernal heat.

Mrs. Bass is at least no worse. The poor girl has suffered. For six weeks she has kept her bed. She may, probably will, pull through. The baby is a fine fellow.

All of our ships have gone. No fourth of July. Not six Americans in town then or now.

My kindest remembrances to Mrs Stewart. I am not likely to forget either of you.

Your Friend,
E. Alexander.

[1] Alexander did not visit England en route home. Upon his return to the United States, he resumed his position as Professor of Greek at the University of North Carolina.

[2] William W. Rockhill (1854-1914), who had served with the American legation in Peking and Seoul, replaced Alexander as Minister to Greece, Rumania, and Serbia. Rockhill served from 1897 to 1899.

325. TO EDMUND B. CRANE

Thomas A. Gullason, "The Letters of Stephen Crane: Additions and Corrections," *American Literature*, 41 (1969), 104-5.

c/o William Heineman
21 Bedford St. W.C.
London.
July 22d [1897]

My dear Ted: Your letter concerning little Bill's death[1] has just reached me after going to Athens and coming here. I knew of it from Helen's[2] letter but I have not written because this is a most difficult letter to write. I dont know what to say to you. I cant say the conventional thing and yet there are so few phrases which I could use to express to you how I feel about the death of brave bold little Bill. Good old Bill and the way he used to smoke my pipes! Give my love to Mame and the kids. Expect to hear from me in the Soudan. The S.A. fight is off.[3]

Yours with love
S.

[1] Edmund's son, William T. Crane, died at two and a half years of age.

[2] Helen Crane, daughter of Stephen's brother, William. Sixteen years old at this time, she would become a rather troublesome ward of the Cranes at Brede Place less than two years later.

³Crane hoped to report the impending clash between the Anglo-Egyptian army in the Sudan and the forces of the Mahdi. Armed conflict between the British and the Boers in South Africa had been temporarily postponed by negotiations over the franchise and other civic rights for the British outlanders. Hostilities on a grand scale did not break out until October 1899. Crane's articles on "Some Curious Lessons from the Transvaal," *New York Journal,* 7 January 1900, p. 27, and "The Great Boer Trek," *Cosmopolitan,* 29 (June 1900), 153-58, are implicitly critical of the British cause in South Africa, but his attitude toward American intervention in Cuba was more positive.

326. TO THE EDITOR OF THE *LONDON DAILY MAIL*
Letterhead: "Telegrams—/ Crane, Oxted./ Ravensbrook,/ Oxted,/ Surrey." ALS, NN.

July 29. [1897]

Dear sir: I am arranging a trip for an American newspaper in the Soudan for the fall—with the troops if possible. I thought perhaps some arrangement might be formed with the Daily Mail.

Yours faithfully
Stephen Crane.

327. TO SYLVESTER SCOVEL
TT, MnU.

Ravensbrook
August 1st ('97)

My dear Harry: Old friends never write to each other. That is almost a law but tonight Cora and I want to speak to you because you are the only one will understand. Velestino has just died—not two hours ago. He died in Cora's bedroom with all the pillows under him which our poverty could supply. For eleven days we fought death for him, thinking nothing of anything but his life. He made a fine manly fight, with only little grateful laps of his tongue on Cora's hands, for he know that she was trying to help him. The V.S. told us that it was distemper. We are burying him tomorrow in the rhododendron bed in the garden. He will wear your collar in his grave.

Yours always
C.

P.S. If any of those pictures of him taken on the boat are at hand send them to us.

328. TO EDMUND B. CRANE
TT, NSyU and OU.

ATTRIDGE'S HOTEL,
SCHULL,
County Cork
Ireland
Sept 9. [1897]

My dear Teddie: I am sorry that I am so careless about writing regularly to you for I am sure you are in my mind very much indeed. In England lately while going to see Harold Frederic I was thrown out of a carriage by a runaway horse and rather badly shaken up. So Frederic and I have come down here on the south coast of Ireland for a little rest.[1] The only result finally of the accident will be a small scar on the side of my nose.

I have a great deal of work to do over here. Next week I am going to Scotland for McClure. I have just finished a novelette of 20000 words—"The Monster."[2] I write considerably for the *Saturday Review*, and *The Westminster Gazette*. I am going to stay over here and lay for another war. As soon as my money gets coming in I will send you some.

The ms you mailed to me was not the one I wanted but I was glad enough to get it. Any odd bits of writing you find at H;[3] please mail to me. Some of them will come in handy. Have you noticed an ms devoted to the adventures of a certain Irishman?[4] Try to get it.

Give my love to all. If it weren't for the silly tariff law I could easily send you nice things from time to time. My address will continue to be at Heineman's.

Yours lovingly
S.

[1] On 19 August Crane and Cora were injured in a carriage accident while driving to the Frederics' home at Kenley, where Frederic had established a second household, apart from his legal wife and children, with Kate Lyon, by whom he had an additional three children. Frederic and Kate nursed the Cranes for about a week, after which the four vacationed at Dunmanus Bay, Ireland. During these three weeks Crane gathered material for the "Irish Notes," which appeared in the *Westminster Gazette,* October-November 1897.

[2] *Harper's Magazine,* 97 (August 1898), 343-76.

[3] Hartwood.

[4] "Dan Emmonds," a fragmentary voyage fantasy that is most likely the opening of a novel Crane began to write sometime before March 1896 but failed to complete. In December 1898, while Crane was in Havana, Cora had a typescript of the holograph manuscript professionally prepared by Crane's English agent, James B. Pinker, and attempted to sell it as a sketch. "Dan Emmonds" did not appear in print until 1963. See R. W. Stallman, "New Short Fiction by Stephen Crane: I, 'Dan Emmonds,' " *Studies in Short Fiction,* 1 (Fall 1963), 1-7; and Thomas Gullason, ed., *The Complete Short Stories and Sketches of Stephen Crane* (Garden City: Doubleday, 1963).

329. TO AMY LESLIE

Letterhead: ". . . Roche's Royal Hotel, Glengariff." ALS, NhD.

[Ireland, 12 September 1897]

My dear Amy: I am sorry to have you write to me in the way that you did because I will always be willing to do anything in the world for you to help you and see that you do not suffer. I never intended to treat you badly and if I did appear to do so, it was more by fate or chance than from any desire of mine. You do not say anything about recieving the $100. I sent you from Greece through Willis. Did you get it?[1] Let me know through Heineman. I am over here in the south of Ireland getting well from a carriage accident. It will be sometime before I get well. I had to leave off work and borrow some money to come here. I was doing very decently in London and would have sent you more money before now if it were not for the accident. As soon as I can I will send some to you if only it is a little at a time.

You know better than to believe those lies about me. You know full well what kind of a man I am. As soon as I get home I shall want to know who told you them.[2]

Keep up heart, Amy. Trust me and it will all turn out right. Go and see Willis and let him always know your address. When you write and tell me that he is still in town and that you got that hundred all right I will rake up more. Dont think too badly of me, dear. Wait, have patience and I will see you through straight. Dont believe anything you hear of me and dont doubt my faith and my honesty.

Yours as ever
C.

[1] Amy Leslie did not receive the Cook's draft for $100 that Crane sent on 18 April to an address where she no longer lived. Crane seems to have forgotten that Hawkins returned and received a receipt from him for the "pony" (£25) he sent on 27 April for Hawkins to disburse to Amy. Disgusted with her inability to obtain further funds from Crane that she felt were due her, Amy Leslie filed suit and obtained a warrent of attachment against him on 3 January 1898 for $550.

[2] Rumors of Crane's relationship with Cora may have reached Amy Leslie.

330. TO E. LESLIE GILLIAMS

ALS on Ravensbrook stationery, Mason City Public Library, Mason City, Iowa.

Sep. 19th 97
England

E. Leslie Gilliams

Dear Sir: My terms for a story of between five and ten thousand words is $500.[1] This does not include the English rights. I would be willing to submit to you a story to be paid for on these terms.

Very Truly Yours.
Stephen Crane

[1] Following the success of *The Red Badge of Courage,* Crane occasionally demanded this amount from quality magazines for his stories, but he seldom received more than five cents a word and in his English years considerably less than that. See James B. Stronks, "Stephen Crane's English Years: The Legend Corrected," *Papers of the Bibliographical Society of America,* 57 (1963), 340-49.

331. CORA CRANE TO SYLVESTER SCOVEL

TT, MnU.

Ravensbrook
Oct. 17th [1897]

My dear Harry: We were very glad to hear from you from those cold, cold regions. We hope by this time that you are safely out of it or safely in it. It is clearly a matter of snow and hills is it not? Stephen thinks your idea of the dog newspaper teams great. Try to get enough gold out of it for a trip to England and come camp with us. Your wife must be a sweet woman and a good one and I am glad Harry. Good women who are not narrow methodists are few. Your a lucky man altogether.

Our place is getting in great shape—you would not know it. The conservatory has been made anew and is now full of beautiful flowers.

And slowly but surely we are furnishing—getting old oak and that sort of thing. The Greeks are still faithful and happy—I have tried an English housemaid with them but it dont go—so I am still chef-housemaid-housekeeper-etc. but I like it and we are happy—very happy—Stephen is working hard at a new book which will be his best I think. We were almost killed in carriage accident in Aug. The same horse and trap you drove home from the Frederics—We had a man driving, horse not properly harnessed and ran away. It was on Harolds birthday and we were going to luncheon party at his place—you can picture our arriving covered with dust and blood. They, dear people, took us in and cured us and then carted us off to Ireland where we had a delightful three weeks in the wilds—

We see much of the Frederic's and of Robert Barr who lives very near us. The former wish to be remembered to you. We are going to dine at their place this week to meet Mark Barr and his bride who later come to us for a few days. So you see we have quite settled down to the English country life and it is sweet and pure.

Now come to us for a long visit when you can. We can do stunts in town and I am sure your wife will pardon our primitive establishment. Stephen says come as soon as possible and write us quickly. This letter is from us both, of course, with best wishes for you both

Ever sincerely
Cora Crane.

P.S. The enclosure is for Pandemonium—from Adoni.

332. TO WILLIAM HOWE CRANE
ALS, NhD.

c/o William Heineman
21 Bedford St, W.C.
London
Sat. Oct 29. [1897]

My dear William: I got your letter this morning. I have been wanting to write you for some time about the library but have been quite too busy. For my part I would gladly give to you power to choose my part of the library. Take an encyclopaedia and as many histories as possible and then let the others have a chance. It cant matter so much to me and I feel that I have not treated the others very fairly in the matter. If you go to Asbury Park, look up my two swords—I wore them at Claverack—and keep them for me.

I have been in England, Ireland, Scotland, Wales France, Turkey and Greece. I have seen Italy but never trod it. Since I have been in England I have been in dreadfully hard luck. I have been here four months and one month I was laid up by the carriage accident. In the working three months I have earned close to 2000 dollars but the sum actually paid in to me has been only £20.17s.3d—about 120 dollars. In consequence I have had to borrow and feel very miserable indeed. I am not sure that I am not in trouble over it.

McClures, with security of over 1000 dollars against my liability of four hundred, refuse to advance me any money. And yet they think they are going to be my American publishers.

I am working now on a big novel.[1] It will be much much longer than The Red Badge. My next short thing after the novelette (The Monster) was The Bride Comes to Yellow Sky. All my friends come here say it is my very best thing. I am so delighted when I am told by competent people that I have made an advance. You know they said over here in England that The Open Boat (Scribner's) was my best thing. There seem so many of them in America who want to kill, bury and forget me purely out of unkindness and envy and—my unworthiness, if you choose. All the hard things they say of me effect me principally because I think of mine own people—you and Teddie and the families. It is nothing, bless you. Now Dick Davis for instance has come to like the abuse. He accepts it as a tribute to his excellence. But he is a fool.[2] Now I want you to promise to never pay any attention to it, even in your thought. It is too immaterial and foolish. Your little brother is neither braggart or a silent egotist but he knows that he is going on steadily to make his simple little place and he cant be stopped, he cant even be retarded. He is coming.

Sometimes I think you and old Ted worry about me and you may well worry! I have managed my success like a fool and a child but then it is difficult to succeed gracefully at 23. However I am learning every day. I am slowly becoming a man. My idea is to come finally to live at Port

Jervis or Hartwood. I am a wanderer now and I must see enough but—afterwards—I think of P.J. & Hartwood.

Ted wrote to me that he wanted to go to Klondike. At least he hinted at a desire. In less than a week, I happened to get a letter from the Bachellers asking me to go there.[3] I do not believe there is exactly too much money in it for me but there will be enough to clear all heavy expenses and so I have accepted the offer in the hope that I may be able to do some small service to Ted—if he really means it.

I go to the Soudan in about a month. The English forces are surely going to Khartoom. Perhaps I may be able to write you from there. That would be nice. I wanted badly to go to India to see the frontier row there but English papers discouraged me. They said it would be all over before I could get there. That was eight weeks ago and the war is still in full blast. The Afridis have thrashed the life out of the Englishmen on one or two occasions but we dont hear about it. That is the Englishman's strong point. However I hope there will be some good fighting in the Soudan before long.[4]

I am sorry about the arm. Perhaps, after a time, it will regain its strength. So Helen has a sweetheart? I got her letter but she didnt mention it. That reminds me—my stamp collection! If Tounley[5] hasn't hocked it, it is now valuable. He had a good claim on it in a way. He gave me the start and, afterward, contributed largely. Try to get it at Asbury Park. Give Helen charge of it and then she and I can be partners. She had better then get a good catalogue that gives valuations.

The Irish Notes and so on, which appear in the Journal are written really for The Westminster Gazette and The Saturday Review.

I suppose it would be the proper thing for me to write long descriptions home of what I see over here but I write myself so completely out in articles that an attempt of the sort would be absurd.

I am just thinking how easy it would be in my present financial extremity to cable you for a hundred dollars but then by the time this reaches you I will probably be all right again. I believe the sum I usually borrowed was fifteen dollars, wasnt it? Fifteen dollars—fifteen dollars—fifteen dollars. I can remember an interminable row of fifteen dollar requests.

Tell Cornelia[6] I still refer to her as the most delicately perfect cook—upon a given material—of the world and I have dined in all the best places of Paris and England. Give her my steadfast love.

I should like to see this famous pony. It appears to me that Edna[7] might write and describe it.

Your loving brother
S.

[1] *Active Service* (1899), Crane's autobiographical novel of the Greco-Turkish War. About two months later, on 20 December (No. 346), he wrote Reynolds that the book was barely begun, but he intended to finish it in April or May 1898; however, the Cuban war intervened, and, although Crane may have worked on the novel in Havana, it was completed at Brede Place in May 1899 and published near the end of the year by Frederick A. Stokes Company in New York and William Heinemann in London.

[2] Crane consistently derided Richard Harding Davis, whom he first met at the Lantern Club and who was his chief rival as star war correspondent in Greece and Cuba. Davis' attitude toward Crane was considerably more complex. He admired Crane's individualistic flair and initiative and described his exploits in a number of articles and books, but he deplored what he considered Crane's loose morality and bohemianism. Davis' short story, "A Derelict," *Scribner's Magazine,* 30 (August 1901), 131-52, depicts a character, Charles Channing, a free-lance writer of genius admired by the English who has written "Tales of the Tenderloin" and excels in "Sunday-special stuff." As early as September 1901, a reviewer in the *Bookman* charged that Crane was the model for Channing, and this allegation has often been repeated since "A Derelict" was collected in *Ranson's Folly* (New York: Scribner's, 1902). There are, however, only superficial similarities between Crane's personality and career and Channing's wayward genius, and it is doubtful that he was modeled upon Crane.

[3] Exceptionally rich gold-bearing gravel was found on Bonanza Creek in the Klondike in 1896.

[4] Crane never went to the Klondike, India, or the Sudan. Fredson Bowers, in *Works,* VIII, p. 960, identifies as Crane's a short satirical piece about the Afridis of northern India, "How the Afridis Made a Ziarat," *New York Press,* 19 September 1897, p. 23. The English campaign against the Afridis began in mid-October. On 14 January 1898, Crane sent Reynolds an article on the fighting to be placed in the *New York Press,* or syndicated, or in the *New York Journal* (See No. 355), but this has not been located.

[5] Stephen and William familiarly referred to their brother Jonathan Townley as either "Tounley" or "Twonley." See Nos. 27, 285, and 585.

[6] William's wife.

[7] William's younger daughter, Edna, wrote a memoir of her childhood experiences with Crane in Port Jervis, "My Uncle, Stephen Crane, as I Knew Him," *Literary Digest International Book Review,* 4 (March 1926), 248-50.

333. TO ELBERT HUBBARD

ALS, Collection of Miriam Roelofs, East Aurora, New York.

c/o William Heineman
21 Bedford St, W.C
London
Oct 29. [1897]

My dear Hubbard: It is a dangerous thing to forget to cummunicate with one's friends. Soon it becomes hard to retrace. I am glad you wrote to me because I have been believing myself an ass in your respect and now I have opportunity to say so.

As for your damned friends I have lost the card but if you send me another one with the address I shall call there as soon as I can afford a top-hat. It is somewhere in Russell Sq I know and I am thinking of calling from house to house.

Sometime ago I sent a thing to The Bookman with instructions in a circuitous way, that if they could not use ($) it, they should forward it to The Philistine. I think you will get it since McArthur[1] cant tell good stuff from hot clam broth. Remember me vividly to Mrs Hubbard, to the docter[2] and his wife and to Marie and to the hoodlums who played Indian on your lawn.

Yours faithfully
Stephen Crane

---

[1] James MacArthur, joint editor of the *Bookman* with Harry Thurston Peck, 1894–1900.

[2] Dr. A. L. Mitchell, a neighbor of Hubbard's in East Aurora, New York. Crane met him in December 1895 at the time of the Philistine Society banquet.

334. TO PAUL REVERE REYNOLDS
Allen, pp. 52-54.

>Ravensbrook,
>Oxsted,
>Surrey.
>[October 1897]

Dear Mr. Reynolds:

Good: Now we can do something. I will allow you ten percent on the sales and refer everything to you, giving you the clear field which is your right. You will have the whole management as in the theatrical business.

Now one of the reasons of this thing is to get me out of the ardent grasp of the S. S. McClure Co. I owe them about $500, I think, and they seem to calculate on controlling my entire out-put. They have in their possession "The Monster" (21,000 words) and "The Bride Comes to Yellow Sky" (4500) both for the American rights alone. The American rights alone of "The Monster" ought to pay them easily, minus your commission. No; perhaps it wouldn't pay them fully but it would pay them a decent amount of it. Then the American rights of "The Bride"—I judge to be worth $175.

As for my existing contracts there are only two. I. To write an article on an engine ride from London to Glasgow for the McClures.[1] II. To give them my next book.[2] Of course these would go on as if I had not called in your assistance.

Robert McClure here in London told me he thought you had "The Monster" in New York but I judge, if that were so, that you would have mentioned it in your letter this morning. I will write to Phillips and ask him to let you have it under the agreement that the money minus your commission shall be paid to them. Then *if* the money for "The Monster" goes far toward paying my debt, you can ask them about "The Bride."[3]

"The Bride Comes to Yellow Sky" is a daisy and don't let them talk funny about it.

Now as for the newspaper business we can do large things. The *Herald* pays me $100 per article of between 3000 and 4000 words. The *World* has never paid me over $50 and expenses but could be brought to $75 or $100, I think. Now that of course is a big graft to play as long as I am here in Europe. As for the *Journal* I have quite a big misunderstanding with them and can't get it pulled out straight. They say I am overdrawn. I say I am not. I have sent them an installment of my Irish Notes that I am doing here for the *Westminster Gazette* and would send them more if it were possible to hear from them. I would send you the Irish Notes and also my London Impressions from the *Saturday Review*—for the *Journal*, if we could get some definite statement from them.[4] My idea was that they would go in with that stuff on the editorial page. Twenty-five dollars per installment would be enough. If the *Journal* will explain why they say I am over-drawn I am the last man in the world to kick and will pay the a/c in work.

Then on the other hand instead of fooling with the big newspapers, here is another scheme. You might go to Curtis Brown, Sunday Editor of the *Press* and say how-how from me. Then tell him this *in the strictest confidence,* that a lady named Imogene Carter whose work he has been using from time to time is also named Stephen Crane and that I did 'em in about twenty minutes on each Sunday, just dictating to a friend.[5] Of course they are rotten bad. But by your explanation he will understand something of the manner of the articles I mean to write only of course they will be done better. Ask him if he wants them, signed and much better in style, and how much he will give. Then if he says all right you might turn up a little syndicate for every Sunday. You can figure out that I should get about £10 per week out of it. Then—you do the business—I do the writing—I take 65 per cent and you take 35. The typewriting expenses in New York we share alike. You do a lot of correspondence, that's all—and keep your eyes peeled for new combinations.

Write me at once. Good luck to you.

Yours very truly
Stephen Crane

---

[1] "The Scotch Express" was published in *McClure's Magazine,* 12 (January 1899), 273-83, and simultaneously in England in *Cassell's Magazine,* n.s. 18 (January 1899), 163-71.

[2] *The Open Boat and Other Tales of Adventure* (1898).

[3] According to Beer, p. 164, Richard Watson Gilder returned "The Monster" to Reynolds with the comment that *The Century* "couldn't publish that thing with half the expectant mothers in America on our subscription list." *McClure's* might also have considered the novelette with its shock effects and grim social realism overly strong for

its family readership. "The Monster," the first of Crane's stories set in Whilomville, appeared in *Harper's Magazine,* 97 (August 1898), 343-76. "The Bride Comes to Yellow Sky" was published in *McClure's Magazine,* 10 (February 1898), 377-84, and in the same month in the English *Chapman's Magazine,* 9 (February 1898), 115-26.

[4] "Queenstown" appeared in the *New York Journal,* 18 October 1897, p. 6. The *Journal* might have been sent more in the series of "Irish Notes" but did not print them. They also declined the "London Impressions," which were not published in the United States in Crane's lifetime. The *Philistine* reprinted two of the "Irish Notes," "An Old Man Goes Wooing" (July 1899) and "A Fishing Village" (August 1899).

[5] This refers only to the unsigned series of "European Letters" published in part by the *New York Press* between 15 August and 10 October 1897. Despite the predominantly feminine subject matter of these articles and the fact that the manuscripts preserved in NNC are largely in Cora's hand, internal evidence suggests that Crane dictated the "Letters" at times and that they should be considered a collaborative effort. The dispatches from Greece to the *New York Journal* under Cora's pen name of Imogene Carter also reveal characteristics of Crane's style, indicating his participation either through dictation or revision.

334a. TO JOHN PHILLIPS

ALS on Ravensbrook stationery, Collection of Stanley and Mary Wertheim, New York City.

[October 1897]

My dear John: I am in hopes to see the railroad article[1] off early next week. What on earth have you done with *The Monster?* I have written to Reynolds to go to you and get the story.[2] He will offer you this arrangement—that he sells the story and pays the money to you on my a/c—minus his 10% of course. For heaven's sake give the story a chance.

I hope you liked The Bride Comes to Yellow Sky but I could see a slight resemblance to some of your other mistakes if you didnt. I have delivered to you over 25000 words against my debt but I dont see myself any better off than if I had asked you to wait until I got damned good and ready to pay. I have worried poor little Robert[3] for money until he wails and screams like a mandrake when I mention it. Now please tell me where I am at. What has happened? Did I write a story called *The Monster*? Did I deliver it to you? And what happened after that?

My American affairs are all to be now in the hands of Reynolds.

Yours faithfully
Stephen Crane.

[1] "The Scotch Express."
[2] See No. 334.
[3] Robert McClure, who was in charge of the McClure Syndicate's London office.

335. TO PAUL REVERE REYNOLDS
ALS on Ravensbrook stationery, NSyU.

Nov 3d [1897]

My dear Reynolds: I am sending you a fifteen hundred word essay on Harold Frederic and his work. The Cosmopolitan begins his new novel in January[1] and I have written this at his request with a definite view of it's going into their December number. However it has not been mentioned to them. Please see them at once. The price is not a particular point this time. I enclose photograph.[2] If Walker[3] will not take it place it where you can.

Yours truly
Stephen Crane

[1] *Gloria Mundi* was serialized in the *Cosmopolitan* from January through November 1898.
[2] The *Cosmopolitan* declined Crane's appreciation of Frederic. It appeared in the *Chap-Book*, 8 (15 March 1898), 358-59, with the photograph of Frederic that Crane had enclosed.
[3] John Brisben Walker, editor and publisher of the *Cosmopolitan*, 1889-1905.

336. TO LOUIS SENGER
ALS, NSyU.

[Ravensbrook] Nov 8. [1897]

My dear Louis: These marital gymnastics on the part of Linson must be hair-raising. Call him off. The halo cant be used as a rim for the domestic stove-lid. Carry him out. It is too much.

Can not you send me a proof of the Scribner's tale? I can have so many people here read it and all that. I congratulate you frankly, completely. It is a pretty sure sign. Blaze away. I heard from Lorrie[1] recently. He is wading around knee-deep in the belief that I am in New York

Your friend S. C.
c/o W. Heineman
21 Bedford St: W. C.
London

[1] Frederic M. Lawrence.

337. FROM JOSEPH CONRAD[1]
Inscribed in a copy of *Almayer's Folly*,[2] NNC.

To Stephen Crane
with the greatest regard
and most sincere ad-
miration from
Jph. Conrad.

9th Nov. 1897.

[1] Crane and Conrad met in October 1897 at a luncheon given by Sidney Pawling, editor and partner in the firm of William Heinemann, their mutual publisher.

[2] Only the flyleaf and half-title have survived. Cora wrote on the flyleaf, "This book belongs to/ Mrs Stephen Crane/ 6, Milborne Grove/ The Boltons/ South Kensington./ 1898." After Crane died, she lived at this address with her friend Mrs. Brotherton from September 1900 to near the end of April 1901, when she returned to the United States.

338. TO JOSEPH CONRAD
ALS on Ravensbrook stationery, NhD.

Nov 11 [1897]

My dear Conrad: My first feat has been to lose your note and so I am obliged to send this through Heineman. I have read the proof sheets which you so kindly sent me and the book is simply great.[1] The simple treatment of the death of Waite[2] is too good, too terrible. I wanted to forget it at once. It caught me very hard. I felt ill over that red thread lining from the corner of the man's mouth to his chin. It was frightful with the weight of a real and present death. By such small means does the real writer suddenly flash out in the sky above those who are always doing rather well. In the meantime I have written to Bacheller and told him to be valiant in the matter of "The Nigger"—I have also written some other little notes to America.[3]

I am afraid you must write to me soon so that I can finally nail your address and put it away in my little book. I was very stupid. Are you quite sure you could not come down for a Sunday luncheon with Mrs Conrad? Say your own date, barring this next one. We could then keep you as long as you would stay.

Did not we have a good pow-wow in London?

Faithfully yours
Stephen Crane

---

[1] *The Nigger of the "Narcissus,"* which ran serially in the *New Review* from August through December 1897. Publication of the English trade edition in December brought renewed charges from reviewers that Conrad had been influenced by the central dramatic conflict of *The Red Badge of Courage.* Crane attempted to deflect potential damage to his friendship with Conrad, who very much resented these aspersions, by praising *The Nigger of the "Narcissus"* in print as "unquestionably the best story of the sea written by a man now alive, and as a matter of fact, one would have to make an extensive search among the tombs before he who has done better could be found" ("Concerning the English 'Academy,'" *Bookman,* 7 [March 1898], 2).

[2] James Wait.

[3] Irving Bacheller secured American copyright under the title *The Nigger of the "Narcissus"* in 1897; but when the book was published by Dodd Mead and Company in America, before the English edition, it was entitled *The Children of the Sea,* in deference, according to Conrad, "to American prejudices."

339. TO HENRY D. DAVRAY[1]
ALS on Ravensbrook stationery, ViU.

England Nov 11. [1897]

M. Henry D. Davray

Dear sir: I am today taking the liberty of sending you a copy of a little book of mine—The Black Riders—in hopes that some happy accident will persuade you to read it. My importunity is not without it's darker side. My dearest wish is to see these simples translanted into French.[2] Some of my other books have recieved German and Russian translations but, let alone translations, the British public nor even my own American public will not look at The Black Riders. Thus my letter to you is in the nature of an appeal. I wish the distinction of appearing just for a moment to the minds of a few of your great and wise artistic public. I do not know if this will appear absurd to you. At any rate, I send you the book. You will tell me? Perchance, there would be a publisher who would print it. What I wish is the distinction. My American publishers, who own the copyrights, would readily agree. I hope I do not bore you too much? If you reply to this letter I shall be delighted.

Faithfully yours
Stephen Crane

[1] Book reviewer for the *Mercure de France*.
[2] Davray reviewed *The Black Riders* in the *Mercure de France*, 25 (January 1898), 330. There is no record of a French translation of the book, but Davray translated *The Red Badge of Courage* (with Francis Vielé-Griffin) under the title *La conquête du courage* (Paris: Mercure de France, 1911).

340. TO HENRY D. DAVRAY
Inscribed in *The Black Riders and Other Lines,* ViU.

To M. Henry D. Davray
From the author
Stephen Crane

London
England, Nov 11, 1897

341. FROM JOSEPH CONRAD
ALS, NNC.

16th Nov. 1897.
Stanford-le-Hope
Essex.

My dear Crane,

I must write to you before I write a single word for a living to-day. I was anxious to know what you would think of the end. If I've hit *you* with the death of Jimmy[1] I don't care if I don't hit another man. I think however that artistically the end of the book is somewhat lame. I mean after the death. All that rigmarolle about the burial and the ship's coming home seems to run away into a rat's tail—thin at the end. Well! It's too late now to bite my thumbs and tear my hair. When I feel depressed about it I say to myself "Crane likes the damned thing"— and am greatly consoled. What your appreciation is to me I renounce to explain. The world looks different to me now, since our long powwow. It was good. The memory of it is good. And now and then (human nature *is* a vile thing) I ask myself whether you meant half of what you said! You must forgive me. The mistrust is not of you—it is of myself: the drop of poison in the cup of life. I am no more vile than my neighbours but this disbelief in oneself is like a taint that spreads on everything one comes in contact with; on men—on things—on the very air one breathes. That's why one sometimes wishes to be a stone breaker.

There's no doubt about breaking a stone. But there's doubt, fear—a black horror, in every page one writes. You at any rate will understand and therefore I write to you as though we had been born together before the beginning of things. For what you have done and intend to do I won't even attempt to thank you. I certainly don't know what to say, tho' I am perfectly certain as to what I feel.[2]

I know it is perfectly right and proper from a ceremonial point of view that I should come to you first. But, my dear fellow, it's impossible. My wife is not presentable just now.[3] And, joking apart, I wouldn't dare let her undertake a journey—even of the shortest. As to myself I would come speedily and I shall come as soon as I can get away with a free mind. Meantime show your condescension by coming to me first. After this week I haven't any engagements. Just drop a postcard saying *I'm coming* and I shall meet the train. From Fenchurch Street you have trains at *11.20* am *1.45* pm *3.28* pm *5.5* pm *5.53* pm *8.13* pm.

Last train to town at night is at *8* arrives in London at 9.30. But we can put you up in a bachelor's quarters I should love to have you under my roof. And come soon for when the circus begins here and then the house is full of doctors and nurses there will be no peace for the poor literary man. Finish to catch the post.

Ever Yours
Jph. Conrad.

---

[1] James Wait in *The Nigger of the "Narcissus."*
[2] Conrad's appreciation is for the praise and encouragement Crane had given him on the afternoon and evening of the day in October when they first met and tramped the streets of London together discussing their literary enthusiasms.
[3] Jessie Conrad was pregnant with her first son, Borys, born 15 January 1898.

342. TO EDWARD GARNETT[1]
ALS on Ravensbrook stationery, CtY.

Nov 16 [1897]

Dear Mr Garnett: I am sorry that I could not get over to you on Tuesday[2] and sorry too that I have let so much time pass without saying so. Will you come over for luncheon at two on Sunday?

Faithfully yours
Stephen Crane

---

[1]Garnett first introduced Crane to Ford Madox Ford (then Ford Madox Hueffer). Garnett's essay, "Mr. Stephen Crane: An Appreciation," *Academy*, 55 (17 December 1898), 483-84, was one of the most perceptive critical studies of Crane in the decade but perpetuated two persistent fallacies: that he is little more than an "interpreter of the surfaces of life" and that "his work is a mass of fragments," lacking in complexity of structure.

[2]16 November was a Tuesday. Crane is referring to an engagement with Garnett he failed to keep on 9 November.

343. FROM HAMLIN GARLAND
ALS, NNC.

23 Grammercy Park
Nov. 29/97.

Dear Mr. Crane:

I was very glad to hear from you and from Mr Conrad. I wish you had written another page to tell me how you were getting on and what you intended to do. I heard you were to make your home in England but this I take to be somebody's lie. I shall not believe it till you write and tell me so.

Mr Conrad's work is not known to me, I am sorry to say, but I shall be all the more delighted to have a copy of the book you speak of. Beeman now has some five of my books.[1] What do you hear of him there? Is he considered a good publisher?

Dont let yourself lie fallow. I do not see much of you lately—This is good if you are working on some larger thing. With best word.

Yours sincerely
Hamlin Garland

[1] The British firm of N. Beeman published Garland's *Rose of Dutcher's Coolly* in 1896 and *Wayside Courtships* in 1898.

344. FROM JOSEPH CONRAD
ALS, NNC.

Stanford-le-Hope, 1st Dec 1897

My Dear Crane

Glad to hear you haven't had your head taken off. We had here on Monday a high tide that smashed the sea-wall flooded the marshes and washed away the Rwy line. Great excitement.

But *my* great excitement was reading your stories. Garnett is right. "A Man and Some Others"[1] is immense. I can't spin a long yarn about it but I admire it without reserve. It is an amazing bit of biography. I am envious of you—horribly. Confound you—you fill the blamed landscape—you—by all the devils—fill the sea-scape. The boat thing[2] is immensely interesting. I don't use the word in its common sense. It is fundamentally interesting to me. Your temperament makes old things new and new things amazing. I want to swear at you, to bless you—perhaps to shoot you—but I prefer to be your friend.

You are an everlasting surprise to one. You shock—and the next moment you give the perfect artistic satisfaction. Your method is fascinating. You are a complete impressionist.[3] The illusions of life come out of your hand without a flaw. It is not life—which nobody wants—it is art—art for which everyone—the abject and the great hanker—mostly without knowing it.

Ever yours
Jph Conrad.

¹In the *Century,* 53 (February 1897), 601-7.

²"The Open Boat," *Scribner's Magazine,* 21 (June 1897), 728-40.

³In a December 1897 letter to Edward Garnett, Conrad commented that Crane's thought was "concise, connected, never very deep—yet often startling. He is *the only* impressionist and *only* an impressionist." This may have suggested to Garnett the judgment in his 1898 *Academy* article that Crane's work lacked depth. But in a later essay Conrad conceded that "His impression of phrase went really deeper than the surface. In his writing he was very sure of his effects" ("Stephen Crane: A Note Without Dates," *London Mercury,* 1 [December 1919], 192).

345. CORA CRANE TO SYLVESTER SCOVEL
TT, MnU.

Ravensbrook
Dec. 18th 97.

Dear Harry: Stephen wishes me to write you acknowledging the receipt of your letter of the 28th Nov. and to tell you he will take great pleasure in doing his best to have your letter printed. It is most difficult to have this sort of thing done in England but he will do his best for his old pal.

We are so pleased that there is a chance of your coming with your wife to England next Summer. Do try to manage it and use Ravensbrook as your headquarters. You would not know the place. We have ever so many more chairs and tables than when you were here. We are going in for old oak which we get from out of the way farm houses. Really we are very comfortable now and oh so happy.

Stephen is fat, for him, and works hard. He is so content and good quite the old married man. We have three dogs, one dog who sort of took Velestino's place, just dog—a mongrel fox terrier and a thoroughbred Russian Poodle which Harold Frederic has just given us. We go a little into society though seldom to London.

Do try to find time to write us of your life and plans. You know how much we are interested and how much Stephen thinks of you. With best wishes from us both for the New Year to give Mr & Mrs Scovell

Sincerely
Cora

Stephen says d— you write to him often.

346. TO PAUL REVERE REYNOLDS
ALS on RavensbrooK stationery, NSyU.

Dec 20 [1897]

Dear Reynolds: I enclose you a short newspaper article on the recent prize-giving by the London *Academy*.[1] Let me know if The Press is taking these articles.

The Harpers terms I perfectly understand and agree to them. I will send over soon, proofs of a lot of stuff of mine which is to appear in the English edition of The Open Boat, but not in the American edition. These stories added to the Monster would make about 40000 or 45000 words. If Harpers does not like this plan, it would be necessary to wait until I had finished more stories. I will soon forward my plan of the book as it could be made from existing stores unpublished and published.[2] Heineman by the way promptly and politely released me from an agreement which would have prevented us from selling the international book-rights to Harper's.

Death and The Child is *not* being sold in England. I am holding it in order to give you a chance with the big fellows. I shall hold it until I hear from you. The Five White Mice however is on the market here.[3]

Now comes the question of the big book. I am writing now a novel which is to be at least 75000 words.[4] It is only started now (12000 words) but it will be finished in April or May and as soon as The Open Boat volume comes out and makes its little hit as I am sure it will, I want you to drop some news of the novel here and there. Perhaps by that time I will be able to send you a third of it and at any rate I will send you a synopsis. We should make a big serial amount and a round sum in advance.

Of course I am awfully hard up. You know of course of my Appleton royalties being attached.[5] They knocked me silly.

The Blue Hotel will come to you in about two weeks. It may be 10000 words.

Why McClure is monkeying around about The Monster I dont quite understand. It might make me come a cropper[6] if I dont get that money directly.

I received the £39.?.?. It came in very handily. Where did you pinch it?

Let me hear from you often and please dont forget to acknowledge the arrival of everything I send you.

Very truly yours
Stephen Crane

---

[1] "Concerning the English 'Academy,'" *Bookman,* 7 (March 1898), 22-24.

[2] The English edition of *The Open Boat* contains nine "Midnight Sketches" not included in the American edition. *The Monster and Other Stories* was published posthumously in England by Harper and Brothers early in 1901 and contained the first book appearance of "Twelve O'Clock," "Moonlight on the Snow," "Manacled," and "An Illusion in Red and White." Crane evidently did not understand that international agreements extended to both periodical and book publication and that he could not publish in Harper's American edition of *The Monster* stories that would appear previously in Heinemann's edition of *The Open Boat*.

[3] Reynolds probably reminded Crane that he had exclusive agency rights, and Crane agreed to give him the opportunity to market "Death and the Child" with one of the important American publisher's magazines, which he did. Nevertheless, the first publication of this story was in an independent English magazine, *Black and White,* 15 (5 March 1898), 332-34; (12 March 1898), 368-70, under the title "The Death and the Child." "The Five White Mice" did not appear in an English periodical but was first printed in a severely cut version in the *New York World,* 10 April 1898, p. 32, of the Sunday Supplement.

[4] *Active Service*.

[5] Amy Leslie obtained a warrant of attachment against Crane for $550 from the Supreme Court of the State of New York on 3 January 1898, but Crane's royalties at Appleton were evidently frozen before this.

[6] Crane felt obligated to send "The Monster" to McClure because he was financially indebted to him, but, as with *The Red Badge of Courage,* McClure delayed decision on the controversial novelette. Presumably, he finally decided to reject it. "Come a cropper" is a slang term referring to a fall from a horse, hence failure in an undertaking.

347. FROM JOSEPH CONRAD
ALS, NNC.

Stanford-le-Hope 24th Dec. 1897.

My Dear Crane.

Just a word to wish—from us both—to you and Mrs Crane all imaginable prosperity and all the happiness that may be found in this merry world.

How are you getting on? I struggle along feeling pretty sick of it all. The New Year does not announce itself very brightly for me—and that's a fact. Well! A bad beginning may make a good ending tho' I don't believe in it much.

Criticisms (!) are coming in. Some praise, some blame, both very stupid.

Yours ever
Jph. Conrad

t.o.p.

ps Have you seen the Daily Tele: Article by that ass Courtney?[1] He does not understand you—and he does not understand me either. That's a feather in our caps anyhow. It is the most *mean-minded* criticism I've read in my life. Do you think I tried to imitate you? No Sir! I may be a little fool but I know better than to try to imitate the inimitable But here it is. Courtney says it: You are a lost sinner and you have lead me astray. If it was true I would be well content to follow you but it isn't true and the perfidious ass tried to damage us both. Three cheers for the Press!

Your
J. C.

[1] W. L. Courtney's review of *The Nigger of the "Narcissus"* in the *Daily Telegraph*, 8 December 1897, p. 4, maintained that Conrad had imitated structural and stylistic techniques of *The Red Badge* in his novel. Subsequent critics have found similarities of characterization and theme between *Lord Jim* (1900) and *The Red Badge*. Nina Galen, in

"Stephen Crane as a Source for Conrad's Jim," *Nineteenth-Century Fiction,* 38 (June 1983), 78-96, suggests intriguingly that Crane himself was the source for the protagonist of Conrad's piece.

348. TO EGAN NEW, ESQ.
ALS on Ravensbrook stationery, ViU.

Dec 27 [1897]

Dear sir: In response to your letter of Dec 22d, I would be glad say that I have new book of nine collected story coming out probably in March. The title story will be The Open Boat. They are all tales of adventure five of them being Mexican and Rio Grande border sketches.[1] We rather expect it to be my most successful book since The Red Badge.

Faithfully Yours
Stephen Crane

Egan New, Esq.

[1] Under "Minor Conflicts" in the English edition of *The Open Boat,* the Western and Mexican stories are "A Man and Some Others," "The Bride Comes to Yellow Sky," "The Wise Men," "The Five White Mice," and "Horses."

349. TO PAUL REVERE REYNOLDS
Allen, p. 55.

[Ravensbrook, December 1897]

Dear Reynolds:

I send you the child story of the Greek business. McClure has a call on it. He should give $300 for it—at least.[1] The English rights are sold.

I have made a proposition to McClure that he advance £200 on the 1st of January for the book rights of my new Greek novel—not yet

347. FROM JOSEPH CONRAD
ALS, NNC.

Stanford-le-Hope 24th Dec. 1897.

My Dear Crane.

Just a word to wish—from us both—to you and Mrs Crane all imaginable prosperity and all the happiness that may be found in this merry world.

How are you getting on? I struggle along feeling pretty sick of it all. The New Year does not announce itself very brightly for me—and that's a fact. Well! A bad beginning may make a good ending tho' I don't believe in it much.

Criticisms (!) are coming in. Some praise, some blame, both very stupid.

Yours ever
Jph. Conrad

t.o.p.

ps Have you seen the Daily Tele: Article by that ass Courtney?[1] He does not understand you—and he does not understand me either. That's a feather in our caps anyhow. It is the most *mean-minded* criticism I've read in my life. Do you think I tried to imitate you? No Sir! I may be a little fool but I know better than to try to imitate the inimitable But here it is. Courtney says it: You are a lost sinner and you have lead me astray. If it was true I would be well content to follow you but it isn't true and the perfidious ass tried to damage us both. Three cheers for the Press!

Your
J. C.

[1] W. L. Courtney's review of *The Nigger of the "Narcissus"* in the *Daily Telegraph*, 8 December 1897, p. 4, maintained that Conrad had imitated structural and stylistic techniques of *The Red Badge* in his novel. Subsequent critics have found similarities of characterization and theme between *Lord Jim* (1900) and *The Red Badge*. Nina Galen, in

"Stephen Crane as a Source for Conrad's Jim," *Nineteenth-Century Fiction,* 38 (June 1983), 78-96, suggests intriguingly that Crane himself was the source for the protagonist of Conrad's piece.

348. TO EGAN NEW, ESQ.
ALS on Ravensbrook stationery, ViU.

Dec 27 [1897]

Dear sir: In response to your letter of Dec 22d, I would be glad say that I have new book of nine collected story coming out probably in March. The title story will be The Open Boat. They are all tales of adventure five of them being Mexican and Rio Grande border sketches.[1] We rather expect it to be my most successful book since The Red Badge.

Faithfully Yours
Stephen Crane

Egan New, Esq.

[1] Under "Minor Conflicts" in the English edition of *The Open Boat,* the Western and Mexican stories are "A Man and Some Others," "The Bride Comes to Yellow Sky," "The Wise Men," "The Five White Mice," and "Horses."

349. TO PAUL REVERE REYNOLDS
Allen, p. 55.

[Ravensbrook, December 1897]

Dear Reynolds:

I send you the child story of the Greek business. McClure has a call on it. He should give $300 for it—at least.[1] The English rights are sold.

I have made a proposition to McClure that he advance £200 on the 1st of January for the book rights of my new Greek novel—not yet begun.[2] If he takes that offer he may want to hold back on payment for this story. I wouldn't have done it if I was not broke. For heaven's sake raise me all the money you can and *cable* it, *cable* it sure between Xmas and New Year's. Sell "The Monster"![3] Don't forget that—cable me some money this month.

S. C.

[1]"Death and the Child" was not accepted by *McClure's Magazine*. Its first American publication was in *Harper's Weekly*, 42 (19 March 1898), 281-82; (26 March 1898), 297-98.
[2]*Active Service* (1899). Frederick A. Stokes Company rather than McClure published the American edition.
[3]*Harper's Magazine*, 97 (August 1898), 343-76.

350. TO LOUIS SENGER

Inscribed in a copy of a German edition of *Maggie*[1] (Leipzig: Georg H. Wigand's Verlag, 1897), NSyU.

[1897]

Dear Louis:
Have this from
S. C.

[1]Two editions of Dora Landé's translation, *Maggie: das Strassenkind* (published by G. H. Wigand and E. Fiedler), appeared in 1897, the subtitle based upon the English *Maggie: A Child of the Streets*. This was the only work of Crane translated into German during his lifetime.

351. TO ELBERT HUBBARD
ALS written at the foot of AMsFr of "A little ink more or less!" NSyU.

[late 1897?]

Oh, Hubbard, mark this well. Mark it well! If it is overbalancing your discretion, inform me.

S. C.

352. TO JOHN NORTHERN HILLIARD[1]
Quoted in the *New York Times,* supplement, 14 July 1900, p. 467.

[1897?]

I have only one pride—and may it be forgiven me. This single pride is that the English edition of "The Red Badge" has been received with praise by the English reviewers. Mr. George Wyndham, Under Secretary for War in the British Government, says, in an essay, that the book challenges comparison with the most vivid scenes of Tolstoi's "War and Peace" or of Zola's "Downfall";[2] and the big reviews here praise it for just what I intended it to be, a psychological portrayal of fear. They all insist that I am a veteran of the civil war, whereas the fact is, as you know, I never smelled even the powder of a sham battle. I know what the psychologists say, that a fellow can't comprehend a condition that he has never experienced, and I argued that many times with the Professor. Of course, I have never been in a battle, but I believe that I got my sense of the rage of conflict on the football field, or else fighting is a hereditary instinct, and I wrote intuitively; for the Cranes were a family of fighters in the old days, and in the Revolution every member did his duty. But be that as it may, I endeavored to express myself in the simplest and most concise way. If I failed, the fault is not mine. I have been very careful not to let any theories or pet ideas of my own creep into my work. Preaching is fatal to art in literature. I try to give to readers a slice out of life; and if there is any moral or lesson in it, I do not try to point it out. I let the reader find it for himself. The result is more satisfactory to both the reader and myself. As Emerson said, "There should be a long logic beneath the story, but it should be kept carefully out of sight." Before "The Red Badge of Courage" was published, I found it difficult to make both ends meet. The book was written during this period. It was an effort born of pain, and I believe that it was beneficial to it as a piece of literature. It seems a pity that this should be so—that art should be a child of suffering; and yet such seems to be the case. Of course there are fine writers who have good incomes and live comfortably and contentedly; but if the conditions of their lives were harder, I believe that their work would be better. Bret Harte is an example. He has not done any work in recent years to compare with those early California sketches. Personally, I like my little book of poems, "The Black Riders," better than I do "The Red Badge of Courage." The reason is, I suppose, that the former is the more ambitious effort. In it I aim to give my ideas of life as a whole, so far as I know it, and the latter is a mere episode, or rather an amplification. Now that I have reached the goal, I suppose that I ought to be contented; but I am not. I was happier in the old days when I was always dreaming of the thing I have now attained. I am disappointed with success, and I am tired of abuse. Over here, happily, they don't treat you as if you were a dog, but give every one an honest measure of praise or blame. There are no disgusting personalities.

[1] This letter to Hilliard illustrates Crane's tendency to repeat or paraphrase statements about his ancestral and literary antecedents and artistic credos in letters to reviewers and editors who requested such information.

[2] In the January 1896 issue of Heinemann's magazine, *The New Review*. Wyndham's essay was solicited by the editor, William Ernest Henley.

353. TO "FRANK"
ALS on Ravensbrook stationery, InU.

[1897-1898]

My dear Frank: Please ask the *Journal* if they owe me anything for the Portsmouth fluke.[1] Explain your advance and ask them, please, if there is any more up their sleeves. Au revoir,

Your uncle[2]
Stephen

[1] Crane had probably submitted an article to the *New York Journal*, which they never published, about the construction of dry docks at Portsmouth in 1896 or the mooring of ships in them in 1897.

[2] A playful allusion. Crane had no nephew named Frank.

1898

354. FROM JOSEPH CONRAD
ALS, NNC.

[Stanford-le-Hope, Essex] Wednesday [12? January 1898]

My dear Crane

I hope you haven't been angry with me. Fact is my dear fellow I've been having a hell of a time—what with one thing and another. Had I come that day I would have been no good at all. I am hardly yet in a decent frame of mind.[1]

I am very curious to know your idea; but I feel somehow that collaborating with you would be either cheating or deceiving you. In any case disappointing you. I have no dramatic gift.[2] *You* have the terseness, the clear eye the easy imagination. You have all—and I have only the accursed faculty of dreaming. My ideas fade—yours come out sharp cut as cameos—they come all living out of your brain and bring images—and bring light. Mine bring only mist in which they are born, and die. I would be only a hindrance to you—I am afraid. And it seems presumptuous of me to think of helping you. You want no help. I have a perfect confidence in your power—and why should you share with me what there may be of profit and fame in the accomplished task?

But I want to know! Your idea is good—I am certain. Perhaps you, yourself, don't know how good it is. I ask you as a friend's favour to let me have a sketch of it when you have the time and in a moment of inclination. I shall—if you allow me—write you *all* I think of it, about it, around it. Then you shall see how worthless I would be to you. But if by any chance such was not your deliberate opinion—if you should really, honestly, artistically think I could be of some use—then my dear Crane I would be only too glad to work by your side and with your lead. And Quien sabe? Something perhaps would get itself shaped to be mangled by the scorn or the praise of the Philistines.

Take your time and answer me. My wife sends kind regards. We are standing by for a regular bust-up. It may come any day. I can't write. The Dly Mail has given a bad notice to the *Nigger.* There is no other news here.

Yours ever
Jph. Conrad.

This letter has been held back and now since I can't come I send it. My sister in law must go away tomorrow,³ and I can't leave my wife all alone here.

Do write your idea. I am anxious

Yours
J. C.

¹Jessie Conrad was at term. Her first son, Borys, was born on 15 January. This event precipitated or coincided with one of Conrad's frequent bouts of depression. To Edward Garnett he wrote, "I hate babies."

²Crane attempted unsuccessfully to induce Conrad to collaborate with him on a play set in the American West to be entitled "The Predecessor." The central situation, as Conrad recalls in his Introduction to Beer, pp. 29-30, involved "a man personating his 'predecessor' (who had died) in the hope of winning a girl's heart. The scenes were to include a ranch at the foot of the Rocky Mountains, I remember, and the action I fear would have been frankly melodramatic." See No. 377, n. 2.

³Jessie Conrad's sixteen-year-old sister, Dora ("Dolly").

355. TO PAUL REVERE REYNOLDS
Allen, pp. 55-56.

[Ravensbrook] Jan. 14 [1898]

Dear Reynolds:

I enclose you a thousand words on the Alfridi business.[1] It might go to the *Press* and be syndicated, or else to the *Journal*.

I received your letter yesterday and promptly cabled you that McClure was not concerned in the matter. When I sent him "The Monster" I owed him a lot of money but when I paid him up, I went to see Robert McClure here and he agreed that "The Monster" was released.[2] He said he would inform the N.Y. office to that effect or even write the same to you, if I liked. I said I did like but it seems the affair was bungled. McClure's claim on the story was one which I gave him through courtesy and honor—no other. Your final manipulation of the novelette I consider very brilliant and I am sorry to see it handicapped by that Scotch ass.

In all the months I have been in England I have never received a cent from America which has not been borrowed. Just read that over twice! The consequences of this have lately been that I have been obliged to make arrangements here with English agents of American houses but in all cases your commission will be protected. This is the best I could do. My English expenses have chased me to the wall. Even now I am waiting for you to cable me my share of the Monster money and if there is a fluke I am lost.

Don't kick so conspicuously about the over-charge on the damned manuscripts.[3] If I was a business man, I would not need a business man to conduct my affairs for me. I will try to do better but if I shouldn't, don't harangue me. The point is of minor importance.

I have withheld the "Death and the Child" story from an English sale because I think you can hit one of the three big fellows with it. "The Five White Mice" is sold in England.[4]

Faithfully yours,
Stephen Crane

[1]In October 1897 the British renewed their campaign against the Afridis of the Northwest Frontier Province of India (now Pakistan) in an effort to keep the Khyber

Pass open. The article Crane sent to Reynolds has not been located, but an earlier humorous piece in the *New York Press*, unsigned, may have been written by Crane. See No. 332, n. 4.

²Robert McClure, the publisher's younger brother, managed the McClure Syndicate's office in London. On 20 December 1897 Crane had agreed to an offer of $450 from Harper's for serial rights to "The Monster" and $250 as an advance toward book publication of the novelette and additional stories Crane was to provide. McClure had decided not to publish "The Monster," but he retained it and other Crane manuscripts as security against a loan of five or six hundred dollars he had made to Crane before he sailed for Greece on 20 March 1897.

³For typewriting. Crane was having his manuscripts typed in London, sending one copy to Reynolds, and billing him for half the expense.

⁴See No. 346, n. 3. "Death and the Child" and "The Five White Mice" were collected in both the American and English editions of *The Open Boat* (1898).

356. FROM JOSEPH CONRAD
ALS, NNC.

Stanford le Hope Essex, 16th Jan 98.

My Dear Crane

Dont you bother about writing unless you feel like it. I quite understand how you feel about it—and am not likely to forget you because you don't write. Still mind that when you do write you give me a very great pleasure.

A male infant arrived yesterday and made a devil of a row. He yelled like an Apache and ever since this morning has been on the war path again. It's a ghastly nuisance.

Look here—when you are coming to town next time just fling a sixpence away on a wire (the day before) to me and I shall try to run up too. If detained shall wire care Heinemann.

Ever yours
Jph. Conrad.

Say—what about *The Monster*. The damned story has been haunting me ever since. I think it must be fine. It's a subject for you.[1]

[1] Crane must have outlined "The Monster" to Conrad after several of his friends expressed reservations about the novelette and Frederic had advised him to discard it altogether. Conrad was more perceptive.

357. TO JOHN PHILLIPS
ALS on Ravensbrook stationery, ViU.

Jan. 21 [1898]

My dear John: I am very anxious to get the originals of the illustrations to The Bride Comes to Yellow Sky.[1] Can you arrange it for me? I am of course willing to pay for them. Will you buy them, send them to me here and charge it all to my a/c? Also will you ask Taber if it is possible to buy his illustrations to The Little Regiment?[2] That's a good boy.

Faithfully yours
S. C.

[1] "The Bride Comes to Yellow Sky," *McClure's Magazine*, 10 (February 1898), 377-84, was illustrated by E. L. Blumenschein.

[2] Isaac W. Taber drew three impressionistic sketches for "The Little Regiment," *McClure's Magazine*, 7 (June 1896), 12-22. Taber illustrated the first edition of Rudyard Kipling's *Captains Courageous* (London: Macmillan, 1897).

358. JOSEPH CONRAD TO CORA CRANE
ALS, NNC.

25 Jan 1898
Stanford-le-Hope
Essex

Dear Mrs. Crane.

My wife shall write as soon as she is allowed to sit up. Meantime let me send you our warmest thanks for the beautiful flowers and for your very kind invitation.

I would hesitate to inflict myself upon you with the tribe—but since you call your fate upon your own head the temptation to please ourselves is too irresistible. So, all being well, we shall descend upon your peaceful homestead on the 19th. I have grounds for hope that by that date my wife shall be able to travel. We shall meantime devote all our energies to the taming of the baby lest he should break out and devastate your countryside, which, I feel, would put you and Crane in a false position vis-a-vis your neighbours. Perhaps a strong iron cage would be the most effective expedient; however we shall judge at the time the exact degree of his ferocity and act accordingly. My most earnest consideration had been also given to the matter of a good reliable keeper—which you with such kind forethought mention yourself. My wife will want some help, not being even at the best of times very athletic. Could we—instead of a nurse—whom we have not—bring Dolly, whom we have. Dolly is a young person with her hair down her back, and of extreme docility. I have the distinction of being her brother-in-law. She is now (and for the next six months) staying with us for the sake of her health and to help my wife. Will you frankly tell me whether there is the slightest objection to this plan. As Crane perhaps told you I am cheeky but easily repressed. You must really forgive me the coolness of my imprudence.

The child is, I am sorry to say, absolutely callous to the honor awaiting him of his very first visit being to your house. I talked myself hoarse trying to explain to him the greatness of the occurrence—all in vain. I want Crane to give it his artistic benediction and call upon its head the spirit—the magnificent spirit that is his familiar—the genius of his work. And then when our writing days are over he who is a child to day may write good prose—may toss a few pearls before the Philistines. I am dear Mrs. Crane your most obedient and faithful servant.

Jph. Conrad.

359. TO ELBERT HUBBARD
ALS on Ravensbrook stationery, Collection of Stanley and Mary Wertheim, New York City.

Jan 29 [1898]

My dear Hubbard: I enclose you some lines.[1] Have you yet recieved "*The Blue Battalions*"[2] and "A man adrift on a slim spar."[3] They are wandering somewhere in America. They were to be sent to you in time. When they arrive let me know.

You sent me two copies of Volume V.[4] I have given one to Harold Frederic. The books are very great feats. Dont forget to mail me continuous Philistines.

The pome[5] enclosed is not the original ms. It is a copy by an outsider. Go on, brave man, and do well. For my part I am heavy with trouble.[6]

Yours faithfully
Stephen Crane

---

[1] "The impact of a dollar upon the heart," *Philistine*, 6 (February 1898), back wrapper, entitled "Some Things." The typed manuscript of this poem was prepared in December 1897 as printer's copy. Hubbard made changes from Crane's typescript, especially bowdlerizing "Whored by pimping merchants" to "Simpered at by pimpled merchants."

[2] "When a people reach the top of a hill," *Philistine*, 7 (June 1898), 9-10, entitled "Lines." The poem was reprinted under the title "The Blue Battalions" (the refrain concluding each of the three stanzas) in *Spanish-American War Songs: A Complete Collection of Newspaper Verse during the Recent War with Spain*, ed. Sidney A. Witherbee (Detroit: Witherbee, 1898), pp. 182-83. This poem was based upon Crane's combat experience in Greece, not in Cuba. Possibly the editor interpreted the initial line literally as referring to the ridges before Santiago.

[3] This poem did not appear in Crane's lifetime. It was first published in the *Bookman*, 69 (April 1929), 120.

⁴Of the *Philistine*.

⁵Although Crane takes second place only to F. Scott Fitzgerald as the worst speller among prominent American writers, he did not err in this instance. Hubbard often affected antiquarian usage, and "pome" was a recognized pronunciation in the seventeenth and early eighteenth centuries.

⁶As indicated in his 14 January letter to Paul Revere Reynolds, No. 355, Crane's expenses at Ravensbrook exceeded his income, and he was beginning to experience the pressures of financial indebtedness that would plague him for the remainder of his life.

360. TO PAUL REVERE REYNOLDS
ALS on Ravensbrook stationery, NSyU.

Jan 31 [1898]

Dear Reynolds: Enclosed is a small sketch which may do for the newspapers. Please send me copies of any articles used.

I am awaiting your letter in regard to the Death and The Child. I expect it on Wednesday steamer.

It turned out that I only owed McClure $71.09 and of course he copped that out of the $200.[1] And at the same time, he has already 53000 words for a book—at least he has as soon as he gets a copy of Death and the Child.[2]

I expect to mail you a story of 10000 words on Saturday. I will keep it open at all ends so that if Harpers want it. They can afterwards put it in the book. Of course I see my mistake about their taking some of the stories that Heineman is to use here.[3]

I am going to write about a thousand or twelve hundred more dollars in short stuff and work only on my big book.[4] In the meantime every hundred dollars is a boon! I enclose you a scheme for a syndicate. I am *sure* you can work it. I could work it from here if you were not my agent.

You have done bully!

Faithfully Yours
Stephen Crane

P.S.: No, I'll not enclose you the syndicate scheme at present. Next week.

—S. C.

[1] Advanced on *The Open Boat and Other Tales of Adventure* (1898).
[2] Despite his understanding, as indicated in the next paragraph, that *Harper's* required both serial and book rights to stories they accepted, Crane was committing "Death and the Child" to *The Open Boat* volume, while Reynolds had already sold the story to *Harper's Weekly*. Crane was free to market the story in England, where it appeared in *Black and White*, 15 (5 March 1898), 332-34; 15 (12 March 1898), 368-70, because *Harper's Weekly* did not publish simultaneously in England and America as *Harper's Monthly* did.
[3] See No. 346.
[4] *Active Service* (1899).

361. TO ROBERT BARR

ALS on Ravensbrook stationery, Altman's Rare Book and Manuscript Division, Altman's Department Store, New York City.

[January-February 1898]

My dear Robert: The Unwin thing was no good. I shall be awfully glad if you should happen to wing either Chatto and Windus or Pearsons. Let me know by wire if anything favorable happens. Of course the point is that £75 advance will be in the nature of a flyer for a publisher who otherwise might not be able to nail one of my invaluable books save at a figure which would be different in altitude.[1] I was tremendously grateful to you for your interest and assistance. I hope to God you have good luck.

Thine
S. C.

[1] Crane's sarcasm fails to conceal his anxiety over mounting debts. Royalties from his books declined appreciably after the brief vogue of *The Red Badge of Courage*, and he enlisted the help of influential friends such as Barr and Conrad to find a publisher who might market his work more successfully than Heinemann. With the exception of *Pictures of War* (1898) and *Bowery Tales* (1900), which contained no new material, *Active Service* (1899) was the last of Crane's productions to be published by Heinemann, and

while Crane was in Cuba, Cora was attempting to find another publisher for this book, as yet unfinished.

362. FROM HAROLD FREDERIC
Letterhead: "Homefield,/ Kenley,/ Surrey." ALS, NNC.

Thursday night. [January-February 1898]

My Dear Boy:

I ran across a little book on Naval names[1] yesterday which impressed me at once as having been made expressly for you—and it leaves by this same post for Ravensbrook.

The scheme of moving the family to Dunmanus Bay in March or the earliest April has reached the point where I have the house. It is a mansion on the sea itself—two boats (one with a lug sail) &c., &c. Seven bed-rooms, bath, hot & cold water, &c. We think of it solely with reference to your sharing it with us.[2] The expenses will be very light. I am going to finish my book there![3] We can work as well as loaf.

Always yours
Harold F.

[1] Louis, Prince of Battenberg, *Men-of-War Names* (London: Stanford, 1897).
[2] A wealthy admirer of Frederic had lent him a mansion at Dunmanus Bay in Ireland. Frederic kindly offered to share the house with the Cranes to relieve their financial plight. On 5 February, however, Frederic and Cora quarreled about the joint household arrangement, and Frederic eventually realized that his well-intentioned scheme was impractical. See No. 366.
[3] *The Market-Place* (1899).

363. FROM JOSEPH CONRAD
ALS, NNC.

5th Febr. 98.
Stanford-le-Hope.

Dear Stephen.

We got home last night. Ever since I've left you I am wondering how you have passed through your crisis. I would like to hear all is well; it hurts me to think you are worried. It is bad for you and it is bad for your art. All the time I was at the Garnetts we have been talking of you. we conclude you must be kept quiet; but who is going to work that miracle?

We trust in Mrs. Crane and in the sagacity of publishers. That last is not much to trust to—I admit. Still! . . .

I've had letters of thanks from Pearson and Blackwood for inducing you to call on them. The Pearson man writes he hopes they shall be able very soon to do something quite satisfactory to Mr. Crane "if he gives us an opportunity." The Blackwood man sends an invite to lunch for the week after next to you and me if you will condescend to accept that invitation through me. It appears old Blackwood is coming to London himself to make your and my acquaintance. He is a good old Scotchman and if you like the idea drop me a line to name the day. It is left to you.[1]

Your whiskey old man has effected a cure and I feel quite fit for work. How long that disposition will last only the devil in charge of my affairs knows. I miss you horribly. In fact Ravensbrook and its inhabitants have left an indelible memory. Some day—perhaps next year—we must take a house together—say in Brittany for 3 months or so. It would work smoothly—I am sure.

Present my respectful and most friendly regards to your wife and assure her of our gratitude for the more than charming hospitality. My wife sends her love to the whole household. She is going to write in a day or two—as soon as we are a little settled.

Give us some news—good, if you can.

Ever yours
Jph. Conrad.

[1]Conrad had arranged with David Meldrum, London consultant of Blackwood and Sons, to bring Crane and William Blackwood together during the week of 14 February. The meeting did not actually occur until 25 March. Through Conrad's importunity, Blackwood's London office lent Crane £60 for his passage to America in April as an advance on articles to be sent from the Cuban war front. *Blackwood's Edinburgh Magazine* published "The Price of the Harness" in December 1898 but rejected "The Clan of No-Name." Meldrum lost confidence in Crane's literary future, and Crane never entirely repaid his debt to Blackwood. When he wished to return to England, Blackwood refused to advance more money.

364. TO PAUL REVERE REYNOLDS
Allen, pp. 56-58.

[Ravensbrook] Feb. 7 [1898]

Dear Reynolds:

I am sending you by the Majestic (Wednesday) a new novelette, "The Blue Hotel." To my mind, it is a daisy. I have left every solitary right free—English book, English serial, American book, American serial—so that you can sell the story to *Harper's Magazine* for the volume.[1] You might gently intimate to them that $500 is about the price I am led to expect for a story of ten thousand words. As for "Death and The Child" it is to go in the McClure book. So is "The Five White Mice."[2]

Besides it would be absurd to conjoin "Death and The Child" with "The Monster." They don't fit. It would be rotten.[3] Now, "The Blue Hotel" goes in neatly with "The Monster" and together they make 32,000. Very little more is needed for a respectably-sized $1.00 book,[4] and that can be readily submitted within the next six weeks.

If the Harpers take this story, try to get them to produce that £50 which is to be paid for the book rights. I shall need every sou for the next two months. And if it hadn't been for your handsome management of the Harpers I would have been stumped absolutely. As you see, I am buckling down and turning out stuff like a man. If you hold your fine gait it will only be a short time before we are throwing out our chests.

There are a few odds and ends of affairs, such as the *Journal* business and so on that I wish you would get settled up. A ten pound note even fills me with awe.

You must understand as my confidential agent that my settlement in England cost me in the neighborhood of $2000. worth of debts. Your payments from the Harpers knocked a comfortable hole in them but I must have about $1200. more. This would have been simple if it were not for that black-mail at Appleton's.[5]

However, now that I am in it, I must beat it and I feel that with your help the affair will not be too serious. I will bombard you with stuff. Then, if you sell *Harper's* "The Blue Hotel," cable the money instantly. I have got big matters to attend to this month. Get me through this and I am prepared to smile.

In a cable-gram, never mind the word "dollars." I will understand that you always speak in U.S. money. My replies should also be understood in U.S. terms.

Yours faithfully
S. C.

---

[1] "The Blue Hotel" was rejected by *Harper's Magazine,* the *Century,* and *Scribner's Magazine.* The *Atlantic Monthly* was willing to publish the story only upon the condition that Crane would agree to submit a novel or a collection of Western stories to Houghton, Mifflin & Co. The first appearance of "The Blue Hotel" was in *Collier's Weekly,* 22 (26 November 1898), 14-16; 22 (3 December 1898), 14-16. It was collected in *The Monster and Other Stories,* published by Harper and Brothers in New York in December 1899 and by the same firm in London in February 1901.

[2] *The Open Boat and Other Tales of Adventure* (1898).

[3] Whatever the aesthetic validity of the judgment, Crane understood only vaguely that Harper's had a valid claim to book rights on "Death and the Child."

[4] The Whilomville story "His New Mittens" was incongruously appended to "The Monster" and "The Blue Hotel" to flesh out the American edition of *The Monster and Other Stories* (1899). The publication price of the book was $1.25.

[5] A warrant of attachment had been obtained on 3 January against Crane by Amy Leslie for the $550 he allegedly owed her, but her suit had frozen his royalties from Appleton since the late fall of 1897.

365. TO PAUL REVERE REYNOLDS
ALS on Ravensbrook stationery, NSyU.

Feb 8. [1898]

Dear Reynolds: Please say to Harpers that it will be very necessary for me to have early proofs of The Monster as I note now, from the original ms, many crudities in style.[1]

The same applies to The Blue Hotel.[2]

Very truly yours
S. C.

[1] Only a single manuscript leaf of "The Monster" survives, preserved in NNC. 68v is virtually a fair copy of the conclusion of the story. On the recto is a canceled earlier version of section XXIII (numbered XXXIII in the manuscript), which indicates that Crane may have significantly reworked what was initially a stark, realistic narrative into a brooding, symbolically charged story.

[2] A fragment of manuscript of "The Blue Hotel," in Cora's hand, taken from dictation, on one side of a single sheet preserved at NNC, reveals considerable polishing of style. In this draft version Scully is named Renigan.

366. HAROLD FREDERIC TO CORA CRANE
ALS on Frederic's Homefield stationery, NNC.

February 8, 1898

My dear Cora:

Forgive the informality of my taking the matter away from Kate,[1] and myself answering your characteristically kind and straightforward letter of Sunday.

I left Ravensbrook on Saturday dismayed at the proportions of the mistake I had made in opening up the Irish business at all. My error arose from my taking as my guide the very delightful memories we both have and cherish of the Irish trip last autumn. I had not at all realized—up to the time of our discussions last week—that so much had changed since then. You see you and Stephen then were still in the chrysalis stage so to speak of house-keeping and you were both relatively fresh from the hap-hazard, bohemian life of the campaign in Thessaly. It was comparatively easy for you both, therefore, to fall in with the general views of the organizer of the picnic. How charmingly you both did so we shall never forget. And you were both ill, too, and that contributed its very sweetening effect, in our minds, to what we look back upon as one of the happiest times of our life.

It has been borne in upon me, however, by practically every word that has been exchanged about the new project, that the conditions are all altered—and I am greatly distressed and angry at my own simplicity in not having seen this in time to avert the unhappy blunder of making the proposition. I am more vexed about my stupidity than you can think—but it never occurred to me that since last Autumn Ravensbrook has defined for itself a system and routine of its own—quite distinct, as is natural, from the system of Homefield—and that an effort to put these two side by side under one roof would necessarily come to grief. There would be the common bond of great and deep personal attachment between the two households, of course—but when it came to a test of strength between that and the divergent impetus of two wholly different sets of habits, I have seen too much of the world to doubt that the bond would be injured much more easily than the habits would be harmonized. And God forbid that that should happen.

I don't want to go any further into the matter. It is all very heart-breaking to me—to us—and I wish with sharp emphasis that Mrs. Rice had never offered me the house at all. As I have said, I take all the blame upon myself for not having realized that under the changed conditions, the things that we had so pleasantly in a community of comradeship would recede into the background, and that our points of difference would rise up and rush forward to monopolize attention. And I think, too, that if we were all off on a holiday, with no necessity of work for either Stephen or me, we could probably take a sufficient number of these differences by the scruff of the neck, and thrust them back where they belong. But with the necessity of work weighing upon us both, I am frankly afraid of the experiment.

Yet I have built so fondly on the prospect of having some long, good fishing days alone with Stephen—and there are such a multitude of like attractions for us all in the first vision of the project—that I want earnestly to set before you a kind of alternative. Do you and Stephen and Mrs. Rudy[2] carve out of your Spring a three weeks of entire leisure (and I will make that period free for myself, or nearly free) and come over and visit us at Ahakista. Everything then will be perfectly simple, and I surely need not waste words in saying how warmly you would be welcome. Bring Adoni[3] with you.

Kate is going to write you tomorrow. Meanwhile I beg you both to read into my letter all the regret and affection which your hearts will tell you I wanted it to contain.

Yours always
Harold F.

[1] Kate Lyon, Frederic's common-law wife and mother of his three younger children: Helen, Héloise, and Barry. When Frederic died of complications following a stroke on 19 October 1898, Kate and Mrs. Mills, the Christian Science practitioner she had called in to treat him in the final week, were arrested for manslaughter. Cora sheltered the children at Ravensbrook and was instrumental in raising a fund in their behalf.

[2] Mrs. Charlotte (Mathilde) Ruedy, Cora's companion and assistant at the Hotel de Dream in Jacksonville. Mrs. Ruedy accompanied Cora to Greece and lived with the Cranes at Ravensbrook and Brede Place. She returned to the United States in June 1899.

[3] Adoni Ptolemy, one of the Greek twins, war refugees, whom the Cranes brought to England. Adoni served for a time as butler at Ravensbrook.

367. FROM ROBERT BARR
ALS, NNC.

London Feb 9 '98

Dear Stephen

Say next Monday or Tuesday & Im wid ye. I have been staying with Julian Ralph[1] in London & did not see your letter till it was forwarded in to me just now.

I enclose a letter to your lawyer which please read seal & post. Remember I am going to America on March 20th so if the suit does not come off before then I shall be glad to go anywhere & testify to what I know for use at the trial.[2]

Ever yours
R. B.

[1] Author and foreign correspondent Julian Ralph (1853-1903) had served with Crane as a member of the *Journal*'s staff in Greece. He was at this time London correspondent for the *Journal*.

[2] Of Amy Leslie's claim against Crane. Amy failed to receive the partial repayments Crane sent to her in April 1897. See No. 329, n. 1.

368. FROM JOSEPH CONRAD
ALS, NNC.

[Stanford-le-Hope] *Tuesday*. [15 February 1898]

My dear Crane.

I've been rather seedy lately—all worry I think. But I am going to put my worries aside and have a real good time with you. I shall wire you on Sat. by what train we are coming; some time in the afternoon but not late.[1] I shall bring a lot of paper and you shall find a pen. I am anxious to know what you have done with your idea for a play. A play to write is no play. I believe you can do anything.[2]

Ever Yours
J. Conrad.

Our kindest regards to Mrs Crane. Baby sends a friendly howl.

[1] Joseph and Jessie Conrad, their infant son, Borys, and Mrs. Conrad's young sister, Dora, visited the Cranes at Ravensbrook for ten days beginning 19 February.

[2] "The Predecessor," a story that Crane wished to transmute into a melodrama of the American West. Conrad wisely declined to collaborate in this venture, and Crane never completed it. See No. 377, n. 2.

369. FROM JOSEPH CONRAD
Inscribed on a flyleaf torn from an unidentified book, probably *The Nigger of the "Narcissus,"* NNC.

To
Stephen and M {*flyleaf torn*}[1]
with the Author's
affectionate regard.

21 Feb 1898

[1] Probably "Mrs Crane," the manner in which Conrad addressed Cora. On the verso of this flyleaf Cora has written: "Joseph Conrad. Both of these names are the Christian names of Joseph Conrad Korzeniowski. He is a Pole of noble family. His father died in Siberia and he was there when an infant with his mother. Their Estates were confiscated. He was educated in France and speaks and acts like a Frenchman. Went to sea when seventeen years of age and has had the most wonderful adventures, particularly in the South Sea Islands. He is a Master in the Merchant Service. In 1898 he lived at Ivy Walls Farm. Stanford-le-Hope Essex. His son Boyes [i.e., Borys] was born there on January 15, 1898. 1899 he moved to Pent Farm Stanford near Hythe Kent." Actually, the Conrads moved to Pent Farm in October 1898.

370. FROM ROBERT BARR
Letterhead: "Hillhead,/ Woldingham,/ Surrey." ALS, NNC.

Feb 23d '98

Dear Stephen;

Glad to see that you've stopped telegraphing & taken to letters. Thus you will become rich, & I shall be the possessor of valuable autographs which I will preserve alongside Kipling's.

I have been waiting to hear from Julian Ralph & have just had a letter. He cant come; I knew he was very busy but he might have let me know sooner. I shall be in town Saturday, Sunday & part of Monday. I shall come right through to Oxted with a whoop, probably on the 5 P.M.

express from Victoria. Tell Mrs Crane to *please* not make any special preparations as I shant have my dress suit on.

If any other day than Monday is handier for you let me know and I'll come that other day to lunch, so that I may climb my accursed hill in daylight.[1] I dont mind meeting ghosts on a level but I hate to meet 'em on a hill where I can't run.

Ever yours
Robert Barr
The Nigger of the Parnessus (Hill)
(Cant spell Parnessus)

[1] Hillhead was an appropriate name for Barr's home, perched upon a steep hill in Woldingham.

371. TO JOSEPH CONRAD
Inscribed in a copy of the first English edition of *The Little Regiment,* NN.

To Joseph Conrad;
With the affectionate remembrances
Of Stephen Crane

Ravensbrooke, Feb 26, 1898

372. TO PAUL REVERE REYNOLDS
ALS on Ravensbrook stationery, NSyU.

March 1st '98

My dear Reynolds: I will forward you this week copies of about thirty "Lines" which are to be issued with about twenty more in a small volumn the size of the Black Riders.[1] In fact I can turn in half the copy. I think we ought to be able to raise a little wind, say £30=0=0 on a contract at once. The stipulations are as follows:—A payment of

£30=0=0 upon the delivery of stuff amounting to half a book the size of the Black Riders. The rest of the copy to be ready in time to have the book on the market for the Xmas sales.² The £30=0=0 to be considered as an advance on the 15/-percent royalty.

I have written to my friend Elbert Hubbard of East Aurora Erie Co. N.Y. that you will give him the first chance. I think he is quite sure to accept this offer.³

Yours Faithfully
Stephen Crane

P.S. Please see MacArthur and get from him a copy of an old number of the Bookman which contans some "Lines" of mine entitled War is Kind.⁴ Make a copy of these lines yourself to include in the stuff which I shall send you and send another copy to me.

---

[1] In the first week of March, Crane sent Reynolds typescripts of most of the "lines" that comprise his second book of poetry, *War Is Kind* (New York: Stokes, 1899), illustrated with flamboyant art nouveau drawings by Will Bradley. A number of poems in this book, notably the last five in the "Intrigue" sequence were written in Havana.

[2] Crane's departure for the Cuban war, somewhat over a month after the date of this letter, interrupted his plan to write additional poems.

[3] Whether Reynolds offered *War Is Kind* to Hubbard is unknown. But the Fra's notorious reluctance to pay royalties would hardly make this prospect appealing to him.

[4] The first publication of "Do not weep, maiden, for war is kind," to which Crane refers is in the *Bookman*, 2 (February 1896), 476, under the title "War Is Kind." This title appears over the poem in the collection, *War Is Kind*, and it is the only single titled poem in the book. Fredson Bowers conjectures that the reason is that the copy text for the book appearance was the typescript that Crane here asks Reynolds to have made from the *Bookman*. The "Intrigue" sequence, however, is also titled. A facsimile of the holograph manuscript of "War Is Kind" in the *Bookman*, 9 (July 1899), 400, has the title "Lines" in an unidentified hand, triple underlined.

373. TO SYLVESTER SCOVEL
TT, MnU.

Ravensbrook
March 5 [1898]

My dear Harry: Cora sent you by today's steamer a copy of the current number[1] (March 5) containing your letter. I also requested MacKenzie, the editor, to send you a personal letter of regret and he today informs me that he is doing so. The delay in publication is owing to the length of the negotiations. From the outset MacKenzie was so frankly sorry that I found it an exceedingly awkward job to drive him. In fact, I was several times quite on the point of compromising in some way—the matter was getting so old. However it came out all right. I don't think you will again receive ungenerous treatment from Black and White.

Yours as always
S. C.

[1] Of the English magazine *Black and White*.

374. TO PAUL REVERE REYNOLDS
ALS on Ravensbrook stationery, NSyU.

England
March 13th '98

My dear Reynolds: I have your letter telling me that Scribner has the blue Hotel. Try to sell it soon as possible. I must have some money by the first of April. Will you collect the numerous small am'ts due me if possible and send to me? Also try to get the book right £50—from Harper.[1]

Yours Faithfully
Stephen Crane

[1]For *The Monster and Other Stories* (1899). On 3 March Reynolds had received $125 from Harper's, half the advance agreed upon for book rights. Harper's ignored Crane's pleas for the balance until nine months after Crane submitted "His New Mittens" to complete the volume.

375. EDWARD GARNETT TO CORA CRANE
ALS, NNC.

The Cearne
Kent Hatch.
Nr Edenbridge
13. March. 98.

Dear Mrs. Crane,

The house is called *Brede Place*. Brede Village. (Postal address Nr Northiam Sussex).

But the best way for you to reach it is to go by train to Hastings, & then be driven there in a fly. It is about 8 miles from Hastings, & the Hastings fly owners & fly men must know it well, as I believe parties drive over from Brede in the summer on purpose to see the house.

If you take train from Westerham to Dunton Green you can catch a South Eastern down train to Hastings.

No doubt a tip to the care taker will gain you admission to *Brede Place*, & information. Or Stephen's eloquence will move even a new tenant to vacate the house, & instal those who respectfully appreciate what they deserve. But *dont go with expectations*. For it is a miracle if something has not happened to it, since the days when I saw that farm baliff encamped in those ancient walls.

I enclose a cutting and a bad map. Heaven help and guide you!

Yours very truly
Edward Garnett

NB. The country round *Battle* (the site of the affair between William the Conquerer & all England in 1066) is very old fashioned. Perhaps the Hastings house agent could put you into some other old houses.

376. JOSEPH CONRAD TO CORA CRANE
ALS, NNC.

Tuesday. [15 March 1898]

Dear Mrs Crane.

I am sorry to say I am not well enough to keep Stephen's engagement for Saturday evening. It is nervous trouble and the doctor advises me to keep very quiet. I think I ought to follow his advice. A dinner in town means sleeping in town and I simply don't feel equal to it. I hope Stephen won't be angry, but really I do not feel at all well. I am writing today to Meldrum saying that Stephen would like to meet Mr Blackwood if it can be managed on Saturday next. If the thing is arranged I shall try to come up on that day for the lunch, but must get home in the afternoon.[1]

I am so glad Stephen is writing; it consoles me from my own inability to work. I haven't written three pages since I left you. I simply *can't*. I am like a man under a fiendish spell cast over the power of thinking.

My wife and Dolly send their love to you all. Believe me dear Mrs Crane your faithful and affectionate servant

Joseph Conrad.

[1] The luncheon with William Blackwood was postponed until Friday, 25 March, but Conrad and Crane attended a dinner at the Savage Club on the evening of the 19th. They did not spend the night in London but returned to their respective homes.

377. TO JOSEPH CONRAD
ALS on Ravensbrook stationery, NNU.

March 17 [1898]

My dear Conrad: I am enclosing you a bit of original ms under the supposition that you might like to keep it in remembrance of my warm and endless friendship for you.[1] I am still hoping that you will consent

347

to Stokes' invitation to come to the Savage on Saturday night. Cannot you endure it? Give my affectionate remembrances to Mrs Conrad and my love to the boy.

Yours always
Stephen Crane

You *must* accept, says Cora—and I—our invitation to come home with me on Sat night[2]

---

[1] "The Five White Mice." In 1912 Conrad gave this twelve-page manuscript (CSmH), which had served as Heinemann's printer's copy, to John Quinn.

[2] After the dinner at the Savage Club that Saturday evening, according to Conrad, he and Crane "sat at Gatti's, I believe; unless it was at a Bodega which existed then in that neighbourhood and talked. . . . Crane told me of a subject for a story—a very exceptional thing for him to do. He called it 'The Predecessor.' I could not recall now by what capricious turns and odd associations of thought he reached the enthusiastic conclusion that it would make a good play, and that we must do it together. . . . We carried on this collaboration as far as the railway time-table would let us, and then made a break for the last train. Afterwards we did talk of our collaboration now and then, but no attempt at it was ever made" (Beer, p. 29). Before he left for Cuba, Crane offered a prospectus of "The Predecessor," recast as a novel and much more credible than Conrad remembered it, to C. Arthur Pearson, Ltd., the publisher of *Pearson's Weekly* and other magazines. When Pearson's declined to offer an advance for his outline, he handed it to George Brown Burgin, literary advisor of the book department, "As Pearson's won't advance anything on this before it's written," he said, "if I don't come back from abroad you can have this plot of a novel and do what you like with it." Burgin reproduces Crane's outline, as he recalls it, in *More Memories (and Some Travels)* (London: Hutchinson, 1922), pp. 170-72. See also Stanton Garner, "Stephen Crane's 'The Predecessor': Unwritten Play, Unwritten Novel," *American Literary Realism, 1870-1910,* 13 (1980), 97-100.

Crane's failure to induce Conrad to collaborate with him on a play, coupled with the furor over "imperialism" precipitated by American reaction to the sinking of the *Maine,* probably motivated Crane to write his closet drama, "The Blood of the Martyr," which satirizes German industrial exploitation of China.

378. TO PAUL REVERE REYNOLDS
ALS on Ravensbrook stationery, NSyU.

March 17/98

My dear Reynolds: Your letter of the 8th with the enclosed one from Mr. Nelson reached me this morning. I regret very much the misunderstanding about the story for Harpers Weekly and apologize to you for my neglect. It will not happen again. I shall write a personal letter to Mr Nelson.[1]

I wrote you last mail to send me what money you could collect by the 1st April as I have heavy obligations to meet.

Yours Very Faithfully
Stephen Crane

[1] Crane had submitted "Death and the Child" to McClure for *The Open Boat and Other Tales of Adventure*. Harper's evidently complained that their prior purchase of the story from Reynolds for *Harper's Weekly* gave them the right to publish it in *The Monster and Other Stories* as well.

379. JOSEPH CONRAD TO CORA CRANE
ALS, NNC.

17.3.98

My dear Mrs Crane

You are both awfully good to me. The only reason why I would hesitate to accept your kind proposal is that I am afraid the company of a wretched creature like me *won't* do any good to Stephen, who is an artist and therefore responsive to outside moods. Now my mood is unhealthy; and I would rather forbear seeing Stephen all my life—(notwithstanding my affection for the man and admiration for the artist)—than bring a deteriorating element into his existence. You, knowing him better than any one, may tell best whether my fear is justified.

However for this time I am inclined to be selfish and say yes. I haven't yet heard from the Blackwood man. I instructed him to write direct to Stephen about the Saturday lunch business. We shall no doubt both get a letter tomorrow (Friday). If *yes* we shall meet where he appoints. If *not* then perhaps Stephen would wire to me on Saturday—as early as possible.

Wife and Dolly send their love to all, and I am dear Mrs Crane always most faithfully your

Jph. Conrad.

380. JOSEPH CONRAD TO CORA CRANE
ALS, NNC.

24th March 98

Dear Mrs Crane

Thanks for your letter. I am glad to hear Stephen is at work. I am not.

I shall be at Heinemann's a little before one. I think it's the best place for us to meet on Friday before going to feed at old Blackwoods expense. The time of feeding is 1.30 and the locality Garrick Club.

Jessie and Dolly send their best love to you and Mrs Rudie.[1] The baby has set up a carriage and is so puffed up with pride that there is no bearing him. He behaved like an accomplished ruffian when Stephen was here and has hurt my feelings so much that we haven't been on speaking terms since.

I am, dear Mrs Crane,

Most sincerely yours
Jph. Conrad

[1] Mrs. Charlotte Ruedy.